the
information on
store

📞 01603 773114
email: ti̶

D0275233

CHILD SEXUAL ABUSE AND ADULT OFFENDERS:
NEW THEORY AND RESEARCH

Already published in this series, in association with CEDR
(Series Editor *Robin Lovelock*)

Changing Patterns of Mental Health Care A case study in the development of local services *Jackie Powell and Robin Lovelock*

Partnership in Practice The Children Act 1989 *ed. Ann Buchanan*

Disability: Britain in Europe An evaluation of UK participation in the HELIOS programme (1988-1991) *Robin Lovelock and Jackie Powell*

The Probation Service and Information Technology *David Colombi*

Visual Impairment; Social Support Recent research in context *Robin Lovelock*

Workloads: Measurement and Management *Joan Orme*

Living with Disfigurement Psychosocial implications of being born with a cleft lip and palate *Poppy Nash*

Educating for Social Work: Arguments for Optimism *ed. Peter Ford and Patrick Hayes*

Dementia Care: Keeping Intact and in Touch A search for occupational therapy interventions *M. Catherine Conroy*

Suicidal Behaviour in Adolescents and Adults Research, taxonomy and prevention *Christopher Bagley and Richard Ramsay*

Narrative Identity and Dementia A study of autobiographical memories and emotions *Marie A. Mills*

In preparation

Community Approaches to Child Welfare International perspectives *ed. Lena Dominelli*

Social Work in Higher Education Demise or development? *Karen Lyons*

Valuing the Field Child welfare in an international context *ed. Marilyn Callahan*

Child Sexual Abuse and Adult Offenders: New Theory and Research

Edited by
CHRISTOPHER BAGLEY
University of Southampton

KANKA MALLICK
Manchester Metropolitan University

Ashgate

Aldershot • Brookfield USA • Singapore • Sydney

Published by
Ashgate Publishing Ltd
Gower House
Croft Road
Aldershot
Hants GU11 3HR
England

Ashgate Publishing Company
Old Post Road
Brookfield
Vermont 05036
USA

British Library Cataloguing in Publication Data
Child sexual abuse and adult offenders : new theory and
    research. - (C. E. D. R.)
    1. Child sexual abuse 2. Sexually abused children 3. Child
    molesters
    I. Bagley, Christopher II. Mallick, Kanka III. University of
    Southampton. Centre for Evaluative & Developmental Research
    362.7'6

Library of Congress Catalog Card Number: 98-73858

ISBN 1 84014 839 X

Printed in Great Britain

Contents

List of Contributors

Dr. Chris Atmore is Lecturer in Feminist Theory, Cultural and Media Studies in the Department of Anthropology and Sociology, Monash University.

Dr. Christopher Bagley is Professor of Social Work Studies, University of Southampton.

Dr. Lee C. Handy is Professor of Counselling Psychology, University of Calgary.

Shirley Jackson is Lecturer in Social Work Studies, University of Southampton.

Dr. Kanka Mallick is Senior Lecturer in Education, Manchester Metropolitan University.

Dr. Susan McIntyre is a Social Work Consultant in Calgary, Alberta.

Dr. Guy Pelletier is Psychologist at Foothills Hospital, Calgary, Alberta.

Dr. Colin Pritchard is Professor of Psychiatric Social Work, University of Southampton.

Elaine Sharland is Lecturer in Social Work Studies, University of Southampton.

Dr. Julia Stroud is Lecturer in Social Work, Brunel University.

Graham Tuson is Lecturer in Social Work Studies, University of Southampton.

Loretta Young is Senior Social Worker at Alberta Children's Hospital, Calgary.

Introduction: Child Sexual Abuse and Adult Offenders

KANKA MALLICK AND CHRISTOPHER BAGLEY

Introduction

This volume contains chapters from Canada, Australia and Britain on the complexities of understanding, preventing and treating child sexual abuse and associated family dysfunctions, including emotional and physical abuse. The themes are diverse, reflecting the wide range of studies now undertaken in the field of child sexual abuse (CSA), ranging from policy analyses to clinical studies of outcomes. These two kinds of studies may in fact be complementary, since potential harms wrought by CSA may well influence how policies are formulated for addressing CSA and associated problems. Indeed, the idea that CSA *is* a social problem has a theoretical underpinning.

This book carries the words "new theory" in its title. No chapter is directly theoretical, but in all there are *implicit* theories: Atmore on the sociology of knowledge; Pelletier and Handy on the hypothetical factors which may influence clinical outcomes for CSA victims; Bagley and Young on the potential for group therapy in the light of a theoretical model built on prior empirical work; Pritchard and Stroud on theories about the possible influences on those who assault and kill children; Bagley on the moral action required to prevent the exploitation of children and adolescents by prostitution; and McIntyre on a qualitatively derived classification of adolescent prostitution in the light of theoretical reasoning about patriarchy. Indeed, the assumption of the editors that theory guides empirical research, and that empirical research generates both working models and new theories which can be put to further test is itself an ideological, theoretical position.

New Perspectives on Child Sexual Abuse

Research on child sexual abuse is now in its "third generation" phase. The first phase involved historical and clinical studies (e.g. Meiselman, 1978; Rush, 1980) drawing attention to the neglected problem of CSA. The second phase

1

involved statistical studies which, whilst informative, were generally descriptive in nature (e.g. Finkelhor, 1984). The third phase has involved both a great volume of studies, and studies using multiple measurements and complex statistical designs (see Bagley and Thurston, 1996 a and b, for review and summary). Major, well-conducted studies (e.g. Wyatt et al., 1993) have sometimes reached the surprising conclusion from non-clinical, community samples that CSA was only harmful for long-term mental health survey when it was combined with other family dysfunctions. The chapters by Pelletier and Handy, and Bagley, Young and Mallick in this volume have confirmed through community mental health surveys, and controlled clinical studies, that this is in fact the case. It follows that child protection and prevention work on behalf of children should focus on those factors associated with CSA which do indeed potentiate or cause psychological harm. Aggressive, punitive interventions which lead to offender suicide (as outlined in the chapter by Bagley and Pritchard) are not amongst those rational and humane interventions.

As the chapters by Sharland and Jackson and Tuson show, social workers intervening for families in which CSA is revealed face multiple pressures and dilemmas in acting in the child's best interests. This is an ideological and procedural minefield, with pressures on social workers to act simultaneously against the "monsters" - the paedophiles who prey on our children; and to act in ways which provide a smooth transit of the child into a family which is supporting and non-abusive.

Theory and research on child sexual abuse has abounded with controversy from the days of Freud onwards. We mention but a few of these interesting debates, in which writings on theory and practice and empirical research cut and thrust with one another in the pages of journals, and in the great volume of books which now accumulate on library shelves. We mention but a few of these controversies which are of interest to us.

Controversy I: The Contributions of Psychodynamic Theories to the Debate on CSA

Rush (1980) exposed a popular view attributed to Freud: that he had repudiated his first views on CSA as a major cause of adult neurosis in favour of a theory of fantasy arising from repressed infantile wishes, which took the form of imagined assaults which adults recollected from their childhoods. However, according to de Mause (1991) pioneer of a discipline called psychohistory (which argues that cultural values both influence and reflect how that culture treats its children) Freud actually abandoned his interpretation that most sexual abuse was based on fantasy by the supposed victim:

> *For the rest of his life in fact, Freud reiterated his belief that these clear memories of incestuous attacks were real. In 1905 he wrote, "I cannot admit that in my paper on 'The Aetiology of Hysteria' I exaggerated the frequency or importance of ... the effects of seduction, which treats a child as a sexual object prematurely." Later he repeatedly wrote such statements as that "The sexual abuse of children is found with uncanny frequency among school teachers and child attendants ... and fantasies of being seduced are of particular interest, because so often they are not fantasies but real memories." ... Therefore, regardless of all that has been written about the subject, an unbiased reading of Freud's work shows that whenever he is confronted with clear evidence of sexual molestation, he called it seduction, not fantasy. There is no "assault on the truth".* (de Mause, 1991, pp. 127-128).

It is important to establish this point, since some writers have gotten themselves into the double bind of using Freud's theory of repression to account for dissociation following sexual abuse, while simultaneously rejecting aspects of Freud's arguments assuming (wrongly) that he gave to the helping professions the idea that children and adults fantasized sexual abuse. It was the professional community itself which had deluded itself in this manner.

Controversy II: Dissociative Personality Disorder and Child Sexual Abuse

This controversy arises indirectly from the critique of Freud's supposed account of child sexual abuse, and the current very heated debate about whether the memory of CSA can be repressed, or forgotten. It is our reading of the work of van der Kolk (1994) that neurological mechanisms do exist through which the negative impact traumatic events can be minimized through a process of repression - actually forgetting. We have reviewed case material which indicates that victims can suddenly remember such repressed events spontaneously, following some significant trigger - oftentimes the death of the abuser (Bagley and King, 1990).

Brandon et al., (1998) argue persuasively that although most memories of CSA recovered during therapy may be real, nevertheless since therapy is never an unbiased or impartial procedure memories recovered in this way are never certain beyond reasonable doubt. And types of therapy practised by some who feel passionately about the wrongs of CSA can as Brandon et al., (1998) show, actually lead to false allegations of sexual abuse. This can have tragic consequences for both the innocent parent accused, and for the victim.

Brandon et al. (1998) also argue that multiple personality disorder (in which the "abused" part of personality hides within broader identity) is over-diagnosed. With this we would agree too, but also from our own research argue for the existence of dissociative personality disorder as an outcome for the worst kinds of physical, emotional and sexual abuse (Bagley et al., 1995). Individuals often cope with unpleasant physical and emotional experiences by dissociation, removing himself or herself from the unpleasant, painful or demeaning situations. Through a process of either repression or of social learning the individual adopts this mantle of dissociation as a protective cloak against many aspects of life later on.

This has implications for the adult recall studies of CSA which we have employed (see Bagley, 1995 for a full review): if the individual cannot remember the traumatic event when interviewed, this technique will *underestimate* the amount of CSA in the population. This under-counting will also diminish the level of correlations of factors associated with memories of abuse.

An interesting British study argues against the repression of memories in adult recall studies: Bifulco et al. (1997) compared accounts of sisters about abusive events, including sexual abuse, when they were children. Those who had experienced, witnessed or knew about various kinds of abuse gave excellent corroboration of one another's accounts, when questioned separately. But is clear too that superficial questions about unwanted sexual events in childhood may significantly undercount the extent of abuse (Widom and Morris, 1997).

Controversy III: Moral Panics, Satanic Scares, Children's Home Panics, and the Distortion of Social Work

Since the "discovery" of CSA in the early 1980s there have been a series of epidemic panics about the widespread nature of ritualized abuse amongst caretakers of children, including eminent members of the community who have access to children (Bagley, 1997). In America a definitive analysis of more than 12,000 allegations (Goodman et al., 1995) indicated that forensic evidence of satanic and ritual abuse has been found in only a handful of cases. Despite

4

widespread allegations of ritual murder, no bodies or evidence of killing has ever been found. La Fontaine (1998) has reached a similar conclusion in Britain.

In Britain the panic over CSA in Cleveland, Rochdale and Orkney is well documented, and again although some children investigated had been abused, none had been ritually abused and there was certainly no organised conspiracy of abuse (Bagley, 1997). Webster (1998) draws a parallel between these groundless panics and "the great children's home panic". It is now alleged that sexual abuse in children's homes was widespread until the recent past. Webster argues that police methods of investigation were fundamentally flawed, asking leading questions and offering thousands of pounds in criminal injuries compensation to any former resident who would allege sexual abuse against an individual against whom police were trying to build a case. Webster offers disturbing evidence that because of this, many innocent men have been imprisoned.

Myers (1994) documents how the backlash against moral fugues about CSA can effect, in turn, the activity of social work investigations of CSA which now have to accommodate a popular mood against external intrusion into family troubles when children may be at risk. This can in fact lead to the failure to protect victims, or to offer them rational and protective social work treatments, as the chapter by Sharland in this volume seems to imply. Indeed, the Children Act of 1989 set up in the wake of the Cleveland enquiry in order to strengthen family powers against arbitrary removal of children now seems to have resulted in an under-serving of the needs of vulnerable children. Ironically, the 1989 Children Act has failed to stop the detention of sexually abused adolescents in secure accommodation for no other reason than that they were suicidal, were running from home and in moral danger, or wanted to return to the home where their abuser was still living (Brogi and Bagley, 1998).

Controversy IV: Are Sex Offenders Treatable?

A current moral panic concerns the alleged propensity of men released from prison or hospital following a sex offence involving a minor, to commit further crimes. Men released from goal following a sex offence, in fear of their lives from the mob have taken refuge in police stations in Britain. But what *are* the chances of a released sex offender reoffending? The evidence on this score is mainly American, and follow-up studies have often not separated out men who offend against adults from those who target minors; and those who offend mainly against boys are sometimes also undifferentiated. This is a pity, since offenders with different targets often have different rates of recidivism.

Evidence reviewed in Bagley and Thurston (1996b) suggests that men released untreated from prison can gave recidivism rates as high as 50 per cent over a decade for all types of sex crimes involving children, adolescents or adults. Treatment in prison or hospital can halve these rates of recidivism however. Self-report measures of reoffending with the guarantee that such reports will remain confidential, support these figures for the relative success of various programmes using a combination of reality counselling, behaviour modification, pharmacology, and relapse prevention in the years following release.

More recent studies indicate the increased success of multi-therapy programmes for sex offenders. Thus Dwyer (1997) in a 17-year follow-up of 180 offenders in USA and Canada found a 9 per cent rate of sexual recidivism, using confidential reports of any further sex crimes. Regular follow-up counselling to maintain the gains in self-control management seem essential for the success of these programmes (Marshall and Anderson, 1996).

In Britain too the most recent study of outcomes for the three high security hospitals (Broadmoor, Rampton and Ashworth) suggests an increased success rate (Buchanan, 1998). Buchanan does not, unfortunately divide his cohort of 425 men and women followed up for 10 years after discharge by type of sex offence, and age of victim. But he does show that only 7.5 per cent of these individuals (mostly men) had been convicted of *any* sex offence in the decade following release. Significant predictors of recidivism were being younger, having a legal category of psychopathic disorder, and having a prior criminal record - but the overall statistical effect was small. However, these are important results when read in conjunction with the chapter by Pritchard and Stroud in this volume, and confirm that only a small minority of men who sexually offend against children are in fact "dangerous", requiring indeterminate sentences. The outcome for male sex offenders released from the prison hospitals in Britain is better than that found by Tennent and Way (1984) in the most recent previous study. But it remains true that there are still some "dangerous" men who after release will go on to sexually assault adults and children. The research by Pritchard and Stroud in this volume offers some additional clues about how to identify those potentially dangerous men. Clearly further work is needed in follow-up work with men convicted of various types of offence involving children, with clear distinctions made between men whose targets are males, females, or both sexes falling into different age categories.

6

Controversy V: Who Are the Resilient Children?

Some children survive quite horrendous episodes of sexual abuse without apparent psychological harm; and most children and adolescents seem to survive milder or briefer forms of sexual exploitation without any abnormal psychological outcomes in the short or long term. The reasons for this could provide important clues for social work and other therapists, who might create the conditions which foster benign outcomes.

For some individuals their resilient psychological survival is a mystery (Higgins, 1994), although factors such as enduring ego-strength and community and religious supports were identified by Higgins as important. Clinical studies focusing on children who have good and poor outcomes following CSA have identified the following factors in psychological survival: high levels of parental support for the victim, including strong support when abuse is revealed; good support by peers; pre-existing high levels of self-esteem; and good intellectual skills which allow the victim to "rise above" the abuse, avoiding self-blame (Draucker, 1995; Liem et al., 1997; Lynskey and Fergusson, 1997; Smith and Carlson, 1997; Freidrich, 1998). Interventions which try to provide the factors which create resilience (removing blame, increasing social supports, giving cognitive restructuring, providing parallel family counselling) are all techniques which can be valuable for social work therapists (Edwards and Alexander, 1992; Bagley and Thurston. 1996 a and b; and Bagley and Young in this volume). More experimental work in this field is clearly needed.

In addition Bybee et al. (1997) show that "conscious repression" in adolescents can be adaptive in the face of a variety of stressors. This may reflect a long-standing psychological ability to belittle or minimize stressful events so that they hardly enter the conscious mind, although they are not actually forgotten or repressed in the sense in which Freudian psychologists use the term "repression". This finding fits well with the work of Himelein and McElath (1996) who in a study of U.S. college students who had experienced CSA, found that resilience and psychological survival was associated with the ability to engage in "creative illusions", minimising the previous experience, reframing it in a positive manner, and refusing to dwell on the past: these are techniques which therapists could focus on with those who are *not* psychological survivors. And, as Himelien and McElrath conclude: "The focus on resilient survivors of CSA is not intended to minimize the potentially devastating impact of an abuse experience ... the fact that some CSA victims not only survive, but thrive, should in no way take attention away from the pain and suffering experienced by the majority of sex abuse victims." (p. 757.)

But, as the chapters by Pelletier and Handy, and Bagley, Young and Mallick in this volume show it is the negative family climate and associated stressors surrounding any events of CSA which are crucial in influencing mental health outcomes: it is the family dysfunction and physical and emotional abuse which surrounds CSA rather than the sexual abuse itself which causes the most psychological harm, as McGee et al. (1997) have also shown.

Selection of Chapters

The selection of chapters for this book has proceeded on the same basis as that of a "special issue" of a journal - potential authors in various centres were invited to submit potential chapters, and these were submitted by KM to external reviewers for comments. Only about two-thirds of the submitted chapters survived this review process, and we thank those whose chapters were not included for their forbearance. We are grateful also to Angela Evans for her patient and skilled editorial work.

PART I
CONCEPTUAL AND POLICY
ISSUES

1 Towards Rethinking Moral Panic: Child Sexual Abuse Conflicts and Social Constructionist Responses

CHRIS ATMORE

Introduction

> 'To understand responses to social problems, we must appreciate how those problems are typified.' (Best, 1990:4)

The late 1980s and early 1990s have seen a cultural concern with child sexual abuse in several western countries, including the US, Britain, Australia, and New Zealand, which although not new (eg Gordon 1988a, 1988b), is unprecedented in degree. There has been an explosion of media representations of various controversies, notably among them conflicts over the truth of 'recovered memories' and claims of cult/ritual/satanic abuse. As part of this attention, there is now a small academic literature which attempts to explain the phenomenon in cultural and societal terms. Most of this work originates from and concentrates on the United States, and takes a social constructionist perspective, focussing on the study of social problems and 'claims-making' - although specific analyses of Satanism scares are also heavily influenced by the sociology of religion and in particular by studies of cults.

My own response comes out of my larger project on the various 'interested stories' that are constructed and interpreted about sexual violences. Stories always emerge from 'a view from somewhere' (Haraway 1988; Rich 1987), according to, although not in any predetermined way, a specific historical and cultural location and the social coordinates of their authors and readers. Such constructions will tend to advance certain interests at the expense of others. A newspaper report that quotes the police warning parents to teach their children not to get into strangers' cars is in many ways a different account from a first-person narrative of childhood incestuous abuse, but both are interested - as are any academic interpretations of them, whether they draw on mass media and cultural theories, feminist critiques of sexual violence, Foucauldian genealogies of disciplinary power or anti-humanist rejections of the 'truth' and transparency of realist representations.

The constructionist analyses may seem like a small and perhaps not very well-known contribution outside the relatively specialised province of 'social problems'. But these approaches share much with contemporary themes in the mass media and in other everyday cultural parlance, including some current post-feminist 'sex war' arguments, and flaming discussions on the Internet.[1] Discursive contexts are complexly interrelated in a multi-dimensional interactive fashion, in a kind of Worldwide Web/home page model. For instance, academic work plays an increasing role in such genres as news coverage and talk shows, and thereby does not simply address the problem of child sexual abuse as already formed 'out there', but helps to construct its very parameters. I use the constructionist work as a point of entry into this web. My concerns are with both academic debate and a more explicitly political commitment to analysing meanings and practices of child sexual abuse in a way that I as a feminist think could be helpful in combatting both sexual coercion *and* unjust forms of meaning construction and intervention.

Analysis and Critique of Social Constructionist Approaches

Western late capitalist societies have reached a new era of sexual politics in which it is becoming increasingly obvious that it is impossible to assume that the truth of any coercion case will be resolved once and for all by an appeal to either science or personal experience. It seems that now for every psychiatrist testifying in favour of the efficacy of recovering memories, there is a similarly qualified expert prepared to refute such techniques and findings as false; for each talk-show confession of traumatic coercion there is a representationally equivalent and opposite claim to victimisation at the hands of a parental state.

The recent constructionist analyses of claims-making activities make important points about this shared discursive terrain, and often, especially in the literature on 'Satanism scares', provide helpful analyses of particular cases and their profound shaping by not only movements like child protection, but also the politics of the American religious right. The best of the literature urges more thoughtful consideration of easy assertions about child victimisation, and begins to ask why concerns over sexual threats to children have become such a preoccupation in not only the news media but in folklore, fiction and cinema (see also Jenkins 1992; Richardson, Best and Bromley 1991; especially Bromley 1991; and Nathan 1991).

While many of the constructionist arguments seem reasonable and indeed important, if a little hard to admit from my position as a former child abuse educator, nevertheless, at the same time there are also tendencies in this field which are highly problematic from the perspective of a feminist analysis of, and opposition to, child sexual abuse. These themes can be pinpointed through supplying a logical but missing element of 'situatedness' to the constructionist accounts, and by focussing on 'what is getting done' in and through them.

Claims-making and Contextual Constructionism

The constructionist analyses tend to define themselves in opposition to their target of research, 'objectivism'. Objectivism is typified by folk wisdom that assumes the recent heightened attention to child abuse reflects real dangers. So for instance, objectivists are said to argue that there has been either a real increase in abuse, or that society has progressed in paying abuse more of the concern it deserves. Constructionism on the other hand, is more interested in how and why threats to children emerge as social issues at specific cultural junctures - especially in how social problems are constructed through successful claims-making. Claims-makers are defined as tending to be

> 'interested parties - individuals who stand to gain something if their claims are successful - but not all claims-makers have similar interest.' (Best 1989c: 75)

What gets studied is not so much simply social conditions and their consequences, but rather, 'the ways in which issues emerge and evolve through discourse' (Best 1994:9).

In one sense then, a constructionist stance begs the question of the relationship between the 'realities' toward more of a Foucauldian relationship between truth, knowledge and power (eg Foucalt 1980): so the truth of child abuse becomes that of the successful claims-maker. Yet the stance taken is somewhat different from stronger, more post-structuralist interpretations affiliated with the 'strict' end of the constructionist spectrum (Kituse and Schneider 1989; Best 1989b, 1989d). Work on child sexual abuse typically locates itself in a more moderate position as 'contextual' constructionism (eg some of Best 1989a; Richardson, Best and Bromley 1991; Best 1990;

Richardson 1994). For example, James Richardson refutes beliefs in and claims about Satanism as almost completely false, by stating that there 'is little hard evidence of the existence of the levels of Satanic activity posited by many anti-Satanists' (Richardson 1984:3).

But there is still a privileged truth about child sexual abuse, to be found via this milder form of constructionism - which brings it closer to the commonsense assumptions of objectivism it criticises. We may acknowledge that the phenomenon feels real for 'the people', but 'we' (as contextualists) know it is not. Consequently, the contextualist stance, although ostensibly independent of any classical positivist notion of objectivity, tends to reserve a neutral space for the text's own arguments,[2] although with occasional hints of unease in the margins. For instance, Joel Best (1990) dedicates his *Threatened Children* to his sons, 'whose father worries anyway'. However in general there is no overt 'I' in his kind of story (cf. Jones 1990).[3]

The more abstract epistemological debates are of less concern to me here, other than that I am persuaded by a feminist 'situated knowledge' argument (Haraway 1988) that a more radical social constructionist stance on child sexual abuse is one which, via postmodernist social science and radical feminism, does not exempt its own account as context-bound, and therefore requires a reflexivity in which it too is self-identified as an interested story. This is therefore a different kind of contextual constructionism. It need not mean that any story about sexual coercion is as good as any other: as many feminists have argued, we can still say that some stories are better because they are less false, and what makes them so is their ongoing commitment to try to explicitly recognise their own stakes, and therefore produce theoretical analysis more open to conversation.

In contrast, the typical contextualist neglect of writing oneself as author into the text sets up several (apparently discrete) groups, such as the media, the general public, various claims-makers, and the contextualist researcher. This last figure, as neutral analyst, knows better than everyone, while anyone who is seen to have an obvious barrow to push is reduced to the status of potential or actual claims-maker, thus keeping them well on the theoretical sidelines. For instance, there are few references in contextualist writing to feminist arguments about child sexual coercion, and what is acknowledged tends to get labelled as a claim in such a way that it is obvious it is to be as seriously considered as the views of anti-Satanist fundamentalists. In fact there is a strong emphasis on the overlap of feminist arguments with those of the moral right.[4]

Such an association is too easily dismissed as simple anti-feminist backlash from ostensibly liberal and even left wing sociologists (Atmore forthcoming). There are certainly grains of truth in the suggestion that there is *some* shared discursive terrain among feminists and the traditionally defined right wing on the subject of violence and its solutions. However, pinpointing the exact nature of what is held in common - and why - is a complex issue deserving an essay in itself. For instance, both conservative and some (but not all) radical feminist arguments may present fairly closed texts about the guilt of an accused perpetrator, and so in some contexts both political stances can reinforce a pre-existing climate of false accusation. Similarly, some feminist accounts share with the religious right certain foundational assumptions about the role of biology in men's propensity to rape (eg Brownmiller 1975).

In both examples however, even where there is overlap the arguments are by no means identical, and much more intellectual and political discussion is needed (see for example, Atmore 1994b, 1997). In contrast, the way that contextualists make their criticisms involves an unhelpful homogenising and rewriting, indeed misreading, of a history of feminist views and debates on sexual violence. Lastly, as I have suggested in relation to the truth of child abuse controversies, discursive overlap among apparently distinct political positions is increasingly typical of late twentieth century cultures. For instance, as I will illustrate, the 'in bed with the moralists' argument is an accusation that can easily backfire on the contextualists themselves.

While the marginalisation of feminist work in sociological theorising more generally is not especially new (and indeed downright boring to point out these days, even if it does seem especially breathtaking when it concerns topics of violence, family, and sexuality), it does have major ramifications for the kind of analysis that results here. The most obvious effect is one less prod towards a more reflexive view of claims-making, as I have suggested. However, there are also important consequences for contextualist arguments about why child sexual abuse in particular has become such an issue at this historical juncture.

Contextualist analyses all draw on a concept of 'moral panic' in explaining and criticising what they perceive as a cultural obsession with sexual threats to children which is out of all proportion to its seriousness and societal impact. The resulting panic is said to be 'safe' because it allows the existing society to rally around its folk devils in a way that leaves basic values and interests in place. Child sexual abuse claims-makers may have their own various interests to pursue, but ultimately their claims are successful because when it comes to the sexual abuse of children, at the broadest level there is not much to disagree about. Joel Best's (1990: 180-181) argument is representative: deviance is an important theme in American culture; flawed individuals - in Best's words, 'just a few villains' - serve as convenient scapegoats in times of social anxiety and uncertainty, and divert attention away from the more complex workings of the social system (see also Jenkins 1992; Bromley 1991; Nathan 1991).

There are several interrelated problems with this explanation. It uses a notion of general and benign consensus, which involves drawing a boundary between the demonised deviant and the positively valued majority, the 'normal' members of society - and thus no obvious interests are threatened. This majority agreement, it seems, therefore excludes only the mainly silent and small minority of paedophilia advocates; and the contextualists, for their diverse reasons. The model of 'just a few villains' also assumes a very small amount of 'real' abuse, which is at odds with not only radical feminist but increasingly mainstream child protection literature and practice.[5] The assertion of 'just a few villains' must also be upheld if a consensus, rather than a conflict, analysis of child sexual abuse and the contests for its meaning is to be supported. A conflict approach to the issue of child sexual abuse is more strongly evident in feminist arguments which are in any case disregarded as theory by contextualists.

Child sexual abusers are then not seen as part of any power complex, but rather are marginal members of society. Gendered and sexualised generational power, if it appears at all, must be (only) personal rather than structural, in contrast to, as for example in contextualist reasoning, issues of class. Hence for instance, Best argues that the efforts of 'child savers' have helped to favour individual pathology solutions rather than structural ones involving addressing poverty (Best 1990: 191-2; see also Nathan 1991: 77-8) - which, among other criticisms, does not make much sense when referring to child *sexual* abuse.[6]

Most pertinently, this kind of moral panic argument again masks the real differences between the moral right and feminist 'child savers' (as just two examples of different groups).[7] Despite constructionists' general insistence on distinctions among different claims-maker interests, there is no consideration that claims-makers can and do *compete* for the meaning of child sexual abuse, and that the demonised molester, still an extremely common cultural typification of abusers, is a figure promoted by the right but *criticised* by feminists.[8] Many feminist analyses of child sexual abuse, like my own (Atmore 1994a, 1996, 1998), argue that perpetrators are more typical of the general (and mainly male) population than otherwise, and that therefore child sexual abuse is 'normal', in the sense of being endemic to and even helping to engender societies which both eroticise dominance and submission and are importantly shaped by power relations of gender and generation. This 'normality' of child abuse then actually helps to prevent it from being treated as socially significant.

Many feminists therefore join the contextualists in criticising some of the same features of public responses to child sexual abuse, for the different reasons. We can then view the tendency toward deviantising, pathologising and individualising of child sexual abuse in policy and mainstream media as due to a conservatism on gender/sexuality processes which cuts across the right, like Christian fundamentalists, and aspects of the left - including the contextualists.

Media/Cultural Framework

Contextualists also tend to favour certain implicit theoretical assumptions about the workings of media and culture. The news media as 'secondary claims-makers' (Best 1990: 87-111) are regarded as essentially conveying the 'paedophile conspiracy' or 'Satanic cult abuse' perspective to a willing public. Despite some suggestion that media have reasons of their own (demands of newsworthiness, 'Satanism sells' - Richardson 1994, it is difficult to avoid an instrumentalism in which the media largely does the bidding of essentially conservative moral crusaders (eg Johnson 1989, Best 1990).[9] Again there is little acknowledgement of any conflict among 'child savers', or between various 'child savers' and the media[10] - or within the media themselves, whose representations are not always exclusively of the deviantising variety (Nava 1988; Skidmore 1995).

The media is implicitly viewed as transmitting a univocal message to an equally helpful audience who overwhelmingly want to and do believe in 'it'.[11] The presumed simple relationship between text and audience is especially jarring because contextualist work on Satanism scares is dominated by sociologists who have some sympathy for would-be 'Satanists', metal fans and 'legend trippers',[12] and who also have done much to dispel conservative notions about 'cults' like the Moonies as dangerous sites for the indoctrination of youth.[13] While politically and intellectually I have as much sympathy for religious fundamentalism as the next unrepentant sinner, contextualist arguments, at least by omission, leave me wondering why the relationship between audience and text is complex for a 'Satanist' but apparently not for an 'anti-Satanist'. There are feminist and other 'progressive' reasons for caution here. Dismissal of a substantial proportion of anti-Satanists or anti-cultists as simply brainwashed, and duped by cultural junk from US sites like the Christian Broadcasting Network, carries an accompanying baggage: the divide of 'low' versus 'high' culture, traditionally used to keep women and 'the masses' in their denigrated position as ignorant and in need of cultural (and cultured) guidance from their social superiors (Modleski 1982, 1986). The textual positioning of the contextualist as rational neutral observer contributes to this opposition, with the author as a figure who tries to be fair but who finds anti-Satanist and repressed memory advocates somewhat incomprehensible and faintly sullying in their hysteria. Here some of the recent work on fan culture might offer alternative understandings,[14] along with broader contributions from audience ethnographies (see also McRobbie 1994: 198-219).

A related issue concerns the way in which the spread of the child saving message is conceptualised, most clearly evident in the literature on 'Satanism scares'. For example,

> 'The development of a virulent anti-Satanist movement in the US has, as one of its consequences, led directly to the spread of the concern to other countries receptive to ideas from the US and culturally attuned to American society. This represents a form of cultural diffusion of an American derived moral panic and hysteria that should give pause for thought to citizens of the US and other societies which are receptive to this American based phenomenon.' (Richardson 1994: 19)

We find at the level of nations the same simplistic model of transmission of the image of the threatened child, from the essentially trashy US to the defenceless and all-too-credulous rest-of-the-west. Again, the idea that non-American audiences might do something different with the message, let alone not receiving 'it' in an identical way in the first place, is not countenanced. The focus of most contextualist analyses on US society would not necessarily in itself be a limitation, but contextualist arguments tend to go on to assume that a cultural product like a moral panic flows from US sources, and is destined to be exported to the rest of the world along with MacDonalds and Coca Cola.[15] This subscribes to a 'cultural imperialism thesis' which is disputed by many cultural critics (eg Lealand 1988; McKinnon 1988; Bell and Bell 1993). While there is no doubt that the American influence on mass media-ted world affairs is strong, it may not be simply a question of passive Australian receptivity to 'cultural diffusion', any more than it can be unproblematically argued that the way Australians play and watch basketball is just a copying of Americans (only not as good as 'the real thing').

Ironically then, the American imperialism argument as it is used here fails to consider the uniqueness of non-American cultures, even if its exponents might see it as a benevolent variant for their particular project. Societies like

Australia do have important similarities to the US, but also require study on their own terms, the influence of the Christian Right being just one important difference.

Rethinking Moral Panic

Given my criticisms of the contextualists, how might child sexual abuse controversies be more effectively analysed as cultural phenomena? It is not simply a matter of rectifying contextualist versions of classic moral panic theory[16] - but nor do I wish to throw out this framework completely.

Here I am in agreement with Angela McRobbie (1994: 198-219), and more recently McRobbie and Sarah Thornton (1995), that the 'new times' of postmodernity require radically new moral panic theories. McRobbie and Thornton argue that the current context, in Britain at least, involves massively expanded (and increasingly tabloid-ised) mass media which can no longer be seen as separate from society, but rather are now sites 'within which the social is continuously being redefined' (McRobbie 1994: 201). The media themselves have taken up as a selling point the term 'moral panic' once solely confined to academic discourse, so that the act of *creating* a moral panic of some kind may now be a newsworthy transgression. A high rate of moral panic turnover has also developed, to the extent that it may be more appropriate to refer to daily panics which are less monolithic than the old model. While panics have historically been inextricably connected with conservatism and social control, they have become increasingly contested by their own folk devils, who are now often highly media-skilled and more likely these days to obtain coverage.

McRobbie and Thornton also suggest that in reconceptualising moral panics (and their labelling as such) as not necessarily hegemonic and totalising, we need to think of them as no longer so predictably associated with traditional conservative interests, but rather as embodying convergences and divergences across the traditional left and right.[17] Postmodern moral panics therefore involve a proliferation of voices and a diversity of speaking positions.

All of these points are relevant to the child sexual abuse example. The increased discursive crossovers, whether actively sought out or not, can be thought of, using the Web model, as involving traffic among different but often overlapping sites: like the contextual constructionists, media, feminists, right wing organisations, the academy, social policy makers and 'grass roots' protest.

As an illustration, after the feminist 'sex wars' of the 1980s, a debate within feminism has at last begun to shift more openly beyond polarities and stalemates (or at least I think so in my more optimistic moments). At the same time though, the way that the academic sector of this arena tends to represent radical feminist theories of sexual coercion actually has elements in common with the assertions of conservatives.[18] We are living in rather different and complicated times when the right wing, anti-'PC', Washington DC-based paper *Campus Report* and the British left journal *Feminist Review* both approvingly cite Camille Paglia as a remedy for feminist excesses over sexual coercion issues (Guy 1996).

In turn, the contextualist discourses overlap with those of the traditional right wing; for example:

> 'The feminist movement has become a powerful force in American society and elsewhere, with influence in many arenas, including politics and the mass media. Concern for feminist values has become a major element in development of the"political correctness" movement in America, making it somewhat difficult to discuss certain issues.' (Richardson 1994: 10)

The themes in the quotation above might just as easily be found in *Campus Report*, and in terms of their attitudes to both sexual coercion and feminisms are increasingly evident in the mass media and popular culture in the US and Australia, while not being immediately taggable as 'conservative' in any simple way.

Certainly the contextualists are a part of McRobbie's and Thornton's broadened range of spokespeople criticising moral panic creation. But might they also be themselves implicated in disseminating panic logic? Looking at how they describe the moral panic and its successful claims-makers, I find rhetoric like 'major outbreaks' (Richardson 1984: 14); and 'the spread of anti-Satanist ideas around the Western world' (ibid:5). I am not necessarily disputing contextualist claims about the organisational strategies of the international anti-ritual abuse movement. But as with the charges levelled at feminists for being 'strange bedfellows' of the right, in critical theory terms we need to 'up the anti' here (de Lauretis 1993), to (following Tania Modleski's [1991: 135-163] representation of her own stance on feminists and porn) something like 'anti-anti-anti-cult'.

Again, too, a critical self-reflexivity in contextualist work would make it more difficult to simply make assertions about 'visits of American "anti-Satanist missionaries" to selected countries' (Richardson 1994: 5), in which

> '[m]aterials were obtained from the US, including printed matter and [video] tapes of presentations by self-proclaimed ritual abuse experts. Next, some of

those so-called experts were invited to come to the UK, to offer seminars and workshops to willing and interested groups of UK social work professionals.' (ibid: 16)

Richardson's own paper was delivered in my department as part of his visit to New Zealand and Australia from his native US, and recent New Zealand sociological writing about a still hotly debated 'ritual abuse panic' refers approvingly to both Jenkins' and Richardson's work.[19]

If it is justifiable to describe 'child savers' as producing moral panic discourse, cannot the same therefore be said of at least some of the contextualists? The panics are by no means fully fledged according to more classical standards, but there are certainly traces of what Simon Watney (1987) describes as 'local intensifications'. At the same time however, there are problems with using Watney's framework to consider child sexual abuse, because it focuses only on the *molester* as folk devil.[20]

This theme underscores the importance of *local* analyses. While the US work gives the impression that there have been no examples where *feminists* or *'child savers'* have been folk devils, my work on two New Zealand controversies in the 1980s (Atmore 1996) found that media representations prominently cast particular feminist child protection professionals in this light. To some extent, depending on the source, this also seemed to be a feature of the Cleveland crisis in Britain, although it was also more contested there in the media itself. Moreover, in NZ two of the leading figures were also singled out as *lesbian* feminists, suggesting again that some kind of *rapprochement* between gay critics like Watney and radical feminists like Catharine MacKinnon would be productive (see also Atmore 1993). The tendency of existing research and theory to defend the falsely accused or the rights of children, but not both at once, is evidence of a failure to address how contemporary panics can be utilised. The fact that both NZ women also had academic affiliations further suggests caution in simply mapping the experiences of northern hemisphere 'core' onto southern hemisphere 'periphery'; rather, while international links are an important subject to investigate, there is a unique web of influence nationally. Aspects of contextualist arguments might therefore be more applicable in *some* specific cultural and historical contexts, with the input of feminist analyses; for instance, day care child sexual abuse conflicts (Best 1990) are different in some important elements from more 'standard' nuclear family charges.

Drawing on my particular historical NZ context, we should also extend McRobbie and Thornton's argument: the issue now is not just about contesting or endorsing traditional panic concerns, even if with different agendas; but also about *creating* different, politically-loaded kinds of 'moral panics' in the first place. In other words, the subjects of panics have also broadened out from traditional conservative concerns, and some of these may emerge from contestations by erstwhile folk devils and their advocates. Here child sexual abuse is in many ways an acid test for interdisciplinary theory; lending itself well to the fuzzing of supposedly time-honoured distinctions between polarised positions like 'left' and 'right', as debates for 15 years have demonstrated (eg Donzelot 1979; Barrett and McIntosh 1982). On the question of state intervention, for instance: if a moral panic is said to traditionally act on behalf of the dominant social order, what do we make of that claim when the issue is child sexual abuse?

When all of this is considered, McRobbie still may give too much to conservatives as engenderers of moral panic discourses, and not enough attention to the role of what we once might have called fairly unproblematically 'the Left'. What is also salient here is a particular, and again always locally inflected, conjunction of *fin-de-siècle* anxieties and representations, involving, for instance: AIDS, serial killers, 'political correctness', and various apocalyptic visions (Atmore forthcoming b). If we are to retain some concept of (moral?) panic, then it seems reasonable not to restrict the willing dissemination and reception of its logic to conservatives as necessarily the only ones who, increasingly desperate over the unsustainability of their favoured way of living, become subject to a more frantic discursive mix in which 'the panics are no longer about social control but rather about the fear of being out of control' (McRobbie 1994: 199).

This opens up possibilities for at least one kind of more feminist-centred explanation. The NZ examples suggest that at least *some* panics, like those about Satanism, however they might be media-led, should be re-examined as expressing in coded form some real and *related* (as opposed to spuriously convenient or downright baseless) anxieties (Atmore forthcoming a). This also applies to the contextualist responses, given traces of panic discourse in their own presentations and arguments. Contextualists' failure to seriously consider feminist challenges then becomes seen as necessary if their version of moral panic argument is to be supported, and more than inertia about reading feminist literature. Rather it involves its own displacements, its own incipient panic responses.

However, I certainly do not wish to imply some sort of conspiratorial, generalising, direct and one-way influence of anti-feminist 'backlash' and thereby construct a new and equally totalising panic discourse of my own which

22

simply tries to rescue radical feminism from theoretical oblivion. Instead, a stronger constructionist attention to claims-making would start from the researcher's own complex home page sympathies and locations, and treat everything as claims and everyone as claims-makers (as I have begun to do here with the contextualists). It would entail tracing non-static lines of influence and investment, and opening up cross-conversations in 'progressive' cultural politics. None of this is possible without more seriously interdisciplinary work, and I suspect that more often than not at present, various contributors do not read each other, let alone engage in conversation. Donna Haraway's (1985) cyborg feminism of twelve years ago is yet to arrive in this field.

Notes

1. See for example the list 'WITCHHUNT', and the participation of some of its contributors in other forums like 'INTVIOL' and 'ABUSE'.
2. 'The relationship between the sociologists and the people being studied is essentially moral: because sociologists have no vested interests beyond uncovering the truth, and are trained to find it, they can and do undermine and criticise other self-interested claims and activities' (Kituse and Schneider 1989: xii, in their critique of contextual constructionism).
3. The most striking example of this tendency comes from a seminar on Satanism as a social problem, given in my department by a visiting academic. I found out by chance several weeks later that the scholar's visit to Australia had been sponsored at least in part by an 'anti-anti-Satanist' group. I am not saying that the seminar should not have been presented, but rather that for the scholar not to state his affiliation seems both intellectually dishonest and ethically dubious.
4. For instance, Best, apart from a brief reference to feminist concern with domestic violence and sexual exploitation, simply attributes feminist theory and activism over child sexual abuse to the fact that:

   > 'feminists argued that women were at the center of family life and child rearing, so that children's issues were women's issues.' (Best 1990: 7)

   He then continues: 'In much the same way, the New Right['s] ...' (ibid). Similarly, Philip Jenkins analyses feminist involvement in child saving not as stemming from his favoured structural analysis but as, in a reversal of feminist logic, a way to make the claims of feminism seem justifiable:

   > 'For example, feminists benefited in this way from the cultivation of the successive panics. Emphasising the threat of sexual violence was a powerful ideological justification for the whole framework of feminist thought. It provided a degree of urgency, by showing that enacting the feminist agenda was not merely a matter of salary or employment opportunities: it was literally a matter of life and death for thousands of women from all social classes.' (Jenkins 1992: 204)

See also Nathan (1991: 80-81).

5. In fact despite his critique of the appeal to the persuasive rhetoric of statistics by claims-makers, Best makes his own specific assumptions about the prevalence of abuse, referring to *'what might seem to be relatively minor offenses* [which were classified as "sexual abuse" when they involved children' (Best 1990: 71, my emphasis). He goes on to give examples like being briefly fondled by a neighbour, and illustrations from Liz Kelly's radical feminist (1988) research with self-defined survivors of sexual violence, which included incidents like exhibitionism, and later refers to 'astonishing statistics' (Best 1990: 72). So Best too is part of an ongoing debate about the definition and cultural significance of child sexual abuse, and the consequent typifications of perpetrators, prevalence and effects. The issue of a justificatory basis for feminist claims in attempting to redefine child sexual abuse is largely unpursued by contextualists, as is the question of what the 'real' (meaning, arrived at in a methodologically approved fashion) incidence of child sexual abuse actually is, outside the much smaller area of Satanic/ritual abuse claims and specific scares.

6. Apart from the problem of collapsing all social structure (in the sociological terms favoured by contextualists - I prefer to refer to technologies of power) into class stratification, child abuse is not in any simple way reducible to an issue of class. Part of the problem with this argument is the tendency to conflate all forms of child abuse as essentially the same phenomenon, when there is much debate over how generalisable research and intervention in, for instance, cases of physical abuse are to other forms like child sexual coercion - the high ratio of male to female perpetrators in the latter, but not the former, being just one illustration (Best [1990: 107] mentions briefly that 'changing family structures contribute to sexual abuse', but does not elaborate). Best devotes more attention to physical abuse, but even here, the salience of class is complex. On the one hand, for 'child savers' to argue that children are battered across the socioeconomic spectrum need not necessarily imply that class factors are irrelevant and therefore rule out a progressive class politics; but conversely, acknowledging the salience of class does not lead to accurate predictions of whether one will be a victim, perpetrator or neither on the basis of class position (cf Best 1990: 106). As with child abuse more generally, it is possible to attribute multiple causes and factors to physically abusive practices, and to argue that perhaps conditions like poverty and overcrowding exacerbate an abusive situation or increase its likelihood of occurring, while at the same time pointing out that children can be and are physically victimised regardless of what class grouping they might be assigned (see eg. Nelson 1982; Pelton 1981; Violence Against Children Study Group 1990).

7. Eg: 'In short, these critics [feminists and moralists] saw dangers to children as one more consequence of a patriarchal society's misplaced values' (Best 1990: 183). There is a brief acknowledgement (ibid: 207 n3) that feminist analyses sometimes challenge basic cultural assumptions, but this is not pursued.

8. Cf Jenkins (1992), who misinterprets the feminist critique of the separation of sex and violence in more conservative conceptualisations, and neglects to discuss important differences between feminists and moralists over 'stranger danger' and law and order strategies, and instead argues that via feminists the left moved from libertarian to more law-and-order attitudes to state and police intervention. This glosses over the diversity of feminist politics (eg lumps in liberal with radical feminisms) and especially Black feminist concerns here (see also Atmore 1994b). Similarly, Best cites Barbara Nelson's (1984) *Making an Issue of Child Abuse* to support his contention that child abuse becomes defined in policy as a question of (safe) individual pathology. For Best, this is due to the success of child abuse claims-makers. But for Nelson, the result represents a *failure* of

claims-making, a problem of translation from child abuse activists to government, and she therefore does not reduce the problem of child abuse to a moral panic in the contextualist sense.

9. Best (1990) states that the original claims of the US missing children movement were distorted into a disproportionate focus on 'stranger danger', but the large work does not explore the implications of this example.

10. For instance, the typical contextualist account pays no attention to feminist-influenced work on media representations of sexual violence, which is critical of the ways in which the media tend to take up the claims of activists (eg Soothill and Walby 1991; Kitzinger and Skidmore 1995).

11. Although Best, for instance, hedges his bets by stating that the mechanism is one of both 'popular culture shaping the audience' and 'popular culture reflecting the audience', how this might actually work is not elaborated. There are similar problems in his discussion of concern and public opinion (Best 1990: 151-175); the (singular) media either reinforces an existing opinion or produces it, rather than being involved in a more active and complex process of negotiation between any audience member, the text, and the rest of their social practices and experiences.

12. 'Legend trippers' from my limited reading seem to be usually (American only? white?) adolescents who plan and carry out excursions to 'known', haunted'/'Satanic' sites, and who might conduct rituals of their own in the process, including scaring other legend trippers. They are generally not regarded by contextualists to be either 'genuine' Satanists or 'genuine' believers in the existence of Satanists (see eg. Richardson et al 1991).

13. See eg. the work of James Richardson and David Bromley. For instance, Bromley (1991) criticises and makes parallels between the anti-Satanist movement and the anti-cult movement.

14. This type of research treats seriously the reception and creation of cultural products which have high value for the consumer even though mainstream culture denigrates these kinds of obsessions (see eg Lewis 1992). For instance, what might groups like fundamentalist Christians gain from talking about suspected Satanists, and writing and reading pamphlets about them - apart from, but not excluding, the obvious instrumental explanation of furthering religious and political aims? A 'progressive' analysed politics of moral right pleasure needs to go beyond the standard simple assertion that 'they're secretly into it'.

15. Even Philip Jenkins (1992), who is an exception in not focussing on US panics, appears to write for an American audience unfamiliar with Britain, his ostensible subject matter. While rejecting a simple Americanisation argument, his work makes backhanded statements like:

> 'The role of the already existing American feminism was to provide theoretical and tactical concepts, and perhaps a range of examples and concerns which affected the emphases of the British movement; but it did not create it.' (ibid: 225)

16. Contextualist explanations relate to a, by now, quite extensive history of the development and use of moral panic arguments in cultural studies, but the contextualists tend to use work like Stanley Cohen's *Folk Devils and Moral Panics* purely as supporting references, rather than giving it a more detailed reading and attempting to integrate it into the overall argument. The contextualists also tend to ignore the less obviously sociological moral panic work concerning sexuality (eg Rubin 1984; Watney 1987; Weeks 1985) - which also links to some of the formers' epistemological problems, although at the same time the

sexuality moral panic work shares with contextualists the marginalisation of gender. Tracing the moral panic theory connections is another essay, although some of them are suggested here in this last section.

17. McRobbie uses the example of both British Tory and Labour responses to the 'new juvenile crime', post-James Bulger.

18. Atmore (1992). This is yet more reason to extend the study of relevant cultural practices to those within university fields, to for instance, the pronounced feminist postmodernist/radical feminist split in academic feminism in Australia at least, if not elsewhere (Atmore 1993a).

19. Eg Barnett and Hill (1993). Thus even those more sympathetic to the contextualist arguments than I, could read not only the literature but the practices of its authors as themselves part of an imperialist project, if perhaps a relatively benign one.

20. These problems are, as I suggest in note 16, a feature of the sexuality panic literature in general to date, and are both evidence for and consequence of a failure to theoretically imbricate technologies of sex *and* gender (cf de Lauretis 1987).

2 Children First: Challenges and Dilemmas for Social Workers Investigating and Treating Child Sexual Abuse

CHRISTOPHER BAGLEY

Introduction

The argument of this chapter is that current policies, frameworks for service delivery, and the implicit values and schemas of harassed front line workers often harm rather than help victims of child sexual abuse. All interventions should have the goal of treating children's interests for therapy and family integration as primary; all other goals, including punitive pursuit of alleged offenders are of secondary importance. Delay of therapy for a child until a criminal trial is over, and requiring a child to undergo cross-examination are often counter productive for the child. Mandatory reporting of alleged sexual abuse has not worked in children's best interests, and may have prevented offenders from voluntarily seeking help, as do the imposition of long prison terms for apparently minor sexual offences. The Quebec legal model is commended, in which Family Service Centres can be the agency of first report, and have the option of deciding whether to ask for criminal prosecution of an alleged offender.

Multiple pressures (legal, organisational and moral) on social workers make the help they are able to give to sexually abused children often imperfect, and may actually do more harm than good for the child. I have been prompted to write this chapter because of a growing unease about the often highly anxious voice of society about child sexual abuse (CSA), sometimes expressed to the point of hysteria (a hysteria to which our own writing - Bagley and King, 1990 - may have contributed). The ambiguities created by this moral climate sometimes influence social work practice in negative ways, as the North American literature reviewed below, seems to indicate.

The immediate stimulus for reviewing this literature comes from a Canadian case discovered in the course of research on role conflicts in young adult gay men (Bagley and Tremblay, 1997):

A man in his late 'twenties, in a severe depression, sought counselling with a social work therapist. In reviewing past events he mentioned that between the ages of 20 and 22 he had a sexual affair with his male cousin, then aged 12 to 14. They met on six occasions over the two year period, and engaged in heavy petting and oral sex, but not intercourse. The adolescent had not made a formal complaint, and gave no indication that the sex was unwanted, or had caused short or long term harm. The therapist informed the client that he was obliged to report these facts to the Director of Child Welfare, who in turn informed police. The man made a full statement of confession, and was informed by police that since he made a full, written apology to his victim he would likely receive a suspended sentence. Unfortunately, the man appeared before a Judge known for his intolerance of homosexuality, and the man was sentenced in 1995 to three years in a Federal Penitentiary. The former 'willing victim', now in his late teens had become confused and guilty over an episode long since forgotten, and which produced no guilt and apparent harm at the time.

The Sociological Literature on Social Work and Child Sexual Abuse

Perhaps defensively, social workers tend to ignore the sociological literature on social work practice, since it sometimes identifies hidden and disturbing ideologies implicit in social work practice. Okami (1990) cites this American literature which shows that child protection workers spend much of their time investigating (and having to discount) allegations of suspected child sexual abuse which are constructed according to prevalent value categories, rather than on rational accounts - at least half of allegations do not lead to intervention, although a veil of confusion may still surround those investigated, including the allegedly abused child, who may also have been subjected to demeaning and painful medical investigations (Bagley and Thurston, 1996b). One price has been the neglect of physical abuse allegations - the number of these reports has actually gone down, since those potentially making referrals now no longer construct physical abuse as a category worthy of intervention, or assume that there is little probability of effective intervention. Okami cites work which argues that the 'hysteria' surrounding sexual abuse, leading to frequent, unwarranted allegations, has also led to the neglect of programmes designed to investigate, treat and prevent the physical and emotional abuse of children.

Detailed support for Okami's critique comes from a sociological analysis of social work practice in the field of child sexual abuse by Margolin (1992) who undertook a content analysis of 120 case records of a child protection agency in Iowa. Margolin argues that harassed social workers when called upon to investigate cases of child abuse, use symbolically constructed, taken-for-granted categories which try and impose a kind of semantic order on the often chaotic lives of their clients. Social workers evolve their own sub-language in dealing with cases, and writing about them. These written records form the basis for further labelling, and decision making which (in hindsight) hardly seems just or rational to the outside observer. Social workers make decisions about clients (and abuse victims) which may have far-reaching (and sometimes deleterious) consequences for parent and child.

A common example is the decision to remove a child following an allegation of abuse: once categories are socially constructed and the symbolic meanings of these categories are shared by colleagues, any new evidence is adapted (or ignored) to fit with the decided-upon categories supporting a particular decision. Margolin illustrates this with a detailed transcript of a social worker questioning an allegedly sexually-abused 8-year-old girl. The social worker seems to be convinced that abuse has taken place, and manipulates (albeit unconsciously) the questions asked of the child into a direction which seems to make it clear that abuse did take place. However, Margolin continues: "I offer this dialogue not as evidence that sexual abuse did or did not occur, but rather to display the means by which equivocal behavior is translated into the 'fact' of sexual abuse. Whatever it is that 'really happened' to the child, we see that her experience of it is not of concern when 'documentation' is being gathered ... as the child learns, even features of the 'event' - such as size, hardness and overall appearance of a penis - can assume critical importance within interviewers' frames of reference" (p. 62). In these interviews the child learns a symbolic frame of reference that is similar to that of the social workers and others who repeatedly question him or her. When the child 'retells' the story of the abuse, the account becomes credible within the frames of references and language often shared by social workers, psychologists, prosecutors and therapists.

In Margolin's (1992) study, social workers' reports contain judgements about the 'credibility' of the child or the adult, based on previously defined symbolic categories. An 18-year-old babysitter (who allegedly assaulted a child) is disbelieved because of a prior conviction for theft. And a 12-year-old who repeatedly denied that anyone had touched her sexually is disbelieved because her account is 'too naive' for a 12-year-old. Once the symbolic categorization has been made, the parties are referred to in case notes as 'victim' and 'perpetrator, abuser or offender' regardless of legal status. In the cases studied by Margolin: "The truth of abuse was problematic since more than half of the suspects either denied the accusations or were not interviewed. Social workers 'made do' without supportive testimony from suspects by routinely defining them as 'non-credible' witnesses. Also, social workers managed to conform to agency regulations requiring proof that suspected abusers intended to do harm or exploit children by agreeing to treat specific observables as if they represented the intent to harm or exploit." (p. 67) Many who write reports about child abuse, Margolin argues, are enmeshed in a syntactical system of shared meanings which are peculiar to the child protection field: when dealing with emotive issues such as child sexual abuse, we often produce anxious agendas and ways of processing clients. Some social workers have been infected with the moral panic prevalent in some sectors of society when faced with increasing reports of child sexual abuse. Not only have case loads of child protection workers increased dramatically in response to widespread concerns about CSA; the actual number of available social workers has been reduced in local government, state and provincial arenas in the face of sometimes massive financial cuts.

Social Work Research Literature

Front-line social workers are caught in a vice: on one side is the moral pressure to do something about child abuse; on the other is the lack of resources to intervene and support the family effectively. It is all too easy for social workers to intervene merely to remove a child, without reference to the child's needs and the actual justice issues involved. Hard-pressed social workers can make wrong diagnoses, or shape facts to fit pre-conceived, symbolic categories which make the role of a social worker pressed almost to breaking point have a semblance of meaning, however much the various categorizations imposed are at variance with reality. Often these categories differ from those perceived or felt by the clients themselves, and by other important people within the client's social or ecological system. This problem is dramatically illustrated in the study of McGee et al. (1995) who reviewed the documentation and personal accounts of a random selection 160 adolescents on the caseload of a child welfare agency in Ontario. Forty social workers involved with these 160 adolescents (many of whom had been on the agency's caseload for many years) completed a questionnaire describing the types of abuse or neglect the adolescents had experienced. The study team also reviewed the written files, while the adolescents themselves completed questionnaires about what actually happened to them, and about their emotional states and behavioural problems. There was poor agreement between what the adolescents perceived, and what social workers thought had happened, in terms of physical, sexual and emotional maltreatment. The social workers claimed that 37 per cent of the young people had been sexually abused: but this did not agree well with what the adolescents said had happened, with imperfect overlap about whether CSA had occurred: thus some half of those whom social workers said had been sexually abused did not confirm this. McGee et al. (1995) cannot explain why the perceptions of the 'victims', and those of social workers about what allegedly happened are often so much at variance. One possible explanation is the that role of social workers in an era of cutbacks is so constrained by constant crisis that good, rational social work which truly does justice to the victim's needs and perceptions is only atypically possible. The more constrained and hazardous the social worker's role, the more likely (in my experience) it is that social workers will use symbolic categories and moral stereotypes in trying to impose order on a chaotic world.

Another way for social workers to cope is to ignore many referrals, only accepting those which fit perceptions of what is an important or deserving case. In the U.S. today some 40 per cent of allegations of child sexual abuse made to social workers are not investigated further (Bagley and Thurston, 1996a). No study has explained why this is so: but hard-pressed social workers may only investigate cases which fit some kind of moral stereotype; or they might have a genuine instinct for identifying cases to investigate in which abuse really did take place. Despite this between 40 and 60 per cent of cases of alleged sexual abuse which social workers do investigate turn out to be false alarms: after extensive interrogations of alleged perpetrators, and interviews with the child and his or her caretakers, no *prima facie* case can be made that sexual abuse did in fact occur.

System-induced Trauma: Inhumane Treatment of Child Victims

Of course, many children are sexually abused, and often experience negative mental health sequels as a result of this abuse: we know this from several adult recall studies carried out in Canada and the U.S.A. (Bagley, 1995 and 1997; Bagley and Thurston, 1996a and b). However, even when sexual abuse really did occur, experience of the way that 'the system' handles the victim can, for some children, be worse than the actual abuse itself. Krieger and Robbins (1985) for example, tracked several hundred female incest victims through the California judicial system. For a girl to make public the incestuous assault is a difficult decision: she is not certain she will be believed and supported; adolescents know too that their family life will be disrupted. Often the girl (not the alleged offender) is removed from home: why should she be punished by being removed from her home, possessions, siblings, school life and friends? Often the group home where she is placed is far from her own home. She is questioned by social workers, police and prosecutors again and again, and is also subjected to humiliating and sometimes painful gynaecological examinations. A long period between the interview and any court hearing reinforces the girl's feelings that she is unimportant, and is being revictimized. Therapy which addresses the details of the abuse cannot begin until court dispositions are over, since this could be construed as coaching (and possibly distorting) a witness's testimony.[1]

The adolescents' main themes in the qualitative research by Krieger and Robins (1985) are ones of insignificance, guilt and hopelessness. These feelings arise not only from the experience of incest and the often impaired sense of self which incest victims develop, but also from insensitive, indeed inhuman processing by the judicial system. The authors argue that all intervention on behalf of the victim should have the purpose of *empowering* him or her from the outset, consulting her at all stages of the process, respecting her wishes, and keeping her fully informed of all the procedures which are being undertaken. If a decision is made not to prosecute an offender she may feel betrayed; if the offender pleads not guilty she may be humiliated in cross-examination. Although young children's testimony is often videotaped, this is much less frequent for adolescents. Even when she is screened from the offender in court, defence counsel may still ask questions which imply that she is lying.

Maddock (1988), a social work researcher and therapist uses a symbolic interactionist framework to address social constructions of abuse, and how these impact not only on the alleged offender, but on the victim as well. Incestuous families are frequently marked by distorted patterns of communication, power and roles; the daughter's sexual experience with a family

---

[1] In Britain one solution to 'protect' the young adolescent who reports sexual abuse in the pre-trial period is to confine them in a secure residential centre, along with disturbed and suicidal adolescents, and young offenders on remand - including young rapists. According to our research with 15 of these centres, CSA victims are frequently raped by the young offenders within the secure units. The rationales for putting CSA victims in such centres are (a) the victim might remain in danger in his or her home, with pressures to retract; (b) they might run from home; (c) the expensive beds in the secure units have to kept at 100 per cent occupancy.

member may be part of the fragile balance of relationships in a pathological family. When seeking outside help, the child must respond to differing contextual cues that are likely to require a different construction of reality. "Thus the stage is set for uncertainty, self-contradiction, and lack of consistency in accounts of alleged abuse" (p. 201). Maddock cites evidence from clinical work indicating that although some children have been victims of brutal and exploitive sexual abuse, many others have been enmeshed in family sexuality which was not brutal or power-driven in its motivations (these typologies are elaborated in Maddock and Larson, 1995). Many cases of incestuous abuse are tied to a loosening of the normal role boundaries of family life, as the child is pulled into a sexual partnership governed by subtle norms of a family isolated from outside moral and social systems. Intervention sub-systems (social workers, police prosecutors, therapists) each have their own moral and procedural agendas, and there may be direct or disguised conflict about how the child who has revealed sexual abuse should be handled.

Maddock argues that in research, clinical work, and public policy we must distinguish carefully between descriptive, explanatory and evaluative accounts of incestuous behaviour. Those with most power in family intervention work should develop a pluralistic sociology of knowledge about incest, and listen carefully to the child's view of his or her family as the most important account. Once the type of family system has been diagnosed, the sexual exploitation of the child should not usually lead to a criminal trial, since the judicial process is generally inimical to the child's best long-term interests. Even when trials proceed, there are strong grounds for not putting a child on the stand as a witness; an electronically recorded interview might be introduced, but asking the child to corroborate this in trial proceedings. But enduring cross-examination is likely to undermine therapy for the child and his or her family, especially in jurisdictions where no therapy can begin until after trial proceedings have been exhausted.

Psychological evaluation of victims should not be servant to the goals of prosecution: its primary purpose should be aimed at assisting in the process of healing the child victim. Any procedures which do not have this direct purpose, Maddock argues, should not be undertaken. Often the family can be healed, and it is this healing, not the process of criminal trial, that should have priority. The only clear legal goal should be to permanently separate an alleged offender from his family when prospects for offender rehabilitation are complex or uncertain.

The evidence of the stress which child sexual abuse investigations have on children is clear from a number of studies (outlined more fully in Bagley and

Thurston, 1996a). For example, Tedesco and Schnell (1987) asked 49 victims, all aged thirteen, how they regarded the whole process of investigation and trial. The respondents reported being interviewed from one to 40 times by an average of seven adults. The interviews by 169 men, and 133 women lasted from 15 minutes to several hours, the average length of interview being about two hours. In only 54 per cent of cases was the trial process completed. Only 48 per cent of the adolescents said that the pre-trial interviews with police and lawyers were helpful; while 19 per cent rated the process as very harmful. Those who had to testify in court were more likely to rate the whole interview process as negative, compared with those whose cases did not go the full course of a criminal trial. Therapists for the adolescents rated the legal interview process as harmful for 71 per cent.

Sauzier's (1989) follow-up study of 115 sexually abused children (mostly girls, average age 10.1 years when abuse was revealed) illustrates further the hazardous process of interrogation and examination imposed on the child. All children received an extensive psychological assessment on referral; two thirds had experienced serious, prolonged or bodily intrusive abuse by a family member. At follow-up 18 months after initial assessment, most showed a significant decrease in symptoms, and an increase in levels of self-esteem: but 24 per cent showed deterioration in mental health and self-esteem levels. This group included most of the girls who regretted having disclosed the sexual abuse. Regret was linked to lack of acceptance of the victim by family members, or actual blaming of her by non-offending parent and/or siblings, and other significant adults. Decline in mental health and self-confidence was also linked to long delays before a court case, and unsympathetic interviewing and processing of the victim. One half of the victims and/or her family found the process of investigation and interrogation by a variety of professionals, unhelpful or traumatic. Overall, 45 per cent of non-offending parents said that the disclosure (rather than the abuse) had harmed the child.

However, the most important factor in poor long-term adjustment of victims was mother's anger at the child for having revealed the sexual relationship. These girls had angry and punitive mothers who were more likely to be chronically unsupportive. Such girls were likely to be removed from their homes by social workers, and felt guilt and shame at the trouble and disgrace they felt they had imposed on their families by revealing the abuse. The clinical case material Sauzier presents makes it clear that sexual abuse often occurs in, or reflects chronic family dysfunction, and a significant minority of the girls who reveal sexual abuse are only atypically given support by her mother and siblings. 'Most of the 19 per cent of adolescents who regretted their disclosure

34

wanted the abuse to stop but ended up feeling that they had destroyed their families. Their disclosure set into motion forces that they could not control any more than they could their abusers' (Sauzier, 1989, p. 468).

Often, it seemed, the bland reassuring words of social workers or clinicians following revelation were at odds with what was really happening. Sometimes this led to recantation, and sexual victimization by another adult. The child who is not supported following revelation of sexual abuse may enter a cycle of promiscuity and running from home or from a residential centre. On the streets these girls are at considerable risk of being pulled into drug and prostitution subcultures (Bagley, 1995 and 1997). In terms of the typology of abuse victims, the victims described by Sauzier (1989) seem similar to those women described by Wyatt et al. (1993) who had been abused within dysfunctional blue collar families, and were at risk for revictimization and later dysfunctional sexual behaviours.

Often, the procedures of criminal trial block or delay therapeutic help for the victim and her family. since therapy can be construed by defence counsel as a process which can distort or colour victim's memory of prior events. In Martone, Jaudes and Cavins' (1996) study police proceeded against 51 per cent of alleged offenders: the average time from first report to the conclusion of the trial took 1.4 years, during which time direct therapy with the victim could not begin. Crucial windows of opportunity for beginning therapy may have been lost. The conclusion for America that that courts trying cases of CSA further victimise children (Dziech and Schudson, 1991) may also apply to Britian (see below).

These findings have some obvious policy implications: the child's needs must come first, and often those needs coincide with those of her mother (who has often herself had an abusive childhood). Social work intervention should protect the child and offer family therapy. Social workers should have the legal power to apply to a court for an order requiring an alleged abuser to remove himself from the household. Therapy for the victim should begin immediately, and should involve both individual and well-established models of family therapy (e.g. Giarretto, 1982; Bentovim et al, 1988; Furniss, 1991; Maddock and Larson, 1995) - therapeutic models which should be applied by skilled, experienced social workers unharried by continued underfunding of child protection and victim therapy services. Alleged offenders should be invited to co-operate in the treatment process (in the case of within-family abuse), in return for probation or suspended sentence. It is important that the process should avoid the trauma of a criminal trial in which the child is aggressively cross-examined, if at all possible.

A Canadian attempt (Sas, 1991) to prepare children for testimony in child sexual abuse trials indicated only limited success: in this Ontario study, 144 alleged victims of child sexual abuse were divided into three groups and given either no pre-trial preparation; verbal explanations about what giving evidence would involve; or five individual preparation sessions including role play, visits to court, and counselling (which for legal reasons could not address abuse issues) to reduce stress and anxiety about the court appearance. These children were in legal limbo for up to two years (the period between revelation of abuse, and the actual trial), and this wait was itself traumatic. The experiment was somewhat successful, in that prosecutors (blind to the experiment) judged those children in the intensive programme to be the most relaxed and assured when giving evidence. Yet the limited success of this experiment can be judged from the fact that the average time in legal limbo was 322 days: in 127 cases this limbo (or period of purgatory) was ended when prosecutors decided not to proceed with the case. [2] Finally, only 37 men (26 per cent of the total) who were charged and pleaded not guilty were finally convicted, with the aid of the child's evidence. The intensive preparation programme made virtually no difference to the actual number of men finally found guilty.

A review of the processing of child sexual abuse cases by the Crown Prosecution Service in England and Wales (1998) reached the extraordinary conclusion that up to eight in ten barristers briefed to prosecute such cases dropped out of the prosecution because of pressure of other (apparently more interesting or lucrative) work. This inevitably means that dates set for trial will be postponed, with the inevitable feelings of frustration and anti-climax for the alleged victim. Yet until the court case is resolved, therapy for a victim cannot begin since such therapy would inevitably address the details of the abuse, which a court would construe as a distortion of the victim's memory of the events.

As Saywitz and Nathanson (1993) have found, court appearances for the sexually abused child continue to be very stressful events. This seems to be an inevitable outcome of a judicial system which pursues the goals of retribution, with often lengthy sentences for sexual offenders found guilty. Faced with a long prison term it is not surprising that the accused man, however guilty, will deny the offence. And of course, in this process the child rather than

---

[2] Because of a lack of Crown prosecutors some cases are now abandoned because the length of time between charge and trial would violate the right to a speedy trial guaranteed by the Canadian constitution.

the offender is likely to suffer, especially when despite the stress the victim has undergone in the trial process, the abuser is acquitted: this happens not infrequently. There must be a better way, a better balance to be struck between goals of justice and therapy. Indeed, the best justice is often for the child to recover his or her psychological equilibrium, rather than being involved in the long process of retribution. In return, we should expect the offenders to admit guilt in return for non-custodial admonition, and partake in the process of family therapy when required (Bagley, 1997).

The Problems of Mandatory Reporting

The North American lobby to enact laws requiring all professionals to report 'reasonable or probable suspicion' of child sexual abuse to police or child protection authorities was supported by a wide range of interest groups. These laws were enacted in all American states and Canadian provinces in the 1980s, but with varying provisions, as in Quebec (see below). Evidence indicates that these legal requirements have not worked well. At first it seemed that the professional who failed to report would be chastised with the same moral vigour with which the alleged malefactors were pursued. This has not happened however, and it is now apparent that many cases are not referred by professional therapists, once they understand that processing of the child by legal and social work systems is often counter-productive, sometimes results in worse harms than the abuse itself, and also impedes the practice of therapy when the child is anxiously waiting for the offender's trial to be over.

Mandatory reporting in the 1980s flooded social work agencies charged with administering Child Welfare statutes with referrals which had to be investigated. In New York State Eckenrode et al. (1988) studied 796 reports which suspected sexual abuse of children. After exhaustive investigations it was determined that only 44 per cent of reports by professionals (mental health workers, physicians, hospital staff, social service agencies, and teachers) were substantiated, compared with 33 per cent of reports from relatives, neighbours or anonymous calls or letters. In reaction to the demands made (at a time when many social service agencies were down-sizing, and caseloads increasing dramatically) some child protection agencies have used their own criteria of what constitutes a *bona fide* complaint that is worth investigating. These decisions are made on the basis of good professional judgement (at best) and stereotypes (at worst). Because of moral and perceptual biases, McGovern (1991) argues, real cases of sexual abuse may be missed. Mandatory reporting, according to Zellman and Antler (1990) creates 'a system in dispair' with confused and bewildered social workers.

The effect which mandatory reporting laws can have on adults voluntarily seeking treatment is illustrated by Berlin, Malin and Dean (1991) who operated a Boston psychiatric clinic which treated sexual abusers, actual and potential. Following the passage of a mandatory reporting law, self-referrals (i.e. voluntary help-seeking) fell to zero. Abusers would no longer seek help, knowing that to do so might well lead to prosecution. The authors conclude that the mandatory reporting law has likely put children at greater risk of sexual abuse, since actual and potential abusers are now afraid to seek voluntary treatment. Hutchison (1993) examined the effects of sexual abuse reporting laws from a U.S. social work perspective, and concludes that on balance they have harmed rather than helped children at risk. She makes the following points:

(1)   Families investigated following abuse allegations are predominantly working class and poor. Yet only about 40 percent of these allegations are founded. The humiliated but innocent family, often with fragile self-esteem, rarely receives an apology and almost never any family support services or counselling. As Thompson-Cooper, Fugere and Cormier (1993) point out 'trauma repair' for the invaded family is rarely possible, given the harassed workload of child protection teams.

(2)   Hutchison (1993) shows that over 12 years in America there has been a 225 per cent increase in allegations of abuse and neglect. States have only been able to contain the economic costs of investigating abuse allegations by decreasing supports for families in which abuse has in fact occurred. At the same time, funding for children's social work services has decreased by at least 10 per cent. Many cases, even when there is *prima facie* evidence of abuse, are not given supportive services: children are often removed to foster care for a short or long period, and then returned to their families without any therapeutic support for the child or his or her family.

(3)   There is evidence that around 60 per cent of American professionals working with children do not comply with compulsory reporting laws, for various reasons: disruption of a therapeutic relationship; an awareness that legal proceedings may actually harm the victim; fear of litigation if their suspicion proves groundless (a danger only when

38

white, middle class families are investigated); and an awareness that if a case is reported, the possibility of effective support for the family and the victim are low. Around 700,000 families in America undergo investigations of unfounded abuse reports each year.

Hutchison argues for a repeal of mandatory reporting laws, focussing instead on educational campaigns which would encourage non-offending parents and children themselves to report abuse, in the expectation that they would be given effective, non-stigmatizing help. Thompson-Cooper at al. (1993) reach similar conclusions, arguing that 'false negatives' (missing abuse when it did actually occur) are much more important than 'false positives' (invading an innocent family on the false assumption that abuse occurred). More research and new practice models are needed in order to provide supportive long-term, non-stigmatizing services for families truly at risk.

Finkelhor and Zellman (1991) agree (from their national U.S. survey of human service professionals) that reporting requirements have often undermined good relations between clients, therapists and social workers. Both families in which abuse is known, and offenders themselves are inhibited from being frank about problems. In order to overcome this dilemma they argue for a special category of professional who would be licensed as an individual not having to report suspected abuse to police. The problem with this proposal (as the authors acknowledge) is that middle class individuals and families might seek out such professionals, knowing that abuse would not be referred. Poor people in contrast would have neither the knowledge nor the resources to consult these high level professionals. The system would continue to stigmatize and label the poor, often removing their children without proper treatment, family support, or permanency planning.

Reporting requirements have in Bernet's (1995) study of mental health professionals created a group of therapists who are 'running scared', with 'excessive concerns about following the rules' about reporting sexual abuse to authorities. As in previous studies, this rule-bound, even ritualistic behaviour was often not in the best interests of the children involved.

Persecuting the Victim: Case 1

This case concerns a 10-year-old girl who was sexually assaulted by five of her male classmates in the boys' lavatory. Her complaint to a teacher led to police investigation, and the charging of the boys (also aged ten) for rape and indecent assault. The boys appeared in the dock at the Old Bailey, England's central court for the trial of malefactors. Charged with indictable offences, the five boys faced imprisonment in secure youth custody. In these adult-type criminal proceedings the ten-year old defendants were each represented by a barrister practised in criminal trial procedures, who vigorously cross-examined the girl for several hours. She was cross-examined in a room separate from the main court (but linked by video camera) so that all could see her distress, and the girl frequently broke down and the questioning took frequent pauses whilst the girl got over her spells of sobbing. The defence counsel accused the girl of making up stories about the assault, and then accused her of going voluntarily into the boys' lavatory in order to have sex with her boy friend. The boys were represented by three different defence lawyers, and each made the girl go over her story again and again, pouncing on inconsistencies. According to a press report (Lee, 1998): "Once she pulled the microphone from her black tracksuit top and refused to continue. She constantly kneaded a set of 'worry balls' in her hands and the judge halted proceedings an hour early when the girl had enough questions" (p. 3).

One of the accused was the child's cousin, and it was from this boy's family that defence counsel learned that the girl had been sexually assaulted by a male relative at the age of six. She described how this man took girls to his home where "... he liked to get his friends and hurt us. He beat us." She was raped twice by this man. Counsel implied that she had enjoyed these assaults, and as a result was always chasing after boys:

Counsel: "Did you go into the boys' toilet and ask them to be your boyfriends?"

Girl: "That is such a lie. I did not ask to be their girlfriend. All I asked for was my coat back."

Counsel: "They were in the boys' toilet, you wanted them to touch you, didn't you?"

Girl: "No, that's a lie. I wasn't playing with them. They forced me to do this. They were going to beat me up."

Later the girl admitted that she had been excluded from school for fighting. Counsel claimed that she had lied to teachers.

40

Is it possible that the experience in court was worse for this girl than the actual sexual assault? Has not in this case the judicial system persecuted an assaulted child? Where is the logic, the decency, the humanity in such action? After five days of legal representations, examinations and cross-examinations the court finally decided that because the girl had given contradictory evidence under cross-examination that her evidence was unsafe. The case was dismissed.

In Canada (where the age of criminal responsibility is twelve, and not ten) such a case if it came to court at all, would have been dealt with in the civil jurisdiction of the family court. The child victim would have made a statement to a social worker, who would have given evidence on her behalf, without the need for the child's court attendance. The boys, on the evidence presented certainly had disrobed and interfered with the child, even though within the strict rules of evidence in criminal trials, this could not be proved to be rape. In a Canadian Family Court the future of the boys would have been considered within a child welfare framework, and the likely outcome would have been support for family supervision and behavioural counselling for the young sexual assailants.

Searching for a reason for the Old Bailey cross-examination and the judicial persecution of the 10-year-old victim I return to the symbolic interactionist account of society. Social action evolves through symbolic rituals in which sexual abuse assumes some kind of totemic value, an end in itself whose emanations are surrounded with a series of rituals which dehumanize the subjects involved, be they malefactors or victims. Indeed, the victims have been smeared with the poison of sexual abuse and, like someone with HIV, must be handled with the protection of rubber gloves and at arm's length. Of course, the victims *may* be innocent, but the soldiers of the judicial army cannot allow such a humane supposition to interfere with the awful majesty of justice. If we are touched by the victim's humanity, like her we may be infected with the disease of sexual abuse.

Persecuting the Victim: Case 2

When children and young adolescents are convicted of rape and sexual assault, but are too young for regular youth detention, some are now confined to a secure residential centre. In 1997 there were 27 such centres in England and Wales, and the majority were fully occupied (by about 3,000 youngsters aged less than 16) for all of the year. These are expensive institutions, and society cannot afford separate centres for separate kinds of children (aged 10 and up).

All of the imprisoned children have a common burden to bear: they must be locked up and not allowed to escape into the body of society. These are children suffering from social and psychological disease, and must be handled at arm's length. According to our study (Brogi and Bagley, 1998) various types of imprisoned children are herded together behind the locked doors and gates of these institutions: youth on remand for serious crimes (arson, rape, murder) too young at aged 14 or less to be remanded to ordinary youth detention centres; children and young adolescents convicted of rape and murder, too young for the company of older adolescents; young adolescents who engage in persistent self-harm and suicidal behaviours for whom no specialist psychiatric beds are available; and sexually abused children waiting to give evidence in trial against their alleged abuser. The reason that victims are locked up is because they are thought to be at risk of either being further abused by a within-family abuser; or it is feared that they may return voluntarily to the abuser. Many of the chronically suicidal adolescents are also victims of sexual abuse. What is the net effect of locking up young rapists with young sexual abuse victims? The question hardly needs asking: we have numerous case study evidence of the effect - the girls (and sometimes the boys) are raped, again and again by their fellow inmates, and now they have nowhere to run. The Managers of the secure centres are frequently unhappy about the mix of children and young people, but they cannot decline to admit children whom social workers require to be admitted under a relevant section of the 1989 Children Act.

Browne and Felshaw (1996) confirm previous research in showing that forty per cent of the males admitted to secure centres have a conviction for sexual assault, while the majority of females admitted have been sexually abused. Is it not fitting that abusers and abused should be locked up together, left to play out their filthiness away from society's gaze? Relax: our own children are safe.

Persecuting the Victim: Case 3

A third example of how British justice persecutes victims concerns the prosecution of juvenile prostitutes for soliciting - a legal nonsense which fortunately does not exist in Canada. Every week dozens of young teenagers are fined for this offence. The men who purchase their sexuality are never prosecuted. The legal system licences sexual abuse by default: if you wish to sexually abuse a 13-year-old all you need to know is which part of the city to frequent, which pub to enter, and have fifty pounds in your pocket.

Interim Conclusion

Interventions in the field of child sexual abuse should meet three standards:

(1)   the needs of children should be paramount;

(2)   interventions should be rational, based on careful enquiries which avoid stereotypical labelling based on symbolic categorizations resorted to by harassed professionals;

(3)   interventions should overall be humane, not only first meeting the needs of children, but also attempting to heal and strengthen families, and also addressing the needs of abusers and potential abusers for support, therapy and forgiveness.

The system of child sexual abuse intervention which has emerged in America, Canada and Britain has been too much based on blind emotion and precipitous action which has put the welfare of children at risk, and has also failed to support abusers in ways which would prevent further children from being sexually victimized. The debacle of mandatory reporting laws well illustrates processing systems (including some social work bureaucracies) which have not been rational or humane, and have not served the interests of children well.

The British system, it its ritual degradation of young victims in courts and secure centres illustrates the horrifying reality of a society which has failed to grasp the humanistic approach to problems of sexual abuse, pioneered by psychiatrists such as Bentovim and Furniss.

A study by Victim Support (a charity for victims of crime) provides evidence of the general failure of British courts to attend to the needs of child witnesses. In a study of 1,000 children in 26 Crown Courts (Gibb, 1996) it was found that children had to wait for hours and sometimes successive days in the court building waiting to give evidence. Judges did not always allow children to give evidence on a closed circuit system, and the case is cited of an 11 year old girl who become incoherent with terror when she was called to give evidence in open court - the case was dismissed.

A survey of CSA cases by the NSPCC (Ghouri, 1997) found that two thirds of workers reported that the Criminal Court process frightened or confused the child. An alternative Family Court procedure was advocated by many workers. A report by the Crown Prosecution Service (Syal, 1998) found that three quarters of barristers dropped the cases assigned to them, often at short notice, causing further postponements of the trial. The report notes that such "returned briefs" are particularly likely to result in distress for children waiting to give evidence in abuse cases.

The Quebec Model

The Quebec model highlights a major dilemma in frontline work with alleged cases of child sexual abuse: the degree to which a full range of professionals should be involved in investigating and processing of cases. If police and crown prosecutors are to be involved, careful co-ordination with child protection and therapy teams is needed. In the USA and Canada some 50 per cent of child sexual abuse complaints turn out to be unfounded (because of mistaken assumptions, rather than because of false allegations.) One solution to the difficult and often wasteful deployment of scarce resources is to leave the matter of police and crown involvement to the discretion of investigating social workers. The merit of the Quebec model is that much of the system-induced trauma which effects a child or adolescent when child sexual abuse (CSA) is investigated, may be avoided.

Quebec has a legal system which has led to child welfare legislation that is rather different from that derived from the common law tradition of Anglophone North America (Pelletier, 1980). Quebec's legal tradition, derived in part from the tradition of the Napoleonic Code of Justice allowed the passage of Bill 24 in the 1980s. In this, the Legislature of Quebec set up an entirely new procedure in the area of youth protection. Instead of requiring mandatory referral of the case in which a child has been allegedly abused to judicial mechanisms, it entrusts each child to a Youth Protection Director in local Social Service Centres, with the task of evaluating the situation and then orienting the person or persons involved towards the proper help or treatment.

It is in this process of dealing with abuse allegations in a non-judicial way that the Youth and Family Counselling Centres have been given the authority to treat incest cases in ways which, in their professional judgement, would serve the child's best interests. Distinctions can be made by these Centres between situations in which incest or sexual assault is a result of a marked sexual deviation (in which case the paedophile abuser will be separated from a family on application to a court) and those in which in the judgement of social workers, incest is a result of a family dysfunction. In this latter case prosecution of the abuser/offender will not usually be sought. (The approach has much similarity to that described by Maddock and Larson, 1995).

Legislation on 'endangered children' was codified in Quebec's Youth Protection Act in 1988 (Sansfacon and Presentey, 1993). Police learning of a case of CSA are required to report this case to the Youth Protection Service (YPS), and not *vice versa* as in other Canadian provinces. The YPS has a specific mandate to avoid criminal processing of individuals involved in CSA whenever possible, particularly when CSA occurs within the family context. However, case histories provided by Sansfacon and Presentey indicate that social workers can and do use criminal prosecution as an instrument of leverage to obtain desired ends in cases of incestuous abuse (e.g. requiring the male abuser to leave the family setting, and desist from sexual abuse). About 25 per cent of cases dealt with by Youth Protection Workers were referred to the criminal justice system when the 'voluntary co-operation' of the offender is in doubt. The sentence imposed in the adult courts for sexual abuse of children was usually probation, regardless of the charge laid. The exceptions included offenders who have required a child to engage in prostitution, and violent rape of a child. In these cases, imprisonment would follow conviction. Several CSA assessment and treatment centres existed in Quebec which provide a family-based therapy model, based on Giarretto's humanistic model.

A systematic evaluation of this important Quebec model, with comparison with an Anglophone Province, has yet to be undertaken. Crucial questions are (a) whether this model results in less trauma to CSA victims; and (b) whether leaving social workers to decide when and if to involve legal sanctions is reflected in greater or lesser amounts of recidivism (i.e. further abuse of the child, or of other children).[3]

---

3   Alas, the hopes for this pioneering Quebec model seem now to be dashed. The anonymous reviewer of this chapter has commented on the current (1998) situation in Quebec, noting four reasons for the demise of Quebec system:

"a)   Over the last five years the ratio of legal versus voluntary treatment plans in child sexual abuse cases reported in Quebec has gone from 1:4 to 4:1 ... meaning the legal options by far dominate the voluntary in current child sexual abuse cases, a complete reversal of practices of five to six years ago.

b)   There is a very strong feminist plus police lobby that is attempting to modify practices so as to require that all cases of child sexual abuse be reported by youth protection services to police. An interministerial committee (COMAS) will deposit recommendations ... by the end of 1998. The arguments marshaled in the chapter under review are very relevant to the debate and were presented in 1996-7 to the commission by various researchers and social workers. Publication of the main thrust of this chapter will be very timely for this type of 'reform' driven debate in North America.

Conclusions

There is ample evidence from child protection workers and therapists of how *not* to address the problems of child sexual abuse. The key maxims for good practice which emerge from this review are:

(1)   Don't panic, don't overreact. Moral panic leads to distorted perceptions, and even witch hunts in which the interests of the children are lost.

(2)   *Everything* that is done must be in the child's best interests; moralistic reactions, and fervour for persecuting the alleged offender should not interfere with the superordinate goal of keeping the child comfortable, safe and happy. Mothers of abuse victims need special support, since their role in supporting their daughter's recovery is crucial.

(3)   Immediate, skilled assessment of a family in which alleged abuse has occurred should be undertaken, as well assessment of the child's need for therapy. Therapy for victim and family should begin immediately, and should not have to wait until trial procedures are over. Helping the child is more important than prosecuting the offender. Support and apology should be given to investigated families where sexual abuse did not occur, but in which other forms of family dysfunction may be present.

---

c)   Sentences for child sexual abuse aggressors in Quebec are now less and less for probation terms.

d)   Specialized child sexual abuse assessment and treatment centers that did exist in may areas up to 1994 are now being disbanded, so that by 1998 only one exists ... Many factors have motivated this radical change, according to the paper by Wright, Lebeau and Perron (1998) to the currently standing Cliche commission on the reform of child protection services in Quebec: (1) a 25 per cent social services budget cut over three years; (b) massive application of the principle of 'get the basic services back to the community' at the expense of specialized central services in all but one center; (c) belief that specialized child sexual abuse services in Quebec were largely ineffective; (d) belief that child sexual abuse often leaves little psychosocial distress; and (e) belief that a massive redeployment of budgets toward prevention is a better investment than curative approaches, reflecting the flawed logic that prevention and cure are somehow at odds."

(4)   The ability to apply to a court for an order to require an alleged offender to leave (where incestuous abuse is suspected) is essential, but is lacking in most Canadian provincial child welfare acts, and in the British Children Act of 1989.

(5)   Work with the alleged offender, offering non-custodial sentences and possible return to his family once a therapist is sure that recidivism will not occur. Enlist the father's co-operation in family therapy, when this is appropriate.

(6)   Reporting laws have not worked, and should be abandoned. Public messages should be addressed to offenders and potential offenders, advising them that they can obtain support and therapy without fear of being turned over to the police.

(7)   Social work teams operating child protection and therapy programmes should be fully staffed, experienced, and not harassed by large caseloads.

(8)   Social workers should have the option not to refer alleged child sex offenders to police for investigation. Judicial referral should only occur (as in the Quebec model) when this is considered to be in the child's best interests, or in cases where society's (and children's) interests require that violent or persistent offenders must be prosecuted.

(9)   Blaming victims of sexual abuse, and persecuting them in the court system and in secure institutions is not the mark of a civilized society.

PART II
CLINICAL ISSUES

3 Is Family Dysfunction More Harmful than Child Sexual Abuse? A Controlled Study

GUY PELLETIER AND LEE C. HANDY

Family Dynamics in Cases of Intrafamilial Sexual Abuse

It is now a well accepted notion that intrafamilial sexual abuse is a problem which generally involves the whole family unit (Alexander, 1985; Friedman, 1988; Pelletier and Handy, 1986; Bagley and Thurston, 1996). The model provided by Steinhauer et al (1984) can be used to generate predictions as to what might be wrong in a family where a member sexually abuses one or many others. Such predictions and the model itself can be further supported by observations of families where CSA occurs. Most of the information available on family process and child sexual abuse has been derived from observations of families where the children were abused by a father figure (father, step-father, or common-law-husband). Thus, the following discussion will be limited to this form of CSA, with the tentative assumption that the processes described bear some similarity to what happens in families where uncle-niece, grandfather-granddaughter, and brother-sister incest occurs.

Many researchers and clinicians agree that families where sexual abuse of a girl by a father figure takes place tend to have many distinctive characteristics. Most obviously, the marital dyad is dysfunctional. The spouses are often dissatisfied with their erotic relationship, they express few feelings, and they have limited capacity for negotiating sexual or other marital and family issues. Often, at least one spouse has opted out of or been incapacitated in his/her functions as a companion and a parent, a situation which sometimes increases the children's vulnerability to abuse (Barnard, 1983; Friedman, 1988; Larson and Maddock, 1986; Mrazek and Bentovim, 1981; Pelletier and Handy, 1986). The dysfunctional marriages are further characterised by unequal and sometimes extreme distributions of power between spouses.

Stern and Meyer (1980) and Trepper and Barrett (1986), apparently quite independently, developed almost identical classifications of interactional patterns in couples which appear to be linked to the occurrence of intrafamilial

51

sexual abuse. Stern and Meyer named their three types possessive-passive, dependent-domineering, and "incestrogenic". Trepper and Barrett described four types which they call father executive, mother executive, chaotic, and 'third generation'. Trepper and Barrett's first three categories are virtually identical to Stern and Meyer's. Trepper and Barrett described their fourth category, the third generation, as characterised by a mother who plays the role of a 'grandparent', and dominates an executive father. She sometimes acts like a distant observer, and occasionally moves closely in order to exert great influence on decisions being made. In this dynamic, the daughter apparently behaves like her father's companion when the mother is emotionally absent, but as a daughter in her presence. Examples of such a dynamic were not found in the literature, and Trepper and Barrett presented no case study. Therefore, this category will be left aside until confirmation at least by case study can be obtained.

However, the first three other categories are well reported by case studies in the literature. Stern and Meyer's (1980) possessive-passive type and Trepper and Barrett's (1986) father executive type are both characterised by a patriarchal husband who dominates a passive wife and dependent children. Such families are often described as conventional, financially stable households where the father controls everything with absolute authority, sometimes imposed by force (Herman, 1981). Men in these types of relationships have often been described as manipulative, domineering, and unpredictable. However, they often present a public persona of conventional and responsible family men. They tend to select immature, ineffective spouses who can be kept financially dependent and isolated. The family functions according to a rigid structure where traditional gender roles are strongly upheld. Examples of cases involving this type of relationship have been given by Bogopolski and Cormier (1979), Groth (1982), and Herman (1981).

The second interactional pattern of couples described by Stern and Meyer (1980) and Trepper and Barrett (1986), and often encountered in the literature is identified as the union of a dependent, inadequate man and a strong, domineering woman. Typically, the mother executive dynamic involves a man who looks to his wife for support and nurturance and appears incapable of meeting her emotional needs. He has little power in the family, but can assert himself with excessive force when he is intoxicated (Groth, 1982). The wives of such men are described as more assertive, educated, and capable than the wives of possessive husbands, and tend to be colder and more rejecting toward their children. Examples of cases showing such patterns are provided by Bigras, Bouchard, Coleman-Porter, and Tasse (1966), Furniss (1983), and Groth (1982).

The 'incestrogenic' (Stern and Meyer, 1980), or 'chaotic' (Trepper and Barrett, 1986; Will, 1983) pattern is characterised by the union of two very dependent adults who cannot meet each other's overwhelming needs. Both are inadequate in their roles as parents and spouse, and all members of the family tend to show poor judgement and low impulse control. CSA is only one aspect of the confusion in roles typical of such households. Detailed studies of such dynamics are presented by Eist and Mandel (1968) and Will (1983).

In addition to marital dysfunction, a second dysfunctional characteristic often observed in families where CSA occurs is that appropriate generational boundaries are broken down. As pointed out by Conte (1986), this fact can be seen as obvious, since by definition, CSA indicates a breakdown in boundaries. However, it seems that most authors describe a process which usually starts before sexual abuse of a child takes place, which might facilitate the offender's access to the child. Appropriate generational boundaries break when roles in the family are blurred or reversed, with the children often in the position of parents or triangulated in parental conflicts. As the parental dyad deteriorates, the breaking down of boundaries can be observed in two ways. First, the adults lack respect for the children's developmental readiness and exploit their body-contact needs in an atmosphere where there is little regard for privacy. Second, the children are drawn into attempts to compensate for their parents' ineffectiveness, and as they continue in roles where they meet inappropriate expectations, they develop 'pseudomature' behaviours in order to prevent the disintegration of the family. Many clinicians have noted the frequent 'role reversal' between mother and daughter in families where intrafamilial CSA occurs. Over time, such roles tend to become fixed and rigidly entrenched in the family system (Alexander, 1985; Barnard, 1983; Friedman, 1988, Larson and Maddock, 1986; Mrazek and Bentovim, 1981; Thorman, 1983).

A third characteristic often observed in families where CSA occurs is an intense commitment to family obligations. A natural consequence of generational breakdown of boundaries in the family is enmeshment and sometimes pathological dependence among family members. Issues of control and fear of loss become paramount and contribute to make families where intrafamilial abuse occurs into very tight units in where individual members lack autonomy. Escape can be very difficult for any member, but especially for the sexually abused child (Alexander, 1985; Barnard, 1983; Friedman, 1988; Thorman, 1983).

There are several other characteristics which may be helpful in the identification of families where there is a substantial risk of CSA. Communication is confused. Families where sexual abuse takes place have difficulties communicating information clearly and resolving differences through negotiation. There is generally little useful discussion of family functioning or of developmental issues such as sexuality. Denial can be an intrinsic part of the family process, and family members expend a considerable amount of energy keeping 'secrets' and maintaining 'myths' which are perceived as essential to the maintenance of the family (Barnard, 1983; Larson and Maddock, 1986; Mrazek and Bentovim, 1981; Thorman, 1983; Maddock and Larson, 1995).

In addition, family affect is distorted, and affective involvement is very limited. Sexually abusive families have difficulties with the open expression of a variety of feelings. Inhibiting anxieties may be exaggerated or reduced, leading either to contained, muffled affect which is clumsily expressed in inappropriate contexts, or to intense displays of anger, rage, and shame, leading to exploitation.

Generally, family members do not empathise easily with each other and tend to be unsupportive at times of stress (Alexander, 1985; Barnard, 1983; Larson and Maddock, 1986; Thorman, 1983; Will, 1983). These families tend to be characterised by extremes in control, with some families being rigidly controlled, usually by the father, and others being rather chaotic. In both cases, physical abuse and/or neglect of the children, and spouse abuse, are not uncommon events (Alexander, 1985; Brooks, 1982; Herman, 1981; Will, 1983).

Finally, families where sexual abuse occurs are frequently socially isolated from the rest of the community, often as a result of the special characteristics described above. They form a closed system where members harbor distorted values and norms about family and social roles. Often, family members are actively discouraged from contacting persons outside the family, thus fostering their excessive dependence on one another (Alexander, 1985; Barnard, 1983; Friedman, 1988; Larson and Maddock, 1986; Mrazek and Bentovim, 1981; Thorman, 1983, Maddock and Larson, 1995).

The 'special' relationship between the father figure and his daughter has serious consequences for the functioning of the family. Siblings may become angry, jealous and resentful of their sister, while feeling rejected by their father. Meanwhile, the level of responsibility, achievement and loyalty (or disloyalty) required from the daughter is often well beyond her capabilities and essentially amounts to developmental exploitation (Pelletier and Handy, 1986). As the daughter lives with the secret of the abuse, the fate of the family rests almost entirely on her shoulders in a climate of isolation, coercion, and possibly violence. Such a situation is likely to be conducive to psychological problems, independently of the sexual contacts themselves.

Verification of the Family Dynamics in Intrafamilial CSA

According to the measures of the dimensions of family functioning outlined by Steinhauer et al (1984), sexually abusive families can be expected to show multiple weaknesses, especially shortly after disclosure and in the early stages of therapy. However, there are no reasons to predict that sexually abusive families should be expected to be very different from other families where there is dysfunctional parent-child conflict. Many families where child or family related problems occur are also characterised by poor communication, inappropriate affective involvement, ineffective role performance, inadequate controls, and values and norms which might differ from those of the community (Minuchin, 1974). It is to be expected that the specific issues of each family would be different, but their functioning might not be.

As observed by Conte (1986), the main problem with the current descriptions of the functioning of sexually abusive families is that they are exclusively based on assumptions and clinical observations. Thus far, there have been few attempts to study the functioning of families where sexual abuse occurs, and compare it to that of other dysfunctional or non-referred families. In one study, family functioning was studied after the clinical families received a course of therapeutic treatment. Levang (1988) compared a group of girls and their families where incest had taken place to a group of girls and their families where the girls were classified as oppositional, with non-clinical families. All groups were made of seven families, and the girls were 12 to 18 years old. Samples of communications in the clinical families were videotaped and analysed using a communication measure based on a circumplex model. The results indicated that the sexually abused girls talked in more parent-like ways to their fathers than the girls from the other groups (an indication of role reversal), and that sexually abusive fathers were more blaming (negatively controlling) than the other groups of fathers. The incestuous families also showed more distance and less emotion than other families. However, the data did not fully support the hypotheses that there is a role reversal between mothers and daughters in incestuous families, that the mothers are overtly rejecting of their daughters, or that sexually abusive fathers are more controlling. Of course, these findings were based on a small sample of families assessed after they received therapy.

Two other studies used questionnaires with demonstrated validity and reliability to compare the functioning of families of CSA victims to other families. Hoagwood and Stewart (1989) asked 30 sexually abused children in a day and residential treatment facility to evaluate the functioning of their families using the McMaster Family Assessment Device, and compared them to evaluations provided by 48 non-abused children receiving treatment in the same facility. The groups were matched for age, gender, and grade level. Results showed that families of sexually abused children functioned significantly more poorly than those of disturbed, non-abused children, and were also less able to solve problems and subject to greater role confusion. Victims of intrafamilial abuse reported poorer general family functioning, more inappropriate expression of affect, and more pathological intimacy and lack of emotional boundaries compared to victims of extrafamilial abuse. Einbender and Friedrich (1989) compared 46 sexually abused girls to 46 non-abused girls and their families using the Conflict, Expressiveness, and Cohesion subscales of the Family Environment Scale which were administered to the children's mothers or female guardians. On the basis of this information, no differences were found between the two groups on the aspects of family functioning mentioned above.

The three studies used rather different samples, instruments, and methodology, which makes them difficult to compare. The only similarity between two of the studies concerned emotional involvement in sexually abusive families, with Levang (1988) observing emotional distance, and Hoagwood and Steward (1989) diagnosing pathological intimacy and a lack of emotional boundaries. Only further studies using a variety of methodologies and instruments will improve and augment this preliminary information.

The Psychological Effects of Child Sexual Abuse

In the last 15 years, sexual abuse has been the subject of two major controversies among professionals. In the early 1980s, the dominant controversy was focused mostly on whether sexual encounters between adults and children were always abusive and damaging, or whether they could be neutral or even enhancing in their psychological effects (Herman, 1981). As clinicians acquired more experience in dealing with child and adult victims who presented themselves for therapy, and as more information was gathered from adult victims in communities (for example, Bagley and Ramsay, 1986; Russell, 1986), it became clear that few children have found sexual contacts with adults

56

at least neutral, if not at times enjoyable (Finkelhor, 1979; Renshaw, 1982; Russell, 1986). Most researchers now agree that CSA usually causes significant damage, in large part because it entails grossly unequal relationships between offenders and children (Finkelhor, 1984; Herman, 1981). Most of the empirical data gathered so far confirms that sexually abused children suffer from more emotional and behavioural problems than non-abused children from the community (Conte and Suerman, 1987; Einbender and Friedrich, 1989; Tufts, 1984).

Although CSA is now increasingly recognised as an exploitative act, perpetrated by an adult who is by definition in an unequal relationship with a child, and thus likely to adversely affect the child's sense of efficacy, the psychological effects of CSA are still being described and verified in the current literature. Indeed, researchers are still not clear as to the nature and extent of the problems presented by young CSA victims. Nevertheless, the increased sophistication shown by researchers has provided a more coherent understanding of the psychosocial difficulties experienced by these children.

Effects Commonly Observed in Child Victims of Sexual Abuse

CSA victims present a wide array of psychological problems, ranging from mild somatic or behavioural problems to severe behaviour disorders, suicidal ideation and behaviour, and extreme aggression (Everstine and Everstine, 1989; Mrazek and Mrazek, 1981). Finkelhor and Browne (1985) have proposed a framework for a more systematic understanding of the affects of CSA. Their suggested taxonomy is presented in terms of four traumagenic dynamics: traumatic sexualisation, betrayal, stigmatisation, and powerlessness. These dynamics are perceived as the conditions which precipitate the psychological injuries inflicted by sexual abuse, as they distort a child's belief system, self perception, and abilities to relate to peers and adults. Although these dynamics are not believed to be related to the problem behaviours shown by CSA victims in a direct causal relationship, they are explanatory in that they facilitate the identification of understanding of behaviours commonly found in such children.

Secondary Stressors and CSA

The sexual abuse of a child does not take place in a vacuum, and like many other child and family problems, it has consequences which reach far into the lives of the victims. As Gelinas (1983) pointed out, sexual abuse is likely to predispose victims to a highly stressful life adjustment, for as family, school, and social lives are increasingly disrupted, sexually abused girls are likely to experience secondary stress. Stressors which may affect these children may include, for instance, separation from parents or family, loss of friends, conflicts with teachers and other authorities, poor marks in school, and changes in living conditions.

These stressors are likely to compound problems already experienced by the child victim, but very few researchers have included them in their research designs. Conte and Shuerman (1987) obtained parental reports of the number of stressful life events in families of sexually abused and non-abused children. These researchers found that the parents of sexually abused children reported more significant stressful events and events generally rated as stressful, and that these events contributed significantly to the behaviour problems experienced by their children. However, Conte and Shuerman do not describe their instruments very well, and it is not possible to know their definition of 'stressful events'.

In another study, Sansonnet-Hayden et al (1987) evaluated the level of stress in the past year according to Axis IV of DSM-III in a group of 54 adolescents, among whom 17 reported sexual abuse. Although the abused adolescents reported significantly more stress in the last year, this factor was not a significant predictor of psychopathology when compared to other factors by means of multivariate analyses. Finally, Einbender and Friedrich (1989) asked the mothers or female guardians of 46 sexually abused girls to complete a 25 item Life Events Checklist as a measure of stress in the children's lives. They found that sexually abused girls had a significantly more stressful background than non-abused controls. However, they gave no indications as to whether stress might have contributed to the children's psychological problems.

Because so little research has been done on this subject, it is obviously premature to draw any conclusions. However, there is a developing trend towards the recognition of secondary stressors as being of lesser but still significant importance in the complex situations brought about by CSA.

Variability in the Psychological Effects of Child Sexual Abuse: CSA as a Form of Stress

Although very few clinicians would dispute the fact that CSA plays a role in the behavioural and developmental problems experienced by young victims, it is also quite obvious that not all children with a history of sexual abuse develop symptoms which require professional intervention. The evidence for this comes mainly from studies of adult populations (reviewed in Bagley and Thurston, 1996b) where in each study, many of sexual abuse victims reported relatively little long-term suffering. Finkelhor (1979), while being cautious about his results, reports that 20 per cent of the sexually abused women in his study reacted in a neutral fashion to incidents of child sexual abuse, and that 8 per cent looked back upon some aspects of their experiences as having been pleasurable. In her study of 930 women living in San Francisco, Russell (1986) discovered that two percent of women who had suffered apparently very severe intrafamilial CSA reported no trauma, as did 10 per cent of women who suffered a level of abuse defined as severe, and 27 per cent of those who suffered the least severe abuse.

Subsequent 'adult recall' studies have produced similar results (Bagley and Thurston, 1996b). For example, the researchers at Tufts New England Medical Centre studied 112 sexually abused children and found that although most of their subjects did present with behavioural or emotional problems, only 17 per cent of four to six year olds met their rigorous criteria on the Louisville Behaviour Checklist for 'clinically disturbed', while the same was true of 40 per cent of the seven to 13 year olds, and 8 per cent of the 14 to 18 year olds. In these studies, it appears that a relatively small percentage of children were affected in such a way that they needed sustained psychological or psychiatric services.

This variability in the psychological consequence of CSA has not escaped researchers. Some have argued that the inconsistencies in the nature and intensity of the effects of sexual abuse are evidence that the harmfulness of the sexual component of CSA has not been scientifically demonstrated (Henderson, 1983; Powell and Chalkley, 1981). However, the variability in effects had led other researchers to investigate the aspects of sexual abuse which are most likely to determine its impact (Bagley, 1995). Thus far, most investigations into the various kinds of CSA have focused on the child-perpetrator relationship and the sexual part of the abuse, with relatively little attention being paid to the characteristics of the individual child, or to the family and social variables which might contribute to the child's difficulties.

However, variability in resistance to stress is not a new observation. Garmezy (1983) mentioned differences in resilience, in that not all children suffer emotional problems following events such as the divorce of their parents, hospitalisation, or war. In fact, Rutter (1985) refers to the 'universal observation that even with the most severe stressors and the most glaring adversities, it is unusual for more than half of children to succumb' (p. 598). In the light of childhood stress theories, the variability in the effects of CSA becomes easier to understand.

Child Sexual Abuse as a Stressor

Sexual abuse is only one of the many types of potentially traumatic stressors to which children are exposed. Although it is unique in some of the relational aspects of its process, and in its sexual nature, there are indications that it may not be very different in its general effects on behaviour from other stressors such as parental discord, divorce and separation from parents, physical abuse and family violence, and illness and hospitalisation.

In order to understand the notion of resilience in adverse situations, Garmezy (1983) proposed a formulation of children's reactions to stress based on three sets of factors which he called predisposing, potentiating and protective factors. Predisposing factors refer to characteristics of individual children and/or environments which increase the likelihood of a child developing an emotional or behavioural disorder in comparison with other children in the general population. Such factors include among others, biogenetic fragility, criminality or mental health problems in a parent, a difficult temperament, low socio-economic status, and family variables such as parental discord, overcrowding, large family size, and family breakdown leading to the child coming into the care of local authorities (Rae-Grant, Thomas, Offord, and Boyle, 1989; Rutter, 1979b).

Potentiating factors (or triggering events) refer to the actual stressful events, such as the events which constitute the sexual abuse of a child and its aftermath. Protective factors are defined as 'those factors that modify, ameliorate, or alter a person's response to some environmental hazards that predispose to a maladaptive outcome' (Rutter, 1985, p. 600). Garmezy (1983) indicated three types of protective factors: positive personal dispositions, a supportive family milieu, and social systems which function in such a way as to support and encourage a child's coping efforts. Thus, factors relevant to the resilience of children include positive temperament (Rutter, 1985), high intelligence, and social competence (Garmezy, Masten, and Tellegen, 1984). Favourable family factors include parental support, family closeness, and adequate rule setting (Garmezy, 1983). Community factors include particularly good peer relationships and success in school (Rae-Grant et al, 1988). As observed by Friedrich et al (1987), CSA victims experience groups of predisposing, potentiating, and protective factors inherent to their situations. It can be hypothesized that it is the variation in these sorts of factors which may account for the variance in the level of trauma observed in the children.

Predisposing, Potentiating, and Protective Factors in Child Sexual Abuse

Recent research has shown that CSA is much more than a sexual interaction between an older offender and a child. Many researchers have focused their attention strictly on the sexual or relational aspects of the sexual abuse, and only a few have looked closely at the child's environment or at the conditions which lead to CSA. However, as will be shown, we are obtaining more information on all aspects of this phenomenon including its associated social and family variables.

Predisposing Factors Associated with Sexual Abuse and Poor Mental Health in Child Victims

Little is known about biogenetic weaknesses prior to the abuse, in sexually abused children. Martin and Walters (1982) have noted that compared to children who had suffered neglect, abandonment, or other forms of family violence, sexually abused children showed a smaller proportion of physical problems. With the exception of low socio-economic status, which is a strong factor predicting the occurrence of sexual abuse, virtually all variables associated with a higher probability of CSA are also family factors associated with poor mental health in children. Risk factors related to the family environment such as the presence of a step-father, having ever been without a mother, a large difference in education between the father and the mother, poor parental mental health, and parental discord, dramatically increase the chances that a child will be sexually abused (Finkelhor, 1979; Gruber and Jones, 1983; Conte, Wolfe and Smith, 1989; Paradise, Rose, Sleeper, and Nathanson, 1994). However, some of these factors also strongly predict poor psychosocial adjustment in children. The absence of a parent, especially a mother, can have direct consequences on the functioning of a family and the mental health of children, especially when the loss follows longstanding parental discord (Rutter, 1979a). Open parental discord and divorce have been abundantly documented as being strongly associated with psychological problems such as conduct disorders, excessive dependency, anxiety, and depression (Dadds, 1987; Emery, 1982; Shaw and Emery, 1987; Sines, 1987; Wallerstein, 1983). The fact that those problems can also be commonly found in sexually abused children suggests that variables related to parental discord may account for part of the difficulties experienced by CSA victims.

The clearest recent evidence outlining the effects of risk factors common to sexually abused children and children suffering other stressors is in the area of family functioning. Family dysfunction has been strongly related to a variety of childhood behaviour problems. In the Ontario Child Health Study, which involved 3,294 children between the ages of four and 16, family functioning as measured by the General Functioning Scale of the McMaster Family Assessment device showed the strongest overall association with internalising and externalising behaviour of all the variables measured in the study (Byles, Byrne, Offord, and Boyle, 1986). Similar relationships were found in smaller scale studies using a variety of measures. Using composite measures of family process, Amato (1989) and Cohen and Brook (1987) found that power assertive punishment was directly related to behaviour problems in children. Smets and Hartup (1988), using the Family Adaptability and Cohesion Scale II, identified fewer symptoms in children of families which were more cohesive and adaptable. Villeneuve and Roy (1984) and Henggeler, Edwards, and Bordwin (1987), analysed family processes where a child or an adolescent presented a problem such as conduct disorder or juvenile delinquency. They found that variables such as excessive distance between family members were strongly associated with those problems.

There is also evidence that the effects of family dysfunction on child behaviour might transcend the impact of stressors such as child abuse. Wolfe and Mosk (1983) found that a group of physically abused children displayed more behaviour problems than a group of non-referred children, but approximately the same level of difficulties as children who experienced parent-child conflict or were considered out of parental control. These researchers concluded that disturbances in the physically abused children's social and behavioural development may have been due more to a negative family environment than to the abuse itself.

A similar relationship has been the object of increasingly sophisticated research in the area of CSA. Initially, the suspected link between family dysfunction and distress in victims of sexual abuse was a matter of clinically based beliefs. LaBarbera, Martin, and Dozier (1980) pointed out that child psychiatrist with more experience considered the factors related to the functioning of incestuous familes to be more relevant to the victim's prognosis than the sexual behaviour itself. Emslie and Rosenfeld (1983), after styding children and adolescents hospitalised for psychiatric problems, concluded that psychopathology serious enough to require hospitalisation may not have been an effect of sexual abuse itself, but a consequence of family pathology which results in ego impairment. In another study, Goodwin, Cormier, and Owen (1983) observed that the nature of the families of girls who were sexually abused by their gransfathers seems to predict the nature and intensity of psychological symptoms in the victims.

More recently, researchers have made a clear effort to measure family functioning as part of increasingly complex research designs. So far, most of the studies investigating family dysfunction and distress in victims of CSA have done so retrospectively, using self reports provides by adult women. Bagley and Ramsay (1986) found that parental separation and parental coldness were independent predictors of poor mental health in adult victims, even when variables related to the sexual assault were controlled. Fromuth (1986) found that poor family background was more strongly related to general adjustment in adult women than sexual abuse itself. Harter, Alexander, and Neimeyer (1988) asked college women with a history of CSA to evaluate their families as they remembered them using a general measure of family functioning (FACES-II). Their results indicated that decreased cohesion and adaptability in the family of origin and increased perceptions of isolation predicted social maladjustment more reliably than sexual abuse. Cole and Woogler (1989) compared the parent-child relations of 21 adult women who had been victims of intrafamilial CSA with 19 women who had been victims of extrafamilial abuse. Although they did not explore mental health issues directly, they found that the women's perceptions of their mothers, combined with CSA, were related to difficulties accepting their own children's dependency and to an unusual portion of child autonomy. Mullen, Martin, Anderson, Romans, and Herbison (1993), in their study of a large sample of women with a history of CSA, found that parental separation, being raised by a single parent, parental absence, or parental discord increased the risk of a child being sexually abused *and* of the adult having poor mental health. Finally, Nash, Hulsey, Sexton, Harralson, and Lambert (1993) asked 105 women with and without a history of CSA to complete measures of psychopathology, hypnotic susceptibility, and family dysfunction. They concluded that family environments as described retrospectively appeared more important than CSA in determining psychological distress in adulthood. They also identified an association between CSA and an excessive use of dissociative defences, although it was unclear to them whether family dysfunction did not play a role there as well.

Only three studies of family dysfunction and child psychopathology have been identified. However, two have large samples and the significant advantage of a prospective design. Friedrich, Beilke, and Urquiza (1987) compared a group of pre-school and school-age sexually abused children to a sample of non-abused children from a psychiatric outpatient clinic and a group of non-referred children. They reported that sexually abused children displayed more behaviour problems than normal, but less than other clinic children, and the difficulties associated with family cohesion, conflict, and support of the child accounted for more of the problems experienced by sexually abused children than the severity of the abuse. It is important to note that Friedrich et al. (1987) relied on staff observations of family functioning rather than on standardised instruments or observational procedures for information on the families. Paradise et al. (1994) studied prospectively 154 children who were brought to urban hospitals following the discovery of CSA. At a six month follow up, the authors discovered that older age of the child, lower educational attainment by the child's mother, mother's poor mental health, and poorer family integration were the better predictors of child behaviour problems. They also noted that neither characteristics of sexual abuse, nor circumstances surrounding its disclosure, nor indicators of the competency of the child's family were associated with the children's problems at follow-up. Boney-McCoy and Finkelhor (1996), on the other hand, interviewed by phone 1433 children age 10 to 16 and their parents as part of a national (U.S.) study of child victimisation. The subjects were interviewed twice at approximately a 15 month interval. The researchers assessed child behaviour problems, family relationships, and victimisation experiences which had occurred in the interim. They found that CSA was related to psychological problems in children, independently of family dysfunction. They also found that family relationships and prior symptoms among the children were strongly related to later symptoms at the 15 month follow-up.

The relative contribution of family dysfunction to the psychological problems experienced by CSA victims, in childhood and in adulthood, remains a source of controversy (Boney-McCoy and Finklehor, 1998; Nash, Hulsey, Neimeyer and Lambert, 1998. However, the findings so far indicate that many aspects of family functioning can have significant consequences for the mental health of sexually abused children, and that some of these factors may be independent of the abuse itself.

Potentiating Factors: Not All Sexual Abuse is the Same

Once it is established that sexual abuse has a negative effect on children's mental health, it becomes important to know which aspects of sexual abuse have the greatest effect on the victims. By definition, sexual abuse varies enormously from a one-time event where a young man might expose himself to his sister to the repeated forcible rape of a daughter by her father over many years. Research in this area has shed some light on the subject, but has also presented many contradictory results. A set of studies which were considered to be methodologically sound have been reviewed by Browne and Finkelhor (1986). They include studies of children recently victimised and studies of adult women who were assaulted as children. The results of some of the studies examined by Browne and Finkelhor will be reviewed here, along with the results of more recent studies.

Age at Onset

One of the more controversial questions in the literature on child sexual abuse concerns whether a child's age at first molestation might affect her reactions to such an experience (Browne and Finkelhor, 1986). Some researchers feel that younger children are more naive and thus less likely to suffer the way a more knowledgeable older child or teenager would. Others have suggested that younger children are more impressionable and less able to make sense of sexual abuse, and that they would be more likely to suffer severe behavioural problems after being abused.

The studies available offer contradictory results concerning this issue. Courtois (1979), who assessed 31 women from the community who had suffered sexual abuse, found that the women who were younger when they were abused showed more difficulties in their relationships with men and in regard to their own sense of self. Meiselman (1978) also observed that pre-pubertal experiences led to greater disturbances in adulthood, although she based her report on clinical observations.

65

As mentioned before, the Tufts (1984) study found that school-aged children who had been sexually abused were more disturbed than either adolescents or pre-school children. However, as observed by Browne and Finkelhor (1986), this seemed to reflect more the time of assessment than the age at onset of abuse. The Tufts researchers observed that the number of developmental periods during which sexual abuse occurred might be more important than the actual age at onset. On the other hand, Paradise et al (1994) found that older children were more likely to show psychological symptoms.

A total of six studies failed to discover a significant relationship between age at onset of abuse and psychological effects in victims. Finkelhor (1979), using a multiple regression, found a non-significant relationship between younger age and trauma. Russell (1986) found the same trend, and reported a small non-significant correlation between experiences before age nine and greater difficulties in adult women. Bagley and Ramsay (1986) discovered a correlation between abuse at a younger age and increased trauma, but the significance of the correlation disappeared when considered along with other factors in a multiple regression. Tsai, Felman-Summers, and Edgar (1979), Friedrich et al (1986), and Briere and Runtz (1988) found no relationship at all between age at onset and psychological effects in children or adults.

Therefore, it appears that only relatively old studies show a connection between age at onset and psychological consequences. More recent studies, which have used larger samples and multivariate analyses which allow for the simultaneous consideration of other abuse variables, have not found such a relationship. The important exception is the Paradise et al (1994) study, which carries significant weight given its prospective design and relatively large sample. The issue of how age is related to behaviour problems in sexually abused children remains unresolved.

Number and Type of Sexual Contacts

Empirical studies suggest that more intrusive sexual contacts are related to greater levels of trauma. The findings are particularly clear in two studies of adult victims by Russell (1986) and Bagley and Ramsay (1986), and one study of girls aged 12 to 18 years by Morrow and Sorrell (1989).

Criminal Proceedings

Some work indicates that testimony in juvenile court may be beneficial to the child, but that protracted criminal proceedings may actually be harmful to the mental health of young CSA victims. The trend which appears in this area is that the consequences of disclosing the abuse (parent's denial or punishing attitudes, being removed from the home, facing legal proceedings) could be more damaging than keeping the abuse secret. It is possible that many children anticipate those difficulties, and it may be that they wait until they have the prospect of better conditions before they talk to a parent or an authority figures. Some studies have, however, identified an 'iatrogenic effect', with protracted criminal proceedings in which the victim has to give evidence reflected in deterioration of mental health in the victim (Bagley and Thurston, 1996b).

Protective Factors in CSA

Protective factors ameliorate or alter a person's response to stress. They differ from risk factors in several ways. They usually become particularly important at crucial moments in a child's life. They function according to a different process from the factor which may have precipitated the child's problems, in that the effect seems to come from the positive end of the variable (Rutter, 1987). Such variables include intelligences, easy temperament, parental support, good peer relationships, and success in school.

Not much is known abut basic variables such as the intelligence and temperament of sexually abused children. Martin and Walters (1982) noted that compared to children who were either abandoned, neglected, physically abused, or emotionally abused, children who had been sexually abused showed very little intellectual impairment. In one study, Mannarino and Cohen (1986) measured the intelligence of 45 CSA victims whose average age was approximately 5 years. On average, these children were found to be at the low end of the average range (92.9). In another study, Einbender and Friedrich (1989) found the IQ of 46 sexually abused girls to be significantly inferior to that of a comparison group. Nevertheless, the median IQ of the sexually abused group was 99.00, which is in the average range. That sexually abused children generally would not show obvious intellectual impairment is in agreement with clinical observations that such children are often expected to accomplish tasks which are within the parental role of normal families. It is unlikely that intellectually disabled children could develop the 'pseudomaturity' observed by the clinicians, with its adaptive and maladaptive consequences.

However, other cognitive factors may come into play in determining a child's ability to cope with such a traumatic event as CSA. One of those factors is a child's attributional style regarding negative life events (Mrazek and Mrazek, 1987; Newberger and De Vos, 1988). Whether a child thinks that the abuse is her fault or the offender's, and whether her attributions are global or specific, stable or unstable, may be relevant to her emotional reactions to sexual abuse. In one study, Wolfe, Gentile and Wolfe (1988) found that the emotional impact of CSA on a sample of 71 victims was mediated by the children's attributional style regarding the causes of positive and negative events. Gold (1986) arrived at similar results when she investigated the role of adult attributional style in 103 adult women who had been victims of CSA and in 88 controls. Morrow and Sorrell (1989) found that older adolescent female victims who blamed themselves for the sexual abuse prior to disclosure also tended to act out more.

Parental support may be the most important protective factor in child sexual abuse. This is particularly obvious at the time of disclosure, which corresponds quite well to Rutter's (1987) notion of a 'key turning point' in a child's life where protective factors are most important. Gruber and Jones (1983) compared 20 CSA victims to 21 non-victims and found that a poor relationship with the mother was characteristic of the victims. Parental responses to disclosure were investigated in a number of studies, including the one conducted at Tufts New England Medical Centre. This study found that negative reactions from the mothers (anger, punishment) were related to worse trauma for the children. These researchers also discovered that being removed from the family following disclosure of CSA also made matters worse, although the children who were removed were, in many cases, the same children who had experienced negative reactions from their mothers. Therefore, the results of these two variables are likely to be confounded.

The findings of the Tufts (1984) researchers are strongly supported by the results obtained by Adams-Tucker (1982), Everson, Hunter, Runyon, Edelsohn, and Coulter (1989), Conte and Shuerman (1987), and Morrow and Sorrell (1989). Adams-Tucker reported that the children in her sample who received support from primary caretakers showed less emotional disturbance than children who did not receive such support. Everson et al (1989) systematically compared maternal support after disclosure of CSA to other variables in a sample of 88 victims. They found that the level of maternal support was a stronger predictor of the child's psychological functioning after disclosure than the type or length of the abuse or the perpetrator's relationship to the child. Morrow and Sorrell (1989) found that a mother's negative reaction at disclosure was related to low self-esteem and depression in sexually abused girls, and that negative perpetrator response was related to more severe acting-out. However, the same researchers failed to find a relationship between the child's removal from the family at disclosure and psychological problems. Finally, Conte and Shuerman (1987) reported that denial of the abuse by the offender was related to negative effects observed by social workers. They also found that when the victims were pressured to retract their stories (possibly by a parent or other relative) and saw themselves as responsible for the abuse, they suffered greater psychological consequences as observed by the parents.

Summary of Factors Related to Mental Health in CSA Victims

When we consider all predisposing, potentiating, and protective factors associated with sexual abuse which might influence the mental health of the victims, the possible interactions are exceedingly complex. Nevertheless, the emerging trends in the research on predisposing factors indicate that children who live in dysfunctional families where there is a step-father or where the natural mother has ever been absent from home are not only at greater risk of being sexually abused, but also might show more pronounced psychological effects. Accumulating evidence suggests that risk factors associated with family functioning may be more important than the sexual interactions itself in accounting for the psychological effects of sexual abuse. However, the methodological limitations of the studies done so far preclude more definitive conclusions. It must also be noted that low socio-economic status, which is not directly a family process variable, is also related both to increased risks of sexual abuse and to more serious psychological problems in children.

The trends associated with precipitating factors are becoming clearer as more methodologically sound studies have been done. A majority of studies indicate that children who are sexually abused by an older offender, especially by a father or step-father, are more likely to suffer serious trauma. Also, children who are molested genitally, who are coerced especially by force into sexual acts, and who later become involved in protracted criminal proceedings, appear more disturbed. Because these findings are based on relatively few studies, they need additional confirmation. However, it must be noted that in three studies (Bagley and Ramsay, 1986; Friedrich et al, 1987; Harter et al, 1988), the effects of precipitating factors were found to be less significant once

69

potentiating and protective family factors were controlled with the exception of fathers as the perpetrator. Such findings should be carefully considered in further research.

Finally, with regard to protective factors, children who have a negative attributional style regarding life events and are not protected by a parent at disclosure are more likely to suffer severe psychological consequences. The latter factor, in at least one study (Everson et al, 1988), has been shown to be more important than variables related to the sexual abuse itself in predicting mental health problems.

A potentially significant missing element in the research on factors related to mental health in CSA victims is the study of constitutional factors which might affect the children's behaviour and interact with environmental factors. So far, no known study has taken into account child characteristics such as temperament and developmental delays, or the presence of mental health problems such as hyperactivity, neurotic behaviours, or psychotic behaviours, which would have occurred prior to the sexual abuse.

Methodology

Clearly, on the basis of available studies, it is not possible to identify a *direct* relationship between the trauma suffered by a child during sexual abuse and the intensity of the psychological problems she might experience. Rather, as observed by Friedrich (1988), it appears that environmental and constitutional factors moderate the psychological outcome over time, and very probably into adult life. It appears that family functioning could be an especially important variable moderating the effects of sexual abuse. Other environment variables such as the extent of marital satisfaction experienced by the children' caregivers, and secondary stressors which are currently affecting a child's life, have been left virtually unexplored. Even when family variables have been studied, they have rarely been the object of formal assessment procedures.

In its design, the present study is very similar to the study of physically abused children done by Wolfe and Mosk (1983), and the study of sexually abused children done by Friedrich et al (1987). As in those studies, one of the main purposes of this present work has been to examine the level of social and psychological impairment of maltreated children in relation to other clinical and non-clinical populations. The importance of the environmental variable of family dysfunction, as a mediating factor in the behavioural problems experienced by sexually abused children, was evaluated by comparing a group of such children to a group of non-abused children from dysfunctional families, and a group of non-referred children from apparently well functioning families.

The study which was most similar to the present study is that of William N. Friedrich at the Mayo Clinic and his associates at the University of Washington (Friedrich et al, 1987). That study involved a comparison of three groups (sexually abused, outpatient, and non-referred) in terms of social competence and behaviour problems. In addition, the importance of family dysfunction and sexual abuse in relation to child behaviour problems was also examined.

After consideration of the weaknesses of various studies, the present study was designed to include features which would introduce some improvements over the work done so far in the field of child sexual abuse. First, it focussed on children of only one gender (girls) who were within a relatively narrow age range (8-15 years old). Second, an important feature of this study was the measurement of environmental variables, including family functioning, marital adjustment, and secondary stressors experienced by the children. Formal measurement of family and marital functioning provided a more refined and complete exploration of the family environment of sexually abuses children in comparison with both clinical and non-referred groups.

Finally, the study made use of a variety of measures based on two sources: the children and their parents or legal guardians. Specifically, the parents or legal guardians were asked to evaluate their families and marriages, and the behaviour of their children, while the children were asked to report on their perceptions of themselves, their levels of depression, and the amount of stress they had experienced in the last 12 months. Although the two sources provided different information (the children were not asked about family functioning, and the parents were not asked directly about their children's self-perception or recent stressors), the bias inherent to single source reporting was at least partially mitigated (Widom, 1988).

Research Population

Three groups of 20 girls between the ages of 8 and 15, and their parents were selected. The first group consisted of girls who had been sexually abused and they and their parent(s), and met the following criteria:

(a)   the sexual abuse involved physical contact between the perpetrator and the victim ranging from fondling to vaginal or anal intercourse;

(b)   the perpetrator was a relative of the child (including in-laws and common-law partners), and at least five years older than she;

(c)   the abuse was substantiated by a therapist and by one other mandated agency such as a child welfare agency, or the police;

(d)   neither the child nor her parents suffered from severe mental, developmental, or physical disabilities;

(e)   the child had lived with her family or had had substantial contacts with her parent(s) over the last six months; and

(f)   the problems presented by the girls in treatment included issues to sexual abuse which had not yet been resolved. The sexual abuse group was recruited through private and public treatment agencies in Calgary, Edmonton, and the Peace River District, Alberta.

In all cases of sexual abuse, the children had been victimised within the last six years (M = 2.5 years, SD = 1.9). The average age of the girls at first molestation was 6.8 years old (SD = 3.0 years). Girls who were molested more than once experienced abuse over an average of 23.3 months (SD = 27.3 months). Characteristics of the sexually abused sample included to the number of incidents, the type of abuse, the number and identity of perpetrators, the use of physical force and verbal threats, court appearances, and protective measures and are presented in Table 1. It should be noted that two children were abused by non-relatives in addition to relatives. Moreover, since many girls were abused by more than one perpetrator, and in more than one way, the sections documenting those aspects of the sexual abuse situations add up to more than 100 per cent.

The sexually abused group represented a non-random sample of families seeking therapeutic assistance. Participation in the study was strictly voluntary, and 17 families which met the criteria for inclusion refused to participate. Very little is known about these families, although their therapists reported that some families did not wish to participate because of the stress they were currently experiencing, or because they had started therapy only recently and had not had enought time to build up a level of comfort which would allow for participation. However, it also appears that many families did not participate because at least one member did not wish to be involved in a research study. In addition, three institutionalised subjects were eventually excluded from the sample because, although the legal guardians consented to the child's participation, the parents refused to become involved.

The second group consisted of twenty girls and their parents who were operationally defined as dysfunctional families. For the purpose of this study, a family was considered dysfunctional when the children exhibited conduct disorders, or when they showed evidence of being out of parental control or being clearly in conflict with their parent(s). The subjects in this group also had to meet the following criteria:

(a)   the child did not have a history of physical abuse, sexual abuse, or neglect, as confirmed by a therapist or a social worker;

(b)   neither the child nor her parents suffered from physical and/or mental disabilities;

(c)   the child had lived with or had had substantial contacts with her parents during the last six months; and

(d)   the problems presented by the girls in treatment included issues related to parent-child conflict and family dysfunction which had not yet been resolved . The dysfunctional families were obtained through public and private treatment agencies in Calgary.

The children in dysfunctional families presented a variety of primary problems including conduct disorders, oppositional disorders, defiant disorders, school refusal and learning problems, adjustment reactions to stressors, suicidal gesturing, dysthymic disorders, enuresis, encopresis, and running away. In all 20 cases, therapists identified a conflict between at least one parent and the girl as part of the problems presented. In 40 per cent of cases, parent-child conflict was actually the primary diagnosis.

Like the sexually abused group, the dysfunctional families were volunteer participants who were not randomly selected. Approximately 14 families which met the criteria for inclusion refused to participate for reasons similar to those given for the families where sexual abuse had occurred. Three families were eventually excluded from the sample when it was discovered that the children had been sexually abused by a non-relative at an earlier point in their childhoods. The incidents of sexual abuse were all 'closed cases' which had received the necessary attention at the time of their occurrences and all therapists concerned knew of the incidents.

The non-referred group of subjects included 20 girls between the ages of 8 and 15 and their parents who were recruited through community networking and a women's resource centre. The criteria for exclusion from this group included either the child or the parents suffering from mental or physical disabilities, and/or the family having received services from mental health professionals for child related family problems in the last two years.

Group means and standard deviations for age, grade, socioeconomic status (SES), time in therapy, number of people in the family, and duration of the parental relationship were compared. SES was determined by rating the parents' occupations according to the Blishen 1981 socioeconomic index for occupations in Canada (Blishen, Carroll, and Moore, 1987). Double income families were given the SES of the parent with the higher rating.

The three groups were compared on each characteristic using univariate tests. After the Bonferroni correction was applied (Kirk, 1982), the results showed that the three groups were matched for the girls' ages and educational grades, the number of people in the family, the number of adults in the family, and the marital characteristics of each parent. However, the three groups were significantly different in terms of SES, and number of natural parents in the home. Student-Neuman-Keuls post-hoc test for SES and an additional chi-square for the number of natural parents in the home showed that the non-referred group accounted for the significance in both cases, with higher values for both characteristics. Although the two clinical groups did not differ significantly in terms of the time they had spent in therapy once the Bonferroni correction was applied, it was judged that the difference on that variable was substantial enough to warrant attention. As a result, time in therapy, SES, and the number of natural parents in the home, were used as a covariates in relevant statistical analyses.

Measures

Five measures were used for this study and were administered to the subjects in the following order:

1)   The general scale of the *Family Assessment Measure* - III (FAM) (Skinner, Steinhauer, and Santa-Barbara, 1983, 1984) was used to assess family functioning in all families. The FAM is a screening instrument based on the process model of family functioning proposed by Steinhauer et al (1984). It provided a description of the families and a comparison of the dynamics and dysfunctions in all three groups of families. The general scale of the FAM consists of 50 items which assess the level of health/pathology in the family from a systems perspective. The scale provides a measure of overall family functioning and scores for the following process-related subscales: task accomplishment, role performance, communication, affective

expression, involvement, control, and values and norms. Two response type subscales, social desirability and defensiveness, are also provided. The scale has established validity (Skinner et al, 1983). The FAM was chosen for this study because it provided an efficient way of measuring family dysfunction over many clinically relevant dimensions. In addition, it is a questionnaire which has been adequately normed on a Canadian population.

2)   The *Child Behaviour Checklist* (CBCL) (Achenbach and Edelbrock, 1983) was used for a general assessment of social and behavioural concerns in all child participants. The use of this test was related to the theoretical expectation that sexually abused girls and girls from dysfunctional families should be equally (or nearly equally) disturbed, but may vary as to the symptoms they show. The CBCL is designed to organise parents' reports of their child's social competence and behaviour problems. Parents provide information on 20 social competence items, and rate their child for 118 behaviour problems using a 0-1-2 scale for how true each item is of the child in the past six months. The parents' responses are then scored on a Child Behaviour Profile which consists of three competence scales and a variety of empirically derived behaviour problem subscales. The test yields normalised $\underline{T}$ scores for each subscale and total normalised $\underline{T}$ scores for the social competence and behaviour problem subscales. Correlations in the normative samples were in the .90's for agreement between mothers' and fathers' ratings (inter-rater reliability) and for one-week test-retest reliabilities of mothers' ratings. The discriminative validity of the checklist has been shown when children referred for mental health services obtained significantly higher scores on all behaviour problem scales and lower scores on all the social competence scales than demographically matched randomly selected children (Achenbach and Edelbrock, 1983).

For the purpose of this study, a sexual behaviour score was obtained by adding the raw scores of the six items in the CBCL which specifically refer to unusual sexual behaviour. These items include: #5 "Behaves like the opposite sex"; #59 "Plays with own sex parts in public"; #60 "Plays with own sex parts too much"; #73 "Sexual problems"; #96 "Thinks about sex too much'" and #110 "Wishes to be of the opposite sex". Such a score was used by Friedrich et al (1986)

75

in their study of sexually abused children although it constitutes only a very approximative measure of such behaviour.

The Child Behaviour Checklist is a very well normed instrument which is used extensively in many clinics in the English speaking world (Achenbach and Edelbrock, 1983).

3)   The *Children's Depression Inventory* (CDI) (Kovacs, 1980/1981) is a 27 item self-report questionnaire designed for use with children 8 to 16 years of age. It was used to assess perceived levels of depression in all subjects and to test the hypothesis that sexually abused girls and girls from distressed families might be depressed. In a study of 594 males and 658 females whose ages ranged from age 8 to 16, the CDI was found to have adequate internal reliability. The test-retest reliability index for the CDI over three weeks was .77 for males and .74 for females (Smucker, Craighead, Craighead, and Green, 1986). The CID has been validated against independent psychiatric and diagnostic evaluations, and preliminary analyses showed its ability to distinguish between child guidance and paediatric out-patient groups, the former receiving much higher CDI scores (Kovacs, 1980/1981). The CDI was chosen for this study because it is a quick and reliable measure of childhood depression which is easy to read for children and has been used in numerous studies (Smucker et al, 1986).

4)   The Children's and Adolescents' versions of the *Self Perception Profile* (SPP-C and SPP-A) (Harter, 1985, 1988) were used to measure each girl's domain specific judgements of her competence, as well as her sense of global self-worth. These instruments were used to test the hypothesis that sexually abused girls and grils from dysfunctional families have lower self-esteem than girls from well functioning families, and to explore which aspects of their self-concepts have suffered the most.

The SPP-C consists of 36 items which tap five specific domains: scholastic competence, social acceptance, athletic competence, physical appearance, and behavioural conduct. The questions are written according to a 'structured alternative format' aimed at reducing bias due to the social desirability of the responses. In addition, there is a global self-worth subscale. The test has established reliability, and was

76

standardised on four different samples of children attending grades 3 to 8, for a total of 1,489 children whose ages ranged from 8 to 13. In the present study, the SPP-C was administered to all subjects aged 8 to 12.

The Self-Perception Profile for Adolescents (SPP-A) is a 45 item questionnaire of a format similar to the SPP-C, which taps eight specific domains: scholastic competence, social acceptance, athletic competence, physical appearance, job competence, romantic appeal, behavioural conduct, and close friendships.

5)   A slightly modified version of the *Life Events Checklist* (LEC) (Johnson, 1986; Johnson and McCutcheon, 1980) was used to assess the children's experiences of important events in their lives, and their emotional reactions to them. The modified version of the scale used 42 of the 46 original items, since items related to pregnancy and abortion were excluded. The child was asked to rate each event on the list as good or bad, and to evaluate the effect it had had on her life. The scale yields a positive change score, a negative change score, and a total score if it is desired. In two studies, Gad and Johnson (1980) and Johnson and McCutcheon (1980) found the negative change scores to be significantly related to numerous indices of behaviour and health problems in children including visits to the doctor, reports of personal problems, depression, anxiety, and reports of emotional maladjustment, while positive change scores showed much weaker relationships to those factors. Those results were taken as a confirmation of the theory underlying the LEC, which is that life stress, and especially negative changes in a person's life, are related to mental and physical health problems. The results were also seen as confirming the construct validity of the checklist. Brand and Johnson (1982) retested 50 children, ages 10 to 17, with the LEC after two weeks, and found that the test-retest reliability of the LEC was .71 for the positive change scores and .66 for the negative change scores.

Development of the Hypotheses

This study was designed to address a number of major issues. Primarily it was intended to address the issue of whether sexually abused girls differ from non-abused girls from dysfunctional families and from non-referred girls in terms of social behaviour, behaviour problems, unusual sexual behaviour, perceived self-worth, levels of depression, and the level of stress attributable to life events. Specific questions related to this general issue are formulated in hypotheses one to six below.

In the areas of behaviour problems and stress, it was expected that there would be very few differences between the sexually abused girls and those who came from dysfunctional families, although important differences were expected between the two clinical groups and the non-referred children. Most comparative studies have suggested this possibility: sexually abused children generally show more behaviour problems, more signs of depression, and lover self-esteem than non-referred children, but are usually comparable with other out-patient children in terms of the intensity of their difficulties, except for the clinical and empirical observation that sexually abused children generally tend to show more sexualised behaviour than any other group of children. Similarly, it can be predicted that sexually abused children will not differ significantly from children of dysfunctional families in terms of the level of stress they have experienced, but will differ significantly from non-referred children with regard to that variable. This is addressed by hypothesis six, with data derived from the Life Events Checklist.

However, despite the general expectation that girls from sexually abusive and other dysfunctional families will be similar in many ways, it is expected that there will be significant differences between these two types of families. The data for the relevant statistical tests were obtained from the Family Assessment measure and the Dyadic Adjustment Scale.

It is hypothesized that families where sexual abuse occurs would differ significantly from other clinical families and non-referred families in areas such as role performance (because of role reversals or role confusion), affective expression (because of problems in self-control or withheld feelings), and affective involvement (either because of enmeshment, or because of excessive distance between family members).

A final statistically complex issue concerns the factors which are most likely to be related to the difficulties experienced by sexually abused children. A number of researchers have now shown that when differences in family functioning are taken into account, the relationships between variables directly related to the incidents of abuse and child behaviour problems are much reduced. In this context, it can be hypothesised that when family functioning, marital functioning, stress attributable to life events, and sexual abuse are taken into account in a multivariate analysis, the first three sets of variables will be significantly related to behaviour problems in children, while sexual abuse variables will not. This hypothesis differs from hypotheses on which similar research has been based, for in addition to family variables, the marital adjustment of the child's caretakers and secondary stressors have been taken into account. This was intended to give a more complete perception of the environmental factors which may have affected the children, in addition to sexual abuse.

In summary, this study was designed to test the following hypotheses:

1) Sexually abused children and children from dysfunctional families will show less social competence than non-referred children, but will not differ significantly from each other with regard to these variables (Child Behaviour Checklist).

2) Sexually abused children and children from dysfunctional families will show more behaviour problems than non-referred children, but will not differ significantly from each other behaviourally (Child Behaviour Checklist).

3) Sexually abused children will differ significantly from children in dysfunctional families and non-referred children with regard to unusual sexual behaviour (Child Behaviour Checklist).

4) Sexually abused children and children from dysfunctional families will have significantly more negative perceptions of themselves and lower self-worth than non-referred children, but will not differ significantly from each other with regard to these variables (Harter Self-Perception Profile).

5) Sexually abused children and children from dysfunctional families will differ significantly from non-referred children in terms of depression, but will not differ significantly from each other (Child Depression Inventory).

6) Sexually abused children and children from dysfunctional families will differ significantly from non-referred children in terms in the amount of stress they have experienced, but will not differ significantly from each other (Life Events Checklist).

7) Sexually abusive and other dysfunctional families will not differ significantly in terms of general family adjustment (Family Assessment Measure, overall score).

8) Families of children who have suffered sexual abused will differ significantly from other dysfunctional families with regard to the

specific variables of role performance, affective expression, and affective involvement (Family Assessment Measure).

9)   When variables such as family dysfunction, marital dysfunction, and stress are taken into account, variables specifically associated with sexual abuse will not be significantly related to the distress experienced by the children as reported by the mothers. (Multiple regression using data from the Life Events Checklist, Family Assessment Measure, Dyadic Adjustment Scale, and a measure of child behaviour problems obtained from the Child Behaviour Check List).

Results

The total scores of all the questionnaires related to child behaviour and stress were included in multivariate analyses of covariance (MANCOVA) in order to obtain an overview of the children's behaviour problems. In a second step, questionnaire subscales were also analysed using MANCOVAs, in order to generate a more detailed description of behavioural issues. All MANCOVAs were done first with SES and the number of natural parents as covariates, since the non-referred group differed significantly from the clinical groups with regard to these variables. MANCOVAs, using time in therapy as a covariate, were repeated in order to compare the sexually abused group and the dysfunctional family group only when tests showed that differences between these two groups were significant. Significant MANCOVAs were followed by univariate analyses of covariances (ANCOVAs) to test the significance of individual variables, and Student-Neuman-Keuls tests were used to determine which of the three groups accounted for the significance.

Data on family and dyadic relationship function were analysed with a slightly different combination of techniques. The family data provided by the mothers were available for all 60 cases, and were analysed in the same manner as the child behaviour data. First, the total scores of the Family Assessment Measure were analysed using an ANCOVA with SES and number of natural parents as covariates. Then, a MANCOVA was used to analyse the subscale scores. When significance was detected, univariate ANCOVAs were done and followed by Student-Neuman-Keuls tests.

Hypothesis 10, concerning relationships between family problems, stress, sexual abuse, and behaviour problems in children, was tested using multiple regression analyses where all variables were entered at the same time. This strategy is know as 'simultaneous solution' and was advised by Briere

(1988) when partialling the effects of family dysfunction and abuse variables under certain conditions, such as when sample sizes are small, and when the causal relationships among various independent variables are not known.

An Overview of Behaviour Problems, Stress, and Child Sexual Abuse

In hypotheses one to six, it was predicted that sexually abused children and children from dysfunctional families would differ significantly from non-referred children in terms of behaviour problems, social competence, general self-worth, depression, and levels of stress, but would not differ significantly from each other. In addition, it was expected that the sexually abused group would show more evidence of sexualised behaviour than the dysfunctional group and the non-referred group.

In order to test these hypotheses, a Multiple Analysis of Covariance (MANCOVA) was conducted on the $\underline{T}$ scores of the total scores of the Social Competence scale and the Behaviour Problem scales of the Child Behaviour Checklist, the sexual behaviour score derived from the CBCL, the Global Self Worth score of the Self Perception Profile, the total score of the Child Depression Inventory, and the total score of the Life Events Checklist. Socioeconomic status and the number of natural parents in the home were used as covariates. By Wilks' criterion, this analysis revealed a statistically significant main effect for the combined group. Univariate ANCOVAs were conducted on each measure to identify which variables contributed to the differences between the groups. Table 2 shows the adjusted means, standard deviations, and univariate $\underline{F}$ values for each measure included in the MANCOVA.

Student-Neuman-Keuls tests revealed that the sexually abused girls and girls from dysfunctional families were significantly less competent than non-referred girls in their general social interactions, and that they suffered more behaviour problems, had lower global self-worth, reported more signs of depression, and suffered more intense stress. The groups did not differ in terms of sexualised behaviour, a finding which was rather unexpected given the trend reported in the literature.

Thus, hypotheses one, two, four, five and six were supported to the extent that, in general terms, problems of social competence, behaviour, self-worth, and stress were not unique to the sexually abused girls; that is, the girls from dysfunctional families suffered to a similar extent. Hypothesis three was not supported for this sample, as there were no significant differences between

81

the groups with regard to sexualised behaviour as measured. Furthermore, the younger girls (age eight to 12) did not differ from the older girls (age 13 to 15) in terms of sexualised behaviour. Finally, hypothesis five was only partially confirmed in that the girls from dysfunctional families reported the greatest level of depression. The sexually abused girls did not differ significantly from the non-referred group with regard to that variable.

Social Competence and Sexual Abuse

Since both clinical groups differed from the non-referred group with regard to social competence, a MANCOVA was done on the subscales of the social competence section of the Child Behaviour Checklist. The subscales measure social activity, participation in activities outside school, and competence in school. By Wilks' criterion, the analysis was statistically significant, and revealed a main effect for group. ANCOVAs were done on all subscales, and the means, standard deviations, and univariate F values are presented in Table 3.

Student-Neuman-Keuls tests showed that according to their mothers' reports, the two clinical groups differed significantly from the non-referred group with regard to school performance, but not from each other. The girls from dysfunctional families and the sexually abused girls obtained lower scores on the school scale of the CBCL. However, the difference between the two clinical groups with regard to school scores was eliminated when time in therapy was controlled by covariance techniques. The MANCOVA done on all CBCL social competence subscales for the two clinical groups was not significant by Wilks' criterion, and indicated that any difference between the two groups on any social competence measure was probably related to the difference in time spent in therapy. It should also be noted that both clinical groups had lower scores than the non-referred group on the Activities subscale of the CBCL, but that they did not differ significantly from each other in that area. Thus, hypothesis one was only partially supported since although both clinical groups differed from the non-referred group in terms of general social competence, activities outside school, and school performance, the three groups did not differ with regard to social involvement with siblings and peers.

Behaviour Problems and Child Sexual Abuse

According to mothers' reports, both clinical groups differed substantially from the non-referred group, with regard to general behaviour problems. In order to investigate whether the sexually abused girls and the girls from dysfunctional families presented a similar profile of inappropriate behaviour compared to the non-referred girls, a MANCOVA was conducted on the T-scores of CBCL subscales shared by all subjects. The subscales included depression/withdrawal, somatic complaints, hyperactivity, delinquent aggressive behaviour, cruel behaviour, and the total T-scores for the internalising and externalising subscales. The 'depressed' subscale for girls aged six to 11 and the 'depressed withdrawal' subscale for girls aged 12 to 16 were judged to be sufficiently similar to each other to be classified together as 'depression/withdrawal'. Social class (SES) and the number of natural parents were used as covariates. The MANCOVA was significant by Wilks' criterion, and was followed by univariate ANCOVAs on all variables. Group means, standard deviations, and univariate F values are provided in Table 4.

All univariate ANCOVAs were significant. Student-Neuman-Keuls tests showed that on three variables (Depression/Withdrawal, Somatic Complaints, and Delinquent), the two clinical groups did *not* differ significantly from each other, although both had significantly higher scores than the non-referred group. On the five other variables (Hyperactive, Aggressive, Cruel, Total Externalising, and Total Internalising), the girls from dysfunctional families had significantly higher scores than the sexually abused girls, who in turn had higher scores than the non-referred girls. Therefore, a MANCOVA was conducted on all eight variables in order to compare the two clinical groups, and time in therapy was used as a covariate. The MANCOVA was not significant by Wilks' criterion, which showed that previous univariate differences between the clinical groups were likely due to the fact that members of the sexually abused group had spent more time in therapy.

Thus, hypothesis two was strongly supported in that the clinical groups were similar to each other with regard to behaviour problems when the difference in length of therapy was taken into consideration, but both clinical groups had significantly more problems than the non-referred group. This was true not only for the total score of the Behaviour Problem section of the CBCL, but also for the subscales of that questionnaire.

Self-perception and Child Sexual Abuse

It has already been found that the sexually abused girls did not differ from the girls from dysfunctional families with regard to global self-worth, although members of both clinical groups had more negative perceptions of themselves than members of the non-referred group. Other aspects of the children's self-perceptions were analysed in a MANCOVA which included the remaining five subscales shared by the child and adolescent versions of the Self-Perception Profile, with SES and the number of natural parents as covariates. The MANCOVA was significant by Wilks' criterion, and univariate ANCOVAs were conducted on each measure. Group means, standard deviations, and univariate F values are shown in Table 5.

Significant main effects for groups were obtained for two of the five subscales: scholastic competence, and behavioural conduct. Student-Neuman-Keuls tests showed that the two clinical groups differed significantly from the non-referred group in terms of their perception of their competence in school, but did not differ from each other. The girls from dysfunctional families perceived themselves as behaving significantly more poorly than the non-referred girls, but there were no significant differences between the clinical groups, or between the sexually abused group and the non-referred group with regard to behavioural conduct. There were no significant differences between the groups on issues such as social acceptance, athletic competence and physical appearance.

Therefore hypothesis four was only partially supported. Although the clinical groups were similar in terms of their appraisal of their own self-worth, and felt less worthy than the non-referred group, they were also expected to have significantly lower scores than the non-referred group on all subscales of the SPP. In fact, the hypothesis was supported only for scholastic competence.

When the results of the Self-Perception Profile and the Child Behaviour Checklist are compared, it is interesting to note that the girls in both clinical groups perceived themselves as being significantly less competent in school, but as similar to the non-referred groups with regard to the extent to which they were accepted by others. This perception of themselves almost exactly matched their mothers' observations of their behaviour. However, it appears that the sexually abused girls did not see their conduct as being very different from that of the non-referred girls. This perception does not correspond to their mothers' observations. On the other hand, the girls from dysfunctional families did perceive themselves as having more conduct problems than the non-referred girls, and their mothers agreed. Overall, it appears that family dysfunction with a parent-child conflict component is more strongly related to both child perception and parental perception of behaviour problems than to a history of sexual abuses.

Stress and Child Sexual Abuse

Sexually abused girls and girls from dysfunctional families perceived a higher level of stress than their non-referred counterparts. A MANCOVA using SES and the number of natural parents in the home as covariates was done to determine whether the groups differed in terms of their experience of negative stress and positive stress. The MANCOVA was significant by Wilks' criterion, and univariate ANCOVAs were conducted on measures of negative and positive stress. Group means, standard deviations, and univariate F values are shown in Table 6.

Student-Neuman-Keuls tests show that members of the non-referred group were aware of relatively little negative stress in their lives compared to the two clinical groups. The clinical groups reported intense levels of negative stress. However, the sexually abused group and the dysfunctional family group did not differ from each other significantly on that variable. As can be seen in Table 6, the three groups differed little in terms of the positive stress they reported in the most recent year of their lives. Thus, hypothesis six was largely supported in that not only did the children in the clinical groups experience greater intensity of stress in the most recent year of their lives, but they also perceived their negative experiences as having a greater effect on their lives.

A Comparison of Family Functioning in Families with a History of Sexual Abuse, Family Dysfunction, and Non-referred Families

It was hypothesised that the parents' perceptions of family functioning in the two clinical groups would be different from parents' perceptions in the non-referred group. Specifically, it was expected that both the mothers and fathers from families with histories of sexual abuse or family dysfunction would perceive their families as experiencing more problems. Furthermore, families where sexual abuse had occurred were expected to report poorer family role performance, less affective expression (expression of emotions) in the family, and less affective involvement (emotional closeness, support) than the dysfunctional families.

In order to test the first hypothesis, an ANCOVA was conducted on the total score of the Family Assessment Measure completed by the mothers, with SES and the number of natural parents as covariates. The ANCOVA showed a significant group effect. A post-hoc test (Student-Neuman-Keuls) found that the two clinical groups reported considerably more family dysfunction than the non-referred group, but did not differ significantly from each other. Thus, hypothesis seven was supported.

The second hypothesis was tested by conducting a MANCOVA on the $\underline{T}$ scores of all the clinical subscales of the FAM, as reported by the mothers. The subscales are measures of task accomplishment, role performance, communication, affective expression, affective involvement, control, and the coherence of the values and norms held by the families. As for other multivariate analyses in this study, SES and the number of natural parents in the home were used as covariates. Group means, and standard deviations are given in Tables 7 and 8. Interestingly, the multivariate $\underline{F}$ value for this analysis was not significant, even though all the univariate values for the subscales were significant, except for task accomplishment. Since the MANCOVA on all the subscales was not significant, another MANCOVA was done only on the three subscales on which the groups were expected to differ, namely role performance, affective expression, and affective involvement. This MANCOVA was significant by Wilk's criterion. Student-Neuman-Keuls tests showed that the two clinical groups were similar on all three subscales, but that they showed more problems than the non-referred group (Table 9).

The Relationship Among Family Dysfunction, Perceived Stress, Sexual Abuse, and Child Behaviour Problems

Hypothesis 9 proposed that when variables such as family functioning, marital functioning, and severity of external stressors are considered, their relationship to child behaviour problems might be stronger than the effects of sexual abuse *per se* or in its major aspects. This hypothesis was tested using two multiple regressions: first, a regression analysis involving the 20 sexually abused subjects was undertaken, using a family dysfunction measure, a measure of stress, and a relevant aspect of sexual abuse, with a measure of child behaviour problems as the dependent variable. Then, a second regression analysis was done involving all 60 subjects, using a family dysfunction measure, a measure of stress, sexual abuse as a dichotomous variable, SES, and the number of natural parents as independent variables, with a measure of child behaviour problems as the dependent variable. Measures of marital functioning were not used since they could not be obtained for all subjects.

The first multiple regression required the identification of which sexual abuse variable(s) were most directly related to behaviour problems in children. Thus, a correlation matrix was designed using sexual abuse variables and the total scores of the child behaviour problem scales used in this study. Correlations significant at the .100 level or less are presented in Table 10. The sexual abuse variable which was most strongly related to distress in children in this sample was the type of perpetrator: sexual abused by a father figure was related to lower social competence, more behaviour problems, and more externalising behaviour on the part of the victims. Surprisingly, the use of physical force by the perpetrator was negatively correlated with difficulties experienced by the children. Children who had been forced by the perpetrator into inappropriate sexual acts reported a higher level of self-worth and fewer indications of depression. Victim's appearance in criminal court was significantly related to more internalising behaviours as observed by the mothers and more depression as reported by the girls. Other sexual abuse variables were only marginally related to measures of behaviour problems in sexually abused girls, when they were related at all. Therefore, the type of perpetrator (a dichotomous variable differentiating father figures from other perpetrators) was entered in the first multiple regression.

The relationship among the variables of family dysfunction as measured by the total score of the mother's FAM, perceived stress as measured by the total score of the LEC, the type of offender, and behaviour problems as measured by the total score of the Behaviour Problem section of the CBCL, was examined with 'simultaneous' multiple regression statistics. Simultaneous regression was used as suggested by Briere (1988) and Briere and Elliott (1993) for conceptual reasons (family dysfunction, stress, and sexual abuse often occur at the same time in a child's life), and to avoid placing too much importance on any given variable, as often happens for the first variable entered in hierarchical or step-wise models. Furthermore, simultaneous regression is considered a better option when the sample size is small and when there is a possible causal relationship among the independent variables (Pedhazur, 1982).

Results of the regression are presented in Table 11. The regression was significant. The variables included accounted for 42 per cent of the variance of child behaviour problems as measured, but only one variable, family dysfunction, contributed significantly and accounted for 16 per cent of the variance of the outcome measure. Therefore, as predicted by hypothesis 11, family dysfunction was a stronger predictor of general behaviour problems in this sample of girls than at least one important aspect of the sexual abuse situation.

In order to examine the relationship between sexual abuse and child behaviour problems in a larger context, two multiple regressions were done on two different groups of subjects. First, the two clinical groups (sexually abused girls and girls from dysfunction families) were pooled and the total score of the Behaviour Problems section of the CBCL was regressed on the following variables: the total score of the FAM as filled in by the mothers, the total score of the LEC, sexual abused as a dichotomous variable, and time spent in therapy. As shown in Table 11, the regression was significant, and the variables entered accounted for 33 per cent of the variance of the outcome measure. Only the total score of the LEC contributed significantly, accounting for 9 per cent of the variance of child behaviour problems for this sample. Thus, the more stress the children reported, the more likely their mothers saw them as experiencing behaviour problems.

The third regression analysis was done on all 60 subjects, with the three groups pooled. Again, measurements of family dysfunction and stress were included, along with sexual abuse as a dichotomous variable, SES, and the number of natural parents in the home since the non-referred group had a higher SES and often had two natural parents in the home. As in the other regressions, the total score of the Behaviour Problem section of the CBCL was used as an outcome measure. The results indicate that the regression was significant, and that the variables included accounted for 38 per cent of the total variance of child behaviour problems. Two variables contributed significantly: the total score of the FAM, and the total score of the LEC. Thus, greater intensity of family dysfunction as reported by the mothers and greater intensity of stress as reported by the children, were more directly related to behaviour problems in children as observed by the mothers, even when sexual abuse and other control variables were taken into account.

Conclusions and Implications for Clinical Interventions

This study produced results similar to the findings of Friedrich et al (1987), in support of the view that sexually abused girls do not differ very much from girls who have known to have other types of family dysfunction and parent-child conflict. In addition, there is now evidence available that at least some aspects of the dynamics of families with a history of sexual abuse may be similar to those of other dysfunctional families. Therefore, many, if not most, of the techniques which have been developed to help children with behaviour problems could probably be applied to sexually abused children with some success. The implication also is that many clinicians who are experienced in working with families with relatively severe problems can probably transfer a good part of their experience to work with sexually abused children and their families.

However, this should not be taken to mean that any experienced clinician can work or should work with sexually abused girls and their families. Sexual abuse remains a unique situation which demands very specific forms of interventions in relation to issues of child protection and support (Handy and Pelletier, 1988; Sgroi, 1982; Trepper and Barrett, 1986). Ethically appropriate interventions in other types of unique situations (for instance, child physical abuse, chemical addictions, custody and divorce) require specialised training, and similarly, a clinician should not begin the treatment of sexually abused children without good preparation.

A second finding of this study is that family dysfunction and, in some cases, secondary stressors seemed to contribute more to the distress of the girls in this sample than certain identified variables related to sexual abuse. This finding suggests that clinicians who work with sexually abused children might do well to identify the difficulties related to the current functioning of these children's families, and the stressors which generally affect their lives. It is possible that when family problems are reduced and the girls' lives have become more predictable and structured, that their individual levels of distress might be substantially reduced. Problems more specifically related to sexual abuse may then become more tractable.

The results of this study, and especially the results of the multiple regressions, may be seen as relevant to the debate as to whether intervention with sexually abused children and their families should start with the family or with the individual child. This issue is often raised when family or marital issues are seen as having a possible causal relationship to child behaviour problems (O'Leary, 1984). It is our experience as clinicians that most agencies who work with sexually abused children adopt at least a two-pronged approach where by children are seen individually and with their families, with different issues being approached in different modalities of treatment. Such approaches are probably well advised, and the issue of where and how therapy should start with these families is probably best decided on a case-by-case basis, after a hierarchy of therapeutic needs has been agreed upon by the therapists and the family.

Any study of a problem as complex as child sexual abuse is bound to have limitations. The results of this study, like those of any other, ought to be considered carefully. The sample for this study was small, and obviously it could not be randomly selected. The design of the study focused on post-abuse functioning, even though sexual abuse was relatively recent in the lives of some of the subjects and parent-child conflicts were current. Factors which could have influenced the lives of the girls in both clinical groups and determined some of the behaviour problems they showed could not be measured prior to the onset of the abuse or of the parent-child conflict. Finally, even though the instruments selected for this study were most suited to the purpose to which they were used, they all measure a rather broad band of symptoms, functions, and stressors. As a result, more subtle or specific aspects of individual, marital, or family functioning in each group may have been missed.

A final word of caution: the results of this study should not be taken to mean that sexual victimisation has no impact of its own on a child's life. Most clinicians would agree that CSA often affects a child, and later a woman, in a very personal manner which ultimately may or may not be measurable. In the same vein, it should be noted that this study was not designed to determine causality between the various factors which were considered. Whether sexual abuse is or is not causally related to child psychopathology, independently or along with factors such as family dysfunction and stress, cannot be inferred from this study. All this study allowed for was the identification of associations between variables. Causal relationships may be the object of future studies.

Summary

Sexually abused children are often described as having a wide range of behaviour problems. Although many studies have been done to investigate the association between sexual abuse and such behaviour problems, a consensus has not yet been achieved with regard to the characteristics of the victims, and their differences from other clinical groups or non-referred children. Also, few researchers have investigated factors which might moderate the effects of sexual abuse.

The present study surveyed behaviour and family problems in a group of twenty sexually abused girls, who were compared to twenty girls from dysfunctional families, and twenty non-referred girls from the community. Behaviour problems were examined using the Achenbach Child Behaviour Checklist, the Child Depression Inventory, and the Self-Perception Profile. The potential mediating factors investigated included family dysfunction as measured by the Family Assessment Measure, and stress in the lives of the girls as measured by the Life Events Checklist.

Results showed that sexually abused girls displayed more behaviour problems and reported more signs of depression than the non-referred girls, but that they did *not* differ significantly in these areas from the girls from dysfunctional families. Surprisingly, there were no differences among the groups with regard to sexualised behaviour. The clinical groups also presented more family dysfunction than the non-referred group. On the other hand, the three groups were very similar in terms of the parents' marital adjustment. Finally, the girls from the clinical groups had experienced more intense stress in the previous year of their lives than the non-referred girls.

Results also showed that family dysfunction and the intensity of stress were significantly related to child behaviour problems. In fact, the strength of the relationship between family dysfunction and behaviour problems exceeded the strength of the relationship between the type of perpetrator and behaviour problems in the sexually abused group. When the two clinical groups were pooled, the strength of the relationship between the intensity of stress and behaviour problems *exceeded* the strength of the relationship between sexual abuse and behaviour problems. When the whole sample was considered, the strength of the relationship between family problems and intensity of stress with behaviour problems *exceeded* the strength of the relationship between sexual abuse and behaviour problems. The results generally agree with a previous report (Friedrich et al, 1987), which described sexually abused children as more disturbed than normal children, but not significantly different from other clinical groups.

Table 1 Abuse characteristics for the sexually abused sample (N = 20)

Abuse variable	Number of cases	%
Number of incidents of abuse:		
One	4	20
Two or more	16	80
Type of abuse experienced:		
Manipulation or fondling of the child's genitals or breast	16	80
Fondling of the child through her clothing	10	50
Attempted intercourse	6	30
Masturbation of the perpetrator by the child	4	20
Vaginal intercourse	4	20
'Dry' intercourse	3	16
Digital penetration or insertion of objects in vagina or rectum	2	10
Fellatio	2	10
Oral stimulation of the child by the perpetrator	1	5
Anal intercourse	1	5
Number of perpetrators:		
One	15	75
Two	2	10
Three	1	5
Four	1	5
Perpetrator:		
Natural father	10	50
Stepfather or common-law husband	6	30
Grandfather	1	5
Uncle	3	15
Brother	2	10
Mothers' boyfriend	4	20
Perpetrator used physical force:		
Yes	5	25
No	15	75

Table 1 Continued

Perpetrator used verbal threats to silence the child:
    Yes   3   15
    No   17   85

Child testified in Family Court:
    Yes   2   10
    No   18   90

Child testified in Criminal Court:
    Yes   3   15
    No   17   85

Child temporarily removed from the home for protection:
    Yes   5   25
    No   15   75

Table 2 Adjusted means, standard deviations, and univariate $\underline{F}$ values of the total scores of six measures of child behaviour problems and stress for sexually abused (SA), dysfunctional family (DF), and non-referred (NR) groups

Variables	SA (N = 20) M	SD	DF (N = 20) M	SD	NR (N = 20) M	SD	$\underline{F}$ values (2,55)
				Groups			
Social competence (CBCL)	39.31	9.24	36.54	11.30	51.90	8.10	10.81***
Behaviour problems (CBCL)	69.43	10.74	75.40	6.73	48.02	6.48	43.33***
Sexualised behaviour (CBCL)	1.01	1.80	.87	1.48	.22	.31	1.20
Global self worth (SPP)	2.93	.81	2.55	.77	3.53	.46	8.74***
CDI	9.17	8.16	13.11	9.40	4.03	3.68	5.84**
LEC (total score)	18.78	14.09	16.49	8.47	9.08	5.05	3.24*

***   p < .001
**   p < .01
*   p < .05

Table 3 Adjusted means, standard deviations, and univariate F values of CBCL Social Competence variables for girls from sexually abused (SA), dysfunctional family (DF), and non-referred (NR) groups

Variables	SA (N = 20)		DF (N = 20)		NR (N = 20)		F values (2,55)
	M	SD	M	SD	M	SD	
Activities	46.81	9.04	45.62	10.08	52.62	2.66	3.14*
Social	39.11	10.11	38.03	11.07	45.61	6.54	2.80
School	39.88	11.83	31.15	9.32	50.12	5.23	17.26***

*** $p < .001$
* $p < .05$

Table 4   Adjusted means, standard deviations, and univariate F values of CBCL behaviour problems subscales for the sexually abused (SA), dysfunctional family (DF), and non-referred (NR) groups

Variables	Groups							F values (2,55)
	SA (N = 20)		DF (N = 20)		NR (N = 20)			
	M	SD	M	SD	M	SD		
Depression/Withdrawal	70.40	10.98	75.15	8.71	56.09	2.75		20.59***
Somatic Complaints	64.19	8.99	68.61	9.78	55.90	4.55		9.84***
Hyperactive	68.13	8.96	73.20	8.70	55.47	.78		23.75***
Delinquent	69.10	9.14	71.82	9.06	58.24	2.95		12.68***
Aggressive	69.19	10.88	75.05	9.18	57.40	3.20		17.24***
Cruel	66.29	9.01	73.65	6.82	59.71	4.54		16.56***
Total Internalising	66.48	9.79	71.80	6.73	49.58	5.51		33.31***
Total Externalising	65.91	10.53	72.18	7.44	48.21	7.27		31.50***

*** $p < .001$

Table 5 Adjusted means, standard deviations, and univariate F values of the Self-Perception Profile subscales for the sexually abused (SA), dysfunctional family (DF), and non-referred (NR) groups

Variables	Groups						F values (2,55)
	SA (N = 20)		DF (N = 20)		NR (N = 20)		
	M	SD	M	SD	M	SD	
Scholastic competence	2.70	.74	2.43	.67	3.27	.62	6.04**
Social acceptance	2.81	.89	2.84	.89	3.42	.48	2.50
Athletic competence	2.82	.66	2.61	.68	2.99	.78	1.25
Physical appearance	2.71	.92	2.80	.85	3.15	.79	1.12
Behavioural conduct	2.88	.65	2.44	.77	3.25	.60	5.97**

** $p < .01$

Table 6   Adjusted means, standard deviations, and univariate F values of Life Events Checklist measures of positive and negative stress for sexually abused (SA), dysfunctional family (DF), and non-referred (NR) groups

Variables	SA (N = 20)		DF (N = 20)		NR (N = 20)		F values (2,55)
	M	SD	M	SD	M	SD	
Positive score	6.86	6.12	5.65	7.23	6.39	3.94	.21
Negative score	11.86	9.37	10.84	7.96	2.70	2.50	6.16**

**   p < .01

Table 7   Adjusted means, standard deviations of the FAM total score (completed by mother) for girls from the sexually abused (SA), dysfunctional family (DF), and non-referred (NR) groups

Variables	SA (N = 20)		DF (N = 20)		NR (N = 20)	
	M	SD	M	SD	M	SD
Family assessment measure (total score)	59.83	9.74	57.05	8.31	48.61	7.38

Table 8

Means and standard deviations for the subscales of the Family Assessment Measure (mothers) for girls from the sexually abused (SA), dysfunctional family (DF), and non-referred (NR) groups

Variables	Groups					
	SA (N = 20)		DF (N = 20)		NR (N = 20)	
	M	SD	M	SD	M	SD
Task accomplishment	62.00	13.14	57.75	10.70	47.75	9.10
Role performance	67.55	14.14	62.65	11.92	48.45	11.12
Communication	60.45	10.26	57.20	7.57	45.70	6.84
Affective expression	62.00	12.27	55.95	9.43	44.35	7.21
Affective involvement	59.15	8.89	55.60	11.21	45.65	8.17
Control	61.90	12.01	57.75	10.29	44.25	9.36
Values and norms	59.70	10.38	57.15	9.71	45.50	9.39

Table 9   Adjusted means, standard deviations, and univariate $\underline{F}$ values of the role performance, affective expression, and affective involvement subscales for the sexually abused (SA), dysfunctional family (DF), and non-referred (NR) groups

Variables	Groups						$\underline{F}$ values (2,55)
	SA (N = 20)		DF (N = 20)		NR (N = 20)		
	M	SD	M	SD	M	SD	
Role performance	66.96	14.14	62.32	11.92	49.37	11.12	7.01***
Affective expression	58.86	12.27	54.99	9.43	48.44	7.32	4.46**
Affective involvement	56.96	8.90	54.87	11.21	48.56	8.18	3.09*

***   p < .01
**   p < .05
*   p < .05

Table 10   Correlations between sexual abuse variables and selected measures of child behaviour problems (N=20)

Sexual abuse variables	Social Competence	Behaviour Problems	Intern[1] Behaviour	Extern[2] Behaviour	Global Self-Worth	Depression
Number of perpetrators				.303*		
Age at first incident						
Monthly frequency					-.321*	
Duration of abuse		.327*				
Type of perpetrator	-.484***	.436**		.579***		
Type of sexual contact					.474**	
Physical force					.431**	-.461**
Verbal threats						
Appearance in Family Court						
Appearance in Criminal Court			.318*			.344*

1 - Internalising   2 - Externalising   *** p < .01   ** p < .05   * p < .100

Table 11   **Regression analyses of the total score of the behavioural problems section of the CBCL**

Group	Variables Entered	r	t	Multi. R.	R²	F
Sexually abused children (N=20)	Type of perpetrator	.436	1.54			
	FAM total scores (mothers)	.483	2.08*			
	LEC total score	.371	1.18	.64	.42	3.80**
Clinical groups (N=40)	Sexual abuse	-.309	-1.85			
	FAM total score (mothers)	.188	2.61			
	LEC total score	.271	2.13*			
	Time in therapy	-.414	-1.95	.58	.33	4.38***
Total sample (N=60)	Sexual abuse	.273	-1.04			
	FAM total score (mothers)	.594	4.13****			
	LEC total score	.473	3.34***			
	SES	-.455	.13			
	Number of natural parents	-.345	-1.31	.70	.49	10.46*****

Significance levels: **** p < .001   *** p < .01   ** p < .05   * p .5

4 The Interactive Effects of Physical, Emotional and Sexual Abuse on Adjustment in a Longitudinal Study of 565 Children From Birth to 17

CHRISTOPHER BAGLEY, LORETTA YOUNG AND
KANKA MALLICK

Introduction

This research represents the culmination of a series of studies of child sexual abuse and other factors in adolescent and adult mental health carried out in the Canadian City of Calgary between 1984 and 1998. The ecological setting of this research and its setting in community mental health surveys is described in Bagley (1995) and Bagley and Ramsay (1997). Calgary is a prosperous North American city whose economy based on oil and natural gas production, ranks it as one of the wealthiest cities in North America. Nevertheless, up to a tenth of the population remain in chronic poverty, living either on minimum-wage incomes, or on government welfare allowances (Bagley, 1992a). Previous community mental health surveys in Calgary (Bagley and Ramsay, 1986; Bagley, 1991; Bagley, Wood and Young, 1994) indicate that up to twelve per cent of women (and about half that proportion in men) have, before the age of 17 experienced more than a single episode of sexual abuse. For both sexes the experience of CSA is reflected in significantly impaired mental health profiles, particularly in the areas of affective disorder and suicidality (Bagley, 1995). However, what potentiates or causes the negative effects of CSA is its co-occurrence with family dysfunction and other forms of abuse, physical and emotional (Bagley, 1996).

The Calgary Longitudinal Survey

This work began in 1980 when a birth cohort of 1,000 children was identified from the records of infant health clinics in Calgary. The study was originally designed to test hypotheses arising from two previous longitudinal studies: the British National Child Development Study (NCDS - Alberman and Goldstein, 1970); and the New York Longitudinal Study of temperamental factors in child development (NYLS - Chess and Thomas, 1984). Half of the sample were selected according to risk criteria for later problems, identified in the NCDS: these risk criteria (Bagley, 1990a) included medical problems during pregnancy and birth, prematurity and low birth weight, potentially disabling conditions observable at birth, mother's under-use of prenatal services, teenaged single parenthood, drug and alcohol use in pregnancy, and many births in conditions of economic poverty. For each 'at-risk' infant a same-sexed control was randomly selected from records of the same infant health clinic attended by the parent of the focus child.

Largest sample loss (315 cases) occurred in the first follow-up when the children were aged three, the major reason for non-participation being mothers' unwillingness to participate. Once mothers were engaged in the study they rarely declined subsequent interviews, and subsequent sample loss in the follow-ups when the children were aged six, nine and 13 was mainly because the family had moved from the city (Bagley 1988 and 1992a; Bagley and Mallick, 1996). However, in the latest data sweep we were able to locate some of these families living in other cities in Canada.

Extensive data were gathered from mothers as well as from children in these various data sweeps, but for ethical and legal reasons questions were not asked about any events of child abuse and neglect of the children until the final data sweep, when the adolescents in the cohort were on average aged 17. Because of problems familiar to researchers (incomplete data because of father absence; and fathers' absence at work etc) we have no direct information from fathers. Questions about sexual and other abuse in their own childhoods were asked of mothers, and in an experimental (wait-list control) design, mothers who had experienced childhood sexual abuse, who currently had poor self-esteem, and who were socially isolated were offered group therapy (Bagley and Young, 1990; Bagley and Ramsay, 1997; and Bagley and Young in this volume). This research showed that women in group counselling made significant gains in self-esteem scores, were less depressed, and had more social support compared with women not enrolled in these groups.

The fact that the mothers of the cohort had been alerted to the possibilities of sexual abuse by reviewing it in their own lives, and that a sub-group who had experienced long-term CSA received relevant counselling means that these mothers may have been able to detect or deter sexual assaults on their own children, including those by step-fathers and cohabitees (who form a particularly numerous group of sexual abusers - Bagley, 1991). Given this, the reports by their children of their own sexual abuse histories may not be representative of the general population, in that they may have experienced less abuse because of their mothers' alertness. A bias working in the opposite direction relates to the special nature of the sampling, since mothers from poverty backgrounds, those from 'multi-problem' families, and single women who were liable to take on partners unrelated to their child were over-sampled. It is known from other evidence (reviewed in Bagley and Thurston 1996 a and b) that children in such families are at elevated risk of abuse.

The Ideas Explored

Sexual abuse research in the late 'nineties has achieved some sophistication, with careful definition of variables and measurement of outcomes, and multivariate designs complemented by sophisticated qualitative studies (Bagley and Thurston, 1996a and b). This research suggests that a single event of sexual abuse is only atypically (e.g. in the case of a forceful rape) associated with long-term psychological harms. Even long-term sexual abuse (i.e. sexual contacts not wanted by the young person) may not be harmful if the child's family life was supportive, and no other kinds of abuse occurred. Conversely, a climate of family dysfunction which surrounds events of sexual (and other) abuse is much more likely to be reflected in adolescent and adult mental health problems. One of the problems in interpreting multiple sources of influence is in deciding the primacy and causal significance of the variables measured. A potentially important way of establishing causal significance is through longitudinal analysis of relevant variables. Such studies are quite rare in the field of child abuse. In the present design, we have asked respondents to establish the date of onset of events of sexual abuse in their lives, attempting to link this onset to the known manifestation of parental factors and behavioural problems in the child observed at various points in the long-term study.

Since previous writers (see Alexander, 1994 for an excellent summary) have pointed to disordered attachments between a child and adult (parental) figures as an important factor mediating the effects of child abuse, a measure of parental bonding has been included in the data sweep at age 17. Other variables included in the analysis are all potential covariants of both abuse and later problems of adjustment. Children with impaired cognitive abilities for example, may be more often targeted for abuse, are least able to resist it, and have fewer cognitive resources which could help them mediate or 'rise above' the abusive events. Children with 'difficult' temperament (which is probably a genetic trait) may be more likely to be scape-goated and rejected, and are known to have elevated rates of conduct disorder (Bagley, 1997b). They may also be targets for abusers, since boys who are estranged from their families are more frequently targets for predatory paedophiles (Bagley, 1997a).

Ethical Issues

In Alberta, any professional who has reasonable or probable grounds for suspecting that a child is being abused is obliged by the Child Welfare Act to report this fact to the Director of Child Welfare for the Province, directly or indirectly. This obligation presents problems for researchers who wish to maintain the confidentiality of information given to them. For this reason we did not ask questions of children and adolescents about abuse of any kind until the young person was aged 17, since at that stage of young adulthood we no longer had a legal obligation to report any accounts of abuse. In fact none of the 17-year-old respondents reported any *current* sexual abuse.

Variables and Hypotheses

Most of the variables in the following statistical analyses are derived from *principal component analyses*, a technique which combines several variables into a single factor or component, with calculation of factor scores for each individual in the analysis. The reason for doing this was to reduce the number of variables in the correlation and regression analyses described below. In all cases the unrotated, general component was used to generate factor scores, since the general component usually groups together a number of measures focussing on the same area of functioning and experience. All of the measures used have previously established validity, and acceptable internal reliability (alpha coefficient at least 0.70) in the present study. For measures which were not normally distributed, a standard z transformation was made.

Central Nervous System (CNS) Problems and Difficult Temperament is based on the principal component which identifies high loading items in the scale of Difficult Temperament (Carey's scale completed by mothers when child aged 3 - see Bagley and Mallick, 1997) and school-identified disability involving the central nervous system at age 6 (Bagley and Mallick, 1997). Since it has been shown with this cohort that both CNS disorders (particularly those causing hyperactivity) and difficult temperament measured early in life are strong predictors of conduct disorder at age 9 (Bagley, 1997b), it is important to control for the effects of this variable, and to examine its interaction with external stressors, which include abusive events in the child's life.

Hypothesis a: Other factors controlled, CNS disorder and Difficult Temperament will remain a significant correlate of self-rated conduct disorder at age 17.

Hypothesis b: Children with CNS Problems and/or Difficult Temperament will react to events of physical, emotional and sexual abuse with increased levels of conduct disorder.

Maternal Stress is based on the general factor in a principal components analysis of Abidin's (1983) Parenting Stress Index completed by mothers when the focus child was aged six. This instrument measures difficulty, depression and disillusionment in child care roles, including the mother's reports of frequencies of physical punishment of the child.

Hypothesis c: Children of highly stressed mothers (based on measure completed by mother when child aged six) will develop increased levels of disturbed behaviour.

Hypothesis d: Children of highly stressed mothers will be at elevated risk of various kinds of child abuse and neglect.

Chronic Poverty was measured by family's total income being at or below the level at which the Province would provide financial support for a destitute family of a particular composition (i.e. income adjusted for number of adults and children in the household). 'Chronic poverty' indicated that family's income was at or below the financial assistance level when the child was aged 6 *and* 9. For correlational analysis this was coded 0 = income above poverty line at both points; 1 = income above poverty line at one point; 2 = income below poverty line at both points.

Hypothesis e: Children from homes stressed by chronic poverty will be (a) more likely to experience abuse and neglect; and (b) will react more adversely to such abuse.

Child's IQ/Achievement combines scores on the Peabody Picture Vocabulary Test (PPVT) when child aged 6 (Bagley, 1988) and measures of reading ability at age 9 (Bagley and Mallick, 1997). In some analyses predicting long-term development, the PPVT score alone was used. The PPVT is an established measure for estimating verbal intelligence, and has produced significant results in explaining why some children are more susceptible to the effects of abuse than others (McGee et al., 1997). The underlying hypothesis is derived from the work of Frodi and Smetena (1984) with younger children: those with relatively impaired cognitive capacities were more likely to be overwhelmed by the everyday verbal (and other) cruelties of an abusive childhood, with more limited resources to negotiate avoidance strategies and to employ the cognitive strategy of self-distancing from the abuser and the abusive events.

Hypothesis f: Children with poorer levels of ability and/or achievement will be (a) more likely to be targeted for abuse; and (b) will react more negatively to such abuse.

Emotional and Physical Abuse were measured by scales contained within two previously validated measures: the Memories of Childhood Rearing Inventory (Arrindell et al., 1983); and the 53-item Childhood Trauma Questionnaire (Bernstein et al., 1994).

Hypothesis g: Emotional and physical abuse will co-occur with CSA to a significant degree, and will be additive or interactive in their potentiation of the negative influence of CSA on mental health.

An example of an emotional abuse item is the invited response to the item 'There was someone in my family who helped me feel important and special' (response 'never true' or 'rarely true': would indicate emotional neglect or abuse). Example of a physical abuse item is the invited response to the statement 'I got hit or beaten with a belt, a board, a cord (or some other hard object).'

Sexual Abuse was measured by scales developed in national and provincial general population surveys in Canada and in Alberta by Bagley (1990b, 1995 and 1997) and Bagley and Ramsay (1986 and 1997). Our working definition of sexual abuse is that of *unwanted* sexual contacts with another person (of whatever age or relationship to the young person) which involved *at least* the touching of the child's and/or the other person's unclothed sexual areas, before the young person's 17th birthday. The information obtained was cross-checked with information provided by a sexual abuse sub-scale in Bernstein et al's (1994) Childhood Trauma Questionnaire. Independent validity for such measures is difficult to obtain, but the measures have structural or face validity in that they correlate strongly with factors thought to be consistent with a history of child sexual abuse, including family disruption, and later mental health problems. For statistical purposes a simple measure of sexual abuse was employed: 0 = none; 1 = one or more events occurring within one week; 2 = multiple and more prolonged events.

Hypothesis h: Multiple events of sexual abuse will have a more negative impact on adolescent mental health than single or brief events.

Hypothesis i: Sexual abuse co-occurring with family dysfunction and/or other types of abuse will be potentiated in its negative impact.

Degree of Sexual Abuse in terms of what actually happened during the abusive events, who the abuser was, and for how long the abuse continued was measured by the instrument described by Bagley (1991). These indicators tend to be inter-correlated, and in statistical analyses are represented by factor scores from a principal component analysis which also incorporated measures of CSA from the Bernstein et al. (1994) scale. The inter-correlations of these elements are presented in Table 4. An item in the Bernstein scale invites responses to 'I believe I was sexually abused'.

Hypothesis j: Prolonged and intrusive sexual abuse will retain a statistically significant and likely causal link to impaired mental health, all other factors controlled.

Conduct and Emotional Disorders at Age 17: These are scales validated with psychiatric populations by Sanford, Offord, Boyle and Pearce (1992), and used in large scale epidemiological work in Ontario. Construct validity for adolescent populations in Alberta (of 2,100 adolescents in a random sample of schools) has been established by Bagley, Bolitho and Bertrand (1997). Because of the high correlation of the emotional and conduct disorder scales with measures of self-esteem in the Alberta normative study, this latter variable has not been operationalized separately in the main analysis. Simply describing oneself as a person with a high frequency of negative emotions and deviant or stigmatized behaviours is an act of self-disparagement, which not surprisingly has high correlations (usually in excess of 0.60) with measures of impaired self-esteem. An example of a question in the emotional disorder or neurosis sub-scale is the invited response to the statement 'I think about killing myself'; example of a conduct disorder statement is 'I get in many fights'.

Attachment and Bonding: The measure used was the Parental Bonding Instrument (Parker, Tupling and Brown, 1979) including the three sub-scales measuring 'Parental Care', 'Denial of Child's Psychological Autonomy' and 'Encouragement of Behavioural Freedom' (Murphy, Brewin and Silka, 1997). Since these three scales all loaded strongly on a single, general factor the scale total was used in statistical analyses. Examples of a scale item is the invited response to the question 'My mother/father ... seemed emotionally cold to me/did not praise me/invaded my privacy.' Responses were asked for each parent in two phases, before and after the child's ninth birthday, parents who were absent for more than two years in either period not being rated. The final score for each scale item was based on the mean rating for all parent figures, at both phases of the child's development. The inference of weak bonding to parent figure(s) carries with it the inference of poor attachments to the parent figure. The alternative would have been to use one of the measures of attachment which involved a lengthy clinical interview, but the research design did not permit this.

Hypothesis k: Adolescents who have experienced various forms of abuse will have weak or negative attachments or impaired bonding to parent figures; and weak attachment will be connected with poorer mental health.

Family Climate was measured by the 12-item summary score in the McMaster Family Assessment Device (Epstein, Baldwin and Bishop, 1983) which asks the individual to describe the degree to which their family life was co-operative, enjoyable and supportive. An example of a question in this scale: responses are invited to the statement 'We don't get along well together'.

110

Hypothesis l: The adolescent's perception of negative family climate will be associated with an increased risk of abuse, and of an increased negative impact of such abuse on adjustment.

Self-Esteem Because of its strong correlation with measures of emotional disorder (at aged 9 and 17), the variable of self-esteem has not been analysed in relation to the variables included in the main correlational analysis (Table 8). Self-esteem is examined in a separate test of self-development in relation to the timing of any sexually abusive events and the identity tasks which in Eriksonian theory (Erikson, 1968) the individual is faced with in the crucial stage of adolescence: in Erikson's schema, the adolescent has to recapitulate successfully achieved role and identity tasks and integrate them in a conception of self in which new roles and psychological tasks are optimistically perceived and integrated as the adolescent readies him or her self for new psychosocial challenges. The longitudinal work of Noam and Valiant (1994) suggests that imposed trauma may subvert the development of the self-system since the adolescent is preoccupied with coping with imposed and unwelcome roles (e.g. that of an unwilling sexual partner or victim of an adult), which may be reflected in the expression of negative role performance, accounting for high scores on measures of emotional and conduct disorder (Westen, 1994). Zimmerman et al. (1997) in a longitudinal study of adolescent self-esteem (SE) show (from cluster analysis) that there are four types of development: SE consistently high; SE moderate and rising; SE steadily decreasing; SE consistently low. Hypothetically, young people experiencing (or who previously experienced) various types of abuse would either have declining or consistently low levels of self-esteem, although a sub-group, recovering from the effects of abuse, could have moderate and rising self-esteem levels.

Three measures of self-esteem have been employed according to their development appropriateness: the brief Piers-Harris measure (Bagley and Mallick, 1978) at age 9; the brief Coopersmith measure (Bagley, 1989) at age 13; and the Rosenberg measure (Bagley et al., 1997) at age 17.

Hypothesis m: Adolescents who experienced sexual abuse spanning the period of early adolescence (ages 11 to 13) will have poorer self-esteem at ages 13 and 17 than (a) those whose sexual abuse did not continue past the age of 11; and (b) those who were not sexually abused, other factors controlled.

Interview setting As in previous data sweeps, most of the interviews when the focus children were aged 17 were carried out in respondents' own homes.

Mothers completed pencil-and-paper questionnaires, while the adolescents (usually in their bedroom) responded to an interactive, computerised questionnaire programmed into a laptop. This format is known to elicit franker responses on sensitive areas such as child sexual abuse (Bagley and Genuis, 1991), and was considered an essential format to protect the confidentiality of information given by the adolescents, who were usually present in the house whilst the mother completed the questionnaire. Qualitative interviews were subsequently conducted in a private setting with 50 of the adolescents with various types of abuse history. Eighteen adolescents who had already separated from their families (living independently, in care, or in a young offenders' institution) were interviewed separately.

Significance levels For the main sample of 17 year olds (275 males and 290 females) an operational correlation coefficient of 0.15 is accepted. This is significant at the one per cent level. While smaller correlations would be statistically significant, they explain so little variance that they have been discounted, since they are effectively meaningless. Accepting a higher level of significance also reduces (but does not eliminate) the possibility of committing 'Type 1 Errors' i.e. apparently supporting a hypothesis when in fact the association of variables was due to random variations in data.

Qualitative analysis Chess and Thomas (1984) have argued persuasively that statistical analyses cannot tell the whole story in accounts of the influence of constitutional factors and their complex interaction with external stressors in explaining the evolution of problems of behaviour and emotion in children. As psychiatrists, they produce frequent clinical case histories to explain or exemplify different pathways through the maze of interacting factors which influence human behaviour. We have followed their example in exemplifying the models of 'spiralling up and spiralling down', in which children with difficult behaviour are blamed and punished, react against this with anger and rebellion, eliciting further punishments (Bagley, 1997b). After the initial interviews using the laptop computerised questionnaire, all adolescents who recorded that they had been victims of prolonged sexual abuse were interviewed in a private setting. In addition, ten individuals who experienced only a single episode of sexual abuse were personally interviewed. Any who had manifest psychological problems were referred for counselling or treatment, in fulfilment of an ethical constraints of this research.

112

Results and Discussion

The kinds of sexual abuse experienced during childhood by the adolescents are outlined in Tables 1 and 2. The proportion of males experiencing prolonged abuse (5.1%) is consistent with previous research in Calgary for males, but the proportion for females (7.2%) is lower than previous estimates for females. This reduced proportion *could* be due to the fact that mothers in our sample were more alert to child sexual abuse issues, and offered their daughters (but not their sons) better protection. It could be too that the various prevention education programmes to counter sexual abuse are having some effect, as we have speculated previously (Bagley, 1990c).

Prolonged abuse for both groups began earlier in the child's life, and inevitably involved more intrusive acts of abuse. Only a minority (less than 30 per cent) of either males or females told anyone about the abuse, and in less than ten per cent of cases were any outside figures (social workers, police etc) involved. No abuser was charged in the case of male victims, and very few in the case of female victims.

Results in Table 3 confirm earlier research (Bagley, 1995), showing that it is *multiple* events of sexual abuse which are associated with profiles on the measures of emotional and conduct disorder which fall into the clinical range of the scores (based on previous normative work with large samples of Alberta and Ontario adolescents). In Table 4 we present the correlation of sexual abuse items which contribute to the sexual abuse factor score. The ranking of the abusers and abuse types variables is based on an examination of the effects of different aspects of abuse on adjustment: thus father-figure as abuser causes more harm than abuser being someone outside of the family; and, as might be expected, penetration of the victim is more harmful than fondling which did not proceed to more intrusive forms of sexual abuse. The use of force or threat was most often used by extra-familial abusers, a type of abuse which is associated with less harm, confirming earlier findings (Bagley and King, 1990). Family abusers tend to use the power of age and structural authority and socialization in seducing the victim, and it is this betrayal of trust which is associated with greater harm.

In Table 5 we show the mental health mean scores for the combinations of abuse types (physical and emotional abuse are measured by the top ten per cent of scorers on the Bernstein scale, in order to give numbers for each abuse category approximately equal to those who experienced prolonged sexual abuse i.e. more than one episode over a period of more than one week). It is clear from this Table that (a) abuse of any kind only atypically occurs on its own; (b) any type of abuse is associated with elevated profiles on measures of conduct and emotional disorder at age 17, often several years after the abuse has ended, implying that the abusive events were associated with chronic impairment of adjustment; (3) types of abuse interact with one another in being associated (probably causally) with elevated profiles on the measures of maladjustment; (d) the combination of sexual and emotional abuse is particularly harmful, with the most harm associated with the combination of all three types of abuse, sexual, physical and emotional. This Table does *not* tell us whether these abuses occurred simultaneously or at different points in time in the child's development; this was explored in personal, qualitative interviews with adolescents reporting a history of sexual abuse.

Tables 6 and 7 present the clinical profiles for emotional and conduct disorder by quintile scores on the principal component measuring emotional and physical abuse (based on quintile divisions of the factor scores for the Arrindell and Bernstein measures' factor scores). Clearly, for both sexes, these 17-year-olds who recall emotional maltreatment by parent figures have significantly elevated profiles on the measures of maladjustment. There are important non-linear trends in these results suggesting that for emotional disorder, in both sexes, the respondents could tolerate a moderate degree of emotional disregard and abuse from their parent(s); but a high level of emotional abuse seems to have precipitated the onset of more severe emotional disorders. This is also true for conduct disorder in females, but not for conduct disorder in males.

The highest levels of physical abuse are clearly associated with elevated risk for clinical profiles for both emotional and conduct disorder, but the trend in all comparisons is more linear in nature. Degree of physical abuse is incrementally matched by steady increases in clinical profiles. The clearest case is for males, for whom the link between physical abuse and conduct disorder is a strong one.

Table 8 presents the product moment correlations between the factor and other scores for the 13 measures; correlations for the sexes have been calculated separately. The large majority of these correlations are statistically significant showing both that problems of behaviour and emotion tend to be generally consistent over time, and also that the numerous correlations require some sort of priorizing procedure in estimating any causal analysis.

The correlations in Table 8 imply a mass of cross-cutting, statistically significant relationships with few clues about direct cause. In order to impose some order on the relationships, and to examine possible causal pathways the technique of hierarchical multiple regression has been employed. This calculates the correlation of a series of predictor variables with a dependent (predicted)

114

variable in a set of steps. One can specify the order in which variables are entered into the regression analysis as part of model fitting or hypothesis testing. We have allowed the variables to enter in order of size of the original correlation with the dependent variable. The statistical programmes employed calculates both beta-weights and partial correlations: in the tables below only partial correlations are presented since these are easier to interpret, and in all cases beta values are quite close to the value of the partial correlations. Statistically significant variables not included in the regression analyses were measures of behaviour and emotional disorder at earlier points in time, and the predictive power of other aspects of behavioural disturbance, including the Somatic Disorders subscale of the Ontario Child Health Scale. This was done to avoid problems of autocorrelation and multicolinearity which can distort the results of regression analysis.

Results of regression analyses Tables 10 and 11 present multiple regression analyses predicting conduct and emotional disorder at age 17, in which the correlations of the three types of abuse are controlled on one another, in relation to their correlations with other identified factors which predict conduct and emotional disorders. With respect to conduct disorder, emotional abuse is the strongest predictor for females, and when the effects of this correlation are controlled for, the effects of both sexual and physical abuse fall dramatically, although the effect of sexual abuse remains significant in the case of emotional disorder.

For most individuals who experienced family problems, a family climate of emotional abuse has been one which enwraps the incidents of physical abuse, which like incidents of sexual abuse tend to be much less frequent than the daily insults of demeaning emotional abuse. Although some young women experienced emotional and physical abuse which was linked to their pre-existing problems of overactivity and difficult temperament, these constitutional factors *retained* their significant contribution to the regression equation in the case of conduct disorder. IQ's effect is eclipsed by the negative emotional factors in family life, as is the influence of physical abuse on conduct disorder in females. All of the regression analyses (in Tables 10 to 13) explain between a fifth and a quarter of the variation in the outcome measures. These explanatory models are based in the main on only three variables: emotional abuse (and associated negative family climate); sexual abuse (in some analyses); and neurological dysfunction (in some analyses).

The most complex picture emerges in the prediction of conduct disorder in males, in which four variables (emotional abuse; weak attachment to parent; sexual abuse; and CNS impairment/difficult temperament) remain significant. Overall, the idea that lower IQ is a vulnerability factor is not supported by these findings for the present population: it appears that IQ's effect is swamped by the effect of CNS problems, which were probably associated causally with poorer cognitive skills.

Predicting risk of prolonged sexual abuse An interesting question is the degree to which demographic and other data collected from mothers at earlier points in time could have predicted the risk of prolonged sexual abuse in females (males show somewhat similar trends in their risk status, but the numbers of sexually assaulted children are too small for this type of analysis to be reliable). In Table 15 these predictors are explored for females in a regression analysis. Surprisingly, mother's years of education emerged as the strongest indicator. This is a proxy measure of social class which was not used in the general correlation analysis; children of mothers with fewer years of completed education were at significantly greater risk of sexual abuse. Chronic poverty and the introduction of a father-figure who was not biologically related to the child retain their statistical significance. An additional risk factor, independent of other factors was child's score on the Peabody Picture Vocabulary Test (a proxy measure of IQ) when the child was aged six. In a separate analysis for males, the same factors were associated with a history of prolonged abuse, but at a weaker level (Table not shown).

Table 16 presents the rates of prolonged sexual abuse in males and females combined, by the demographic risk factors which have emerged in combination for the two sexes. When two or more of these risk factors combine, there is at least a thirty per cent chance that a child will have to endure prolonged sexual abuse. This is a rather different type of analysis from that deployed in the regression equations (Tables 11 to 14); the focus on demographic variables did not include the measures of emotional abuse, impaired attachment and poor psychological climate in the family. It may be inferred (and can be shown statistically) that the risk factors identified in Table 16 are often associated with emotional and interactional dysfunctions in the family.

Qualitative Exploration of Hypotheses

All of the adolescents who reported in the computerized questionnaire that they experienced unwanted, prolonged, and intrusive sexual contacts were later interviewed about the intertwining of events in their lives, and how they felt that these factors had influenced them. Case histories given below generally tend to support the hypotheses elaborated above. The Biblical names are pseudonyms.

Case 1 - illustration of hypotheses a, b and f: Adam's mother was known from other information gathered in the study to have consumed alcohol and smoked heavily throughout the pregnancy with Adam, her third child. Adam was born a month prematurely weighing four pounds. He remained in hospital with jaundice and other neonatal conditions for six weeks following birth, and continued to attend hospital for treatment and eventual surgery for a cranio-facial deformity. His intellectual achievements while in the normal range, were below average and this combined with his hyperactivity led to his placement in a special education class. His single mother had two further pregnancies by different men, and finally cohabited with a third. Adam continuously rebelled against his step-father, and was soundly beaten as a result. He was emotionally rejected by his mother, and at the age of 17 recalled his family (from whom he was now separated) as one marked by conflict and strife. At the age of 12 during one of his many truancies he was picked up by a neighbourhood paedophile who engaged Adam for the next three years, until the man was arrested and imprisoned for sexual assault on another boy (Adam was not involved in this court case). At age 17 he had marked conduct disorder, and was serving time in a young offenders' institution. He attributed the beginning of his stealing and house-breaking to his sexual victimization which he saw as 'the final blow'. He specialized in defiling the houses he broke into, a reflection of his earlier behaviour problem of encopresis.

Case 2 - illustration of hypotheses c, d and e: Judith was the fourth in a family of five children, whose father was frequently sick, philandering, or in jail. The family frequently lived below the poverty line, and on one occasion mother had been cut off benefit for failing to inform welfare authorities that her husband (whom she steadfastly loved, despite his infidelities with other women and with his daughters) had returned from jail. The children were encouraged to shop-lift, and operated rather successfully in groups of three or four. Judith like her two sisters was intermittently raped by her father. Judith's father encouraged her entry to prostitution at the age of 14. At age 17 Judith had minimal self-esteem and a high score on the measure of emotional disorder. She said that there was never a time when she remembers not being worried or scared, and took life passively, as it came. But being forced to become a prostitute was she thought 'the final straw', an observation like Adam's, which occurred several times in the

117

interviews: children were stressed but just about coping, but then some final, bitter blow devastated their adjustment and self-regard.

Case 3 - illustration of hypotheses g, h, i, j and k: Miriam is the oldest daughter in an intact but dysfunctional family. Father experienced an industrial injury and had not worked for several years, staying home and marginalising the role of his wife, who was the main income earner. He jealously guarded the intimate care of his daughters, whom he groomed for sexual abuse which in Miriam's case lasted for six years from when she was 8 until 13. Miriam thinks her mother may have known about the abuse, since the girl gave many verbal clues. Miriam attempted suicide at age 13, but did not tell her psychiatrist about the abuse. She claimed that her mother was cold and rejecting, her father hot and domineering, wheedling and exploitive. Mother insisted on sleeping alone, and at one stage he shared a bedroom with his two daughters. In mid-adolescence Miriam had markedly acting out behaviour, frequently stayed away from home overnight, was involved in street life and the drug scene. At 15 she had a termination of pregnancy, and may have been involved in prostitution.

Case 4 tends to confirm hypothesis l, in that it was family dysfunction and not sexual abuse which was the cause of adolescent unhappiness. *Joel* was the subject of harsh discipline as far back as he could remember. He was resentful at both his parents for not providing comfort and sympathy when his leg was broken in a traffic accident. He confided to the researcher that he deliberately ran in front of a car, hoping to gain sympathy from his parents. By 13 he was spending much of his time away from home, and proved an easy recruit into sexual activities by a man running a sex ring. Despite guilt about sexuality, Joel said that he had actually enjoyed the close emotional relationship with this paedophile, since it gave him a sense of warmth and belonging he never had at home. He felt that the sex was a small price to pay for the love and affection from this man. Joel seemed to have made a satisfactory transition beyond his sexual exploitation, and was engaged in heterosexual dating. He said that he had no interest in sex with younger boys, disconfirming the idea of a 'victim-to-abuser' process in his case.

A Typology Derived from Qualitative Interviews

Phenomena in social science are often heterogenous in nature. Take suicide for instance - sociologists and psychologists from Durkheim onwards have tried to classify suicide and suicidal behaviour into different types, as an aid to heuristic understanding, treatment and prevention. Classification can take two basic forms - an intuitive classification based on an understanding and interpretation of a large amount of information on individuals or the subject matter; and numerical taxonomy, using the techniques of component and cluster analysis. We have preferred the latter type of approach in classifying suicidal behaviours (Bagley and Ramsay, 1997), and have also used this technique in classifying adult women survivors of sexual abuse (Bagley, 1996), showing that some types of sexual abuse (particularly that associated with systemic family problems) is more harmful to long-term mental health than other types of abuse. In that analysis we had enough subjects to divide the sample into two and check the emergent classification in each half of the sample. In the present study there are (fortunately) just not enough victims of sexual abuse for this to be done. Instead however an intuitive classification is presented, based on the qualitative interviews.

Three types of sexual abuse victimology seem to emerge. The *first type* is marked by families in which the mother, often a lone parent who had not completed the final years of high school, lived in poverty for a long period in the child's life. While casual cohabitees were often the purveyors of within-family sexual abuse, the children from these families (boys and girls alike) who were sexually abused were as likely to be victimized outside of the immediate family circle as within in it. Five children in this type of CSA had been sexually abused both within their family and in the wider community.

Case example: Ruth was born to a single mother who had two subsequent children by different fathers. The family often survived on welfare income, but at a time of relative affluence Ruth's step-father sexually assaulted her several times over the period of three months, when she was 8-years-old. She was later sexually assaulted by a teenaged cousin living in the neighbourhood over a period of three weeks when she was eleven. Like other children classified in this group, her recollection of emotional and physical abuse was of greater punishment and emotional rejection than by most children in the study. According to her recollection, emotional and physical abuse both preceded and was contemporary with her experience of sexual abuse.

The *second type* involves children who experienced particularly high levels of emotional abuse, with high scores on the measure of negative family climate (the Epstein et al. FAD). For most, it was their step-father in a reconstituted family who was the sexual abuser.

Case example: Rebecca experienced the divorce of her parents when she was four, and had no further contact with her biological father. Her mother remarried when Rebecca was seven, and her step-father brought two children into the marriage, including a boy five years older than Rebecca. It was this boy who sexually assaulted Rebecca for a period of four years, when she was aged eight to eleven. Rebecca had not told anyone about the assaults. Family life was marked by frequent parental arguments and fights, and Rebecca's mother left with Rebecca when she was twelve.

The *third type* is marked by high levels of physical abuse in families with a child displaying a difficult temperament, often associated with early-onset CNS problems. Mothers tended to be highly stressed in the child's early years, and parents often resorted to physical punishments as an increasingly ineffective method of control. Three of the five boys in this group had entered a victim-to-abuser cycle. It is of note that in a study of adolescents in Calgary who were sexually assaultive it was found that they were significantly more likely than controls to have a history of early-onset CNS problems, with medication for overactivity or seizure disorder (Bagley and Sewchuk-Dann, 1991).

Case example: Aaron was a sickly infant, and experienced several febrile convulsions in his first year of life. He was a difficult baby to feed and to hold. He screamed for long periods in infancy, and as a toddler reacted badly to any kind of frustration, or novel situation. He had frequent temper tantrums, and by the age of three was extremely hyperactive. His grand mal seizures were effectively controlled by medication, but with definite side effects of slowing him into apathy. He found school work difficult, and hated school. At the age of nine he was barely literate. His stressed mother often smacked and otherwise hit him, and locked him in a 'time out' cupboard. He was recruited by a gang of older boys when he was ten as a 'packer' (carrier of drugs - someone unlikely to be searched by police, and too young to be prosecuted). This delinquent gang also prostituted him. He graduated into senior membership of this gang, and was eventually arrested on a number of charges including sexual assault of younger children.

Because of the small numbers allocated to each type, the typology must remain tentative, awaiting numerical taxonomy of a larger sample for confirmation or rejection. Nevertheless, these types do seem meaningful for about half of the adolescents in this study who recalled prolonged sexual abuse.

Why Some Children Avoid Prolonged Abuse: A Qualitative Exploration

An interesting question is why some children's sexual abuse does not become prolonged. This has been explored both from statistical analyses, and from qualitative materiel. First it is clear from comparison of mean self-esteem scores that although the children who experienced long-term abuse had significantly poorer self-esteem than the main sample, the children who were sexually abused on one occasion only (or whose abuse was endured within a single week) did not have impaired self-esteem. The ten extended interviews with adolescents who recalled only a single episode of abuse indicated that although they usually felt outraged or hurt by the abuse, they were able either to tell a parent or other adult about the abuse, were able to threaten the abuser with exposure telling him in no uncertain terms to get lost, were able to avoid the situation where the abuser had access to them, or a combination of these strategies. What united these children was their adequate sense of self and their lack of self-blame for the abusive incident.

In contrast, the children who had to submit to prolonged sexual abuse frequently had impaired self-esteem at the outset, which often reflected a negative family climate in which physical punishments and emotional rejection were common. These children were, so far as we can reconstruct events from personal accounts, sometimes selected for sexual abuse *because* they had poor self-esteem, or because they were vulnerable in other ways which were associated with poorer self-esteem. In other words, the prolonged victim group usually had poorer self-esteem at the onset of abuse, and the abuse itself merely confirmed the self-picture of themselves as bad or worthless children, a portrait originally painted by parents who beat these children frequently, or emotionally rejected them. In this 'spiralling down' initially poor mental health became worse because of the events of sexual abuse.

Two case examples illustrate these processes: *Noah* was sexually assaulted at age ten by an uncle whilst staying with the man at his invitation. The uncle masturbated Noah in the bath, and required the boy to reciprocate. Noah telephoned his mother who arrived immediately to remove the boy. All contact with the uncle was terminated by the family, who provided an atmosphere of loving and non-blaming support for their son. *David* was also sexually abused by a relative at the age of ten, but his background was markedly different. Prior to the sexual abuse he was frequently punished, and was suspended from school for physical attacks on other children. At age nine he had a marked conduct disorder, and very low self-esteem. The sexual abuse in the relative's house continued for two years, following which David was sexually abused by several men following recruitment to a paedophile ring.

Does Sexual Abuse Extending Across the Period of Adolescent Identity Development Impair Self-esteem?

In this analysis (Table 16) we have combined the sexes, since trends were broadly similar when males and females were compared; since numbers in particular groups were small this combining of data for sexes was particularly necessary. A comparison group of young people, experiencing similar levels of physical and emotional abuse but who were not sexually abused, have been included in the analysis. The trends are interesting, but are not in conventional reckoning, statistically significant (with a 1 in 5 probability of chance occurrence). For children whose prolonged sexual abuse ended before their eleventh birthday self-esteem made some recovery in adolescence, but was still somewhat impaired at age 17. For those whom prolonged sexual abuse began or continued between ages 11 and 13, self-esteem levels did decline, being particularly poor at age 17. Levels of self-esteem at the three age points in the comparison groups although impaired, show a different trend. While these results are suggestive, indicating that abuse beginning or continuing during the crucial phases of adolescent identity formation identified by Erikson (1968) may be particularly harmful in terms of self-esteem development, numbers are too small for firm conclusions. Replication with a larger sample is needed.

A case example illustrates a possible pattern of self-esteem development: *Zachariah* lived in a strict religious household, marked by frequent beating for small transgressions. He recalled his mother as an emotionally cold person who rarely comforted him. At age nine he displayed signs of conduct disorder for which his parents 'tried to beat the devil out of him'. His sexual abuse (by a church minister) began when he was twelve, and continued for two years. His self-esteem level, low at age nine deteriorated (indicated by the percentile position of his self-esteem score, relative to the remainder of the cohort) at ages 13 and 17. Ironically, his parents relaxed punishments during his adolescence, approving of his frequent overnight stays at the minister's house. His conduct disorder problem faded, but he developed problems of emotional disorder, and made a serious suicide attempt at age 16 when his parents, aghast and disbelieving of his accusations of sexual abuse against the church minister, rejected him. When interviewed, he was suffering a burden of guilt and self-disgust. After initial counselling by the research interviewer, he was referred to a therapist.

Conclusions and Policy Proposals

First of all, there are limitations to this study. The sample on which the study is based is only partially random, and is over-weighted by children whose early histories have been marked by difficult pregnancy and birth, low birth weight, early illness affecting the central nervous system, and early backgrounds marked by unsupported single parenthood, or by poverty. This has however had the indirect advantage of including groups of children at elevated risk of sexual abuse. Since mothers were alerted to the possibility of sexual abuse by questions asked during the course of the longitudinal survey, and since some mothers were offered therapy for long-term problems associated with their own sexual abuse, increased maternal sensitivity may have allowed them to protect their children against such abuse. If this is the case, then the children who were sexually abused may represent a higher risk group in terms of failure by a parent to understand that their child was being abused. Indeed, the findings show that highly stressed mothers who frequently resorted to physical and emotional punishments were much more likely to have children who became sexual abuse victims.

The adult recall method has advantages in that it identifies cases of abuse many of which have never (as in our survey) come to the notice of any agency. This type of recall survey will miss cases of sexual abuse which the individual chooses not to reveal, perhaps because of a pervading sense of guilt or shame. It will also miss those incidents of abuse which the individual has dissociated from to the degree that they are lost to present memory. It is clear from our clinical work (Bagley, Rodberg and Wellings, 1994) that victims of early, severe and prolonged abuse can dissociate from abusive events as the psyche attempts to protect itself from the cruel implications of abuse. There are also examples in adult recall surveys of individuals who when interviewed, report that they had lost the memory of sexual abuse for part of their lives (Bagley and King, 1990). One of the events which precipitates a recovered memory is the death of the abuser. These are *not* memories recovered in the course of therapy, and are certainly not 'false' memories. It is important to stress that to the extent that the present survey has missed some cases of sexual abuse, this is a conservative bias working *against* the possibility of obtaining statistically significant results.

The regression analyses show that although sexual abuse is often an important factor underlying later adjustment, its impact is often enfolded within the negative emotional climate of a household. While acts of sexual exploitation can take on a profoundly negative symbolic importance for an individual, sexual abuse is very unlikely to take place in households with relatively normal types of socialization and social interaction. This is a welcome finding, and does point to the possibility of early intervention on behalf of families struggling with dysfunctional relationships, and incipient problems of behaviour disorder in children which can lead to later labelling and victimization. In interpreting these statistical trends it is important to avoid the fallacy of composition which leads to the following (fallacious) argument: 'there is strong relationship between emotional abuse and maladjustment; children who are emotionally abused are maladjusted'. This is not the case: the combination of emotional and other abuse factors including various forms of family pathology can explain less than third of the variance in the maladjustment measures. Indeed, multiple correlations in psychology rarely explain more than a third of variance in designs such as this. Factors which can explain the failure to be more powerfully predictive are the imperfection of the measures used; the failure to include measures which could explain more variance; and the (merciful) failure of a deterministic model of human thought and action. Some individuals are able to *choose* how they might react to adverse factors, even in adolescence. This proposition has implications too for social casework: one needs to know a great deal about an individual in order to counsel the best adaptive strategies for them, including ways of helping them to be self-determining in the face of adverse life stresses.

The intuitive typology, heuristically derived from an analysis of case material gives a somewhat similiar picture to that which emerged in the more formalistic regression analyses, and deserves replication.

If validated, it could be that correlations of variables *within* these sub-populations of abuse victims are much higher than in the sample as a whole. Both the findings of the typological analysis and from the general statistical analyses do point to certain risk factors for physical, emotional and sexual abuse: children with hyperactivity or difficult temperament, with poor social skills, poor achievements and fewer cognitive resources are scapegoated and punished in some highly stressed families, in ways which lay them open to sexual abuse both within and outside of their families. Children in families stressed by multiple partnerships and chronic or intermittent poverty are also at elevated risk of the various kinds of abuse. Sexual abuse in 'ordinary' middle class families in these families was conspicuous by its absence, according to the information given by our 17-years-old informants. In this respect, the pictures

124

of sexual abuse revealed resembled those located in an earlier British study (Bagley and McDonald, 1984).

There is an ecological dimension to the Calgary findings, in that sexual and other kinds of abuse were significantly more likely to occur in families living in two areas of the city marked by either poor quality private housing, or low-rent public housing. Both areas had and high rates of crime and other indicators of social deprivation. Date from the longitudinal and community mental health surveys had already identified the two neighbourhoods as potential targets for community work interventions (Bagley and Kufeldt, 1989; Bagley, 1992c). In such neighbourhoods paedophiles prowl, and it is here too that a disproportionate number of paedophile sex rings operate, identified in Bagley (1997). The proposals we made then remain valid today: these are neighbourhoods which cry out for a concentration of social and community supports and recreational facilities for youth, which can both divert young people from delinquency and sexual victimization, and also provide early intervention and support for families under stress.

The psychological findings from this study also have important implications. We have shown as have others (Manly et al, 1994; McGee et al., 1997) that sexual, physical and emotional abuse often occur in the same family, or to the same child. These abuse types may occur sequentially or concurrently, and their effect is both additive and interactive in increasing or causing levels of behaviour disorder and emotional distress. Family work on behalf of victims of child sexual abuse must look at psychosocial processes within the whole family, if a complete healing is to be achieved. Youth (particularly boys) abused outside of their immediate family often have previously experienced within-family physical and emotional abuse. While the negative impact of sexual abuse is contained within the negative effects of emotional abuse for many adolescent women, sexual abuse emerges as an independent predictor of impaired psychological functioning for adolescent men.

These are statistical trends, not deterministic patterns and do not necessarily apply to any particular individual. This is illustrated by a final case history: *Naomi* was sexually abused by her step-father from her earliest memory until she was twelve. Her abuser would invent excuses to punish her, and engaged in sadistic beating which was often associated with sexual assaults. Her mother was often subjected to violent assault by her alcoholic husband. Naomi recalled the sexual abuse as far worse than the beatings, or her step-father's insults (calling her a slut etc). She ran from home at age twelve, moved into care but left a group home and survived for several months on the street, and had been a sex trade worker. Her mother (enrolled in a group run by the research team, for women who had been sexually abused in childhood) finally left her brutal husband, and rescued her daughter from the street. By the age of 17, after two years of individual and group therapy, Naomi had made a good psychological recovery, and the measures of adjustment completed at age 17 were in the normal range.

Both Naomi and her mother seem to have broken the bonds created by sexual abuse and violence.

Table 1 Types and frequencies of sexual abuse recalled by 275 males in a community, longitudinal study

	Single event or events < 7 days (N=17)	Multiple events (N=14)
WHO ABUSED		
Father figure	6%	29%
Other adult relative	29%	36%
Juvenile (<17) relative/acquaintance	35%	18%
Other male adult	29%	43%
Female adult	0%	7%
ABUSE DURATION (WEEKS)		
< one week	100%	0%
1 - 4 weeks	0%	25%
4 - 12 weeks	0%	29%
12+ weeks (range 12 to 240)	0%	43%
TYPES OF ABUSE		
Fondling of genitals/buttocks	86%	100%
Oral sex on victim	23%	79%
Oral sex by victim	6%	53%
Anal insertion/intercourse	12%	50%
AGE WHEN ABUSE BEGAN		
Up to 5 years	0%	14%
6 to 8 years	23%	36%
9 to 10 years	35%	43%
10 to 11 years	23%	7%
12 to 16 years	18%	0%
ACTION TAKEN		
Told no-one	76%	71%
Told someone, abuse continued	0%	14%
Told someone, abuse was stopped	12%	7%
Action by social workers	6%	7%
Abuser charged	0%	0%

Note: Percentages total more than 100% when multiple abusers and/or types of abuse occurred.

Table 2 Types and frequencies of sexual abuse recalled by 290 females in a community, longitudinal study

	Single event or events < 7 days (N=64)	Multiple event (N=21)
FEMALES - WHO ABUSED		
Father figure	6%	24%
Other adult relative	36%	48%
Juvenile (<17) relative	22%	24%
Juvenile (<17) Acquaintance	17%	9%
Other male adult	19%	38%
Female adult	0%	5%
FEMALES - ABUSE DURATION (WEEKS)		
< 1 week	100%	0%
1 - 4 weeks	0%	24%
4 - 12 weeks	0%	19%
12+ weeks (range 12 to 500+)	0%	57%
FEMALES - TYPES OF ABUSE		
Fondling of genitals/breasts/buttocks	77%	100%
Oral sex on victim	8%	71%
Oral sex by victim	3%	62%
Vaginal insertion/intercourse	3%	48%
Anal insertion/intercourse	0%	19%
AGE WHEN ABUSE BEGAN		
Up to age 5	3%	14%
6 to 7 years	8%	24%
7 to 8 years	25%	19%
9 to 10 years	33%	33%
11 to 12 years	19%	5%
13 to 16 years	12%	5%
ACTION TAKEN		
Told no-one	70%	76%
Told someone, abuse continued	0%	14%
Told someone, abuse stopped	23%	9%
Action by social workers	2%	9%
Abuser charged	2%	5%

Note: Percentages total more than 100% when multiple abusers and/or types of abuse occurred.

Table 3 Incidence of unwanted sexual contacts up to age 16 in 275 males and 290 males by clinical categories

Proportion above clinical cut-off point for Emotional Disorder:

MALES	No abuse	Abuse in < 1 week	Abuse prolonged
	N=244 (88.7%) 9.0% in clinical group	N=17 (6.2%) 11.8% in clinical group	N=14 (5.1%) 35.7% in clinical group
FEMALES	No abuse	Abuse in < 1 week	Abuse prolonged
	N=205 (70.7%) 9.8% in clinical group	N=64 (22.1%) 9.4% clinical group	N=21 (7.2%) 33.3% in clinical group

Proportion above clinical cut-off point for Conduct Disorder:

MALES	No abuse	Abuse in < 1 week	Abuse prolonged
	N=244 (88.7%) 13.9% in clinical group	N=17 (6.2%) 17.6% in clinical group	N=14 (5.1%) 35.7% in clinical group
FEMALES	No abuse	Abuse < 1 week	Abuse prolonged
	N=205 (70.7%) 7.8% in clinical group	N=64 (22.1%) 10.9% in clinical group	N=21 (7.2%) 38.1% in clinical group

Note: Scheffé post-hoc comparisons of no abuse plus one time abuse versus multiple abuse, $p < .05$ for all comparisons (Emotional Disorder and Conduct Disorder) for both sexes.

Table 4 Intercorrelation of aspects of sexual abuse with behaviour profiles at age 17 in 275 females and 290 males, and general factor loadings for abuse items

	1.	2.	3.	4.	5.	A	B	GF
1. Abuser other/adult family member/ father figure	-	20	27	27	43	18	31	41
2. Abuse type: fondling/ oral/penetrative on victim	50	-	35	49	50	19	29	58
3. Abuse type: fondling/ oral/penetrative on abuser	43	70	-	36	41	16	30	59
4. Force or threat by abuser	-13	04	17	-	19	-07	09	18
5. Duration: 1 week/1-12 weeks/13 or more weeks	61	52	44	00	-	19	35	60
A Conduct disorder	26	25	27	09	57	-	-	-
B Emotional disorders	29	34	35	13	35	-	-	-
General factor loadings	69	71	74	05	60	-	-	-

Note: Decimal points omitted. Correlations for females below the diagonal, for males above the diagonal. Correlations of 0.15 < .01. GF equals general factor combining sexual abuse items based on unrotated, orthogonal principal component analysis, generated factor scores for each individual.

130

Table 5 Combination of types of physical, sexual and emotional abuse with onset before age 17, by mean scores of maladjustment at age 17 in 565 adolescents

Types of abuse	Physical abuse	Sexual abuse (Prolonged)	Emotional abuse	Conduct Disorder Mean (SD)	Emotional Disorder Mean (SD)
All three types of abuse (9 children)	N=9	N=9	N=9	9.7 (4.5)	12.9 (5.3)
Physical & Sexual (9 children)	N=9	N=9	N=0	6.6 (5.6)	9.1 (6.9)
Physical & Emotional (21 children)	N=21	N=0	N=21	7.8 (5.6)	10.1 (7.2)
Sexual & Emotional (14 children)	N=0	N=14	N=14	8.5 (5.5)	10.8 (6.1)
Physical (17 children)	N=17	N=0	N=0	6.0 (4.9)	8.8 (5.7)
Sexual (3 children)	N=0	N=3	N=0	5.4 (3.5)	8.7 (3.2)
Emotional (12 children)	N=0	N=0	N=12	5.1 (4.9)	9.0 (6.6)
No abuse (480 children)	N=0	N=0	N=0	2.1 (3.5)	4.1 (4.6)

Note: Emotional and Physical abuse categories defined by the top 10% on Bernstein et al's (1996) scales in Childhood Trauma Questionnaire. Sexual abuse defined as abuse occurring 2 or more times over a period of more than 1 week. Emotional and Conduct Disorders based on responses to standardized self-completion measures (Sanford et al., 1992).

Eta (non-linear measure of association based on analysis of variance) of Conduct Disorders across three categories (3 types of abuse vs. 2 types of abuse vs. 1 type of abuse vs. no abuse) 0.39, p <.001 for Conduct Disorder. Eta for Emotional Disorder 0.40, p <.001.

Table 6   **Proportions who experienced emotional abuse, by clinical categories for emotional and conduct disorder**

Proportions above clinical cut-off point for Emotional Disorder:

MALES	Emotional Abuse lowest quintile N=55 3.6% clinical	Emotional Abuse middle quintiles N=165 6.6% clinical	Emotional Abuse highest quintile N=55 27.3% clinical
FEMALES	Emotional Abuse lowest quintile N=58 5.1% clinical	Emotional Abuse middle quintiles N=174 9.7% clinical	Emotional Abuse highest quintiles N=58 22.4% clinical

Proportions above clinical cut-off point for Conduct Disorder:

MALES	Emotional Abuse lowest quintile N=55 9.1% clinical	Emotional Abuse middle quintiles N=165 15.1% clinical	Emotional Abuse highest quintile N=55 21.8%
FEMALES	Emotional Abuse lowest quintile N=58 5.2% clinical	Emotional Abuse middle quintiles N=174 8.0% clinical	Emotional Abuse highest quintile N=58 25.4% clinical

Note: Scheffé post-hoc comparisons (from analysis of variance) of variation of Emotional and Conduct Disorder scores across low and middle quintiles (80% of respondents) versus highest quintile (20% of respondents) $p < .01$, for both sexes.

Table 7 Proportions who experienced physical abuse, by clinical categories for emotional and conduct disorder

Proportions above clinical cut-off point for Emotional Disorder:

MALES	Physical Abuse lowest quintile N=55 5.4% clinical	Physical Abuse middle quintiles N=165 9.1% clinical	Physical Abuse highest quintile N=55 18.23% clinical
FEMALES	Physical Abuse lowest quintile N=58 5.1% clinical	Physical Abuse middle quintiles N=174 11.5% clinical	Physical Abuse highest quintiles N=58 17.2% clinical

Proportions above clinical cut-off point for Conduct Disorder:

MALES	Physical Abuse lowest quintile N=55 9.1% clinical	Physical Abuse middle quintiles N=165 12.1% clinical	Physical Abuse highest quintile N=55 31.0% clinical
FEMALES	Physical Abuse lowest quintile N=58 6.9% clinical	Physical Abuse middle quintiles N=174 9.2% clinical	Physical Abuse highest quintile N=58 19.0% clinical

Note: Scheffé post-hoc comparisons (from analysis of variance) of variation of Emotional and Conduct Disorder scores across low and middle quintiles (80% of respondents) versus highest quintile (20% of respondents) $p < .01$, for both sexes.

Table 8 Correlations between variables antecedent to conduct disorder and neurosis at age 17 in 275 males and 290 females in a longitudinal study of an 'at-risk' cohort

	1	2	3	4	5	6	7	8	9	10	11	12	13
1. CNS/temperament	-	36	15	-40	43	22	38	13	27	21	12	-02	09
2. Maternal stress	39	-	47	-24	31	26	30	24	37	16	10	17	22
3. Chronic poverty	21	51	-	-19	37	30	33	25	37	20	05	16	24
4. Child's IQ/ach.	-46	-30	-24	-	-48	-32	-46	-29	-28	-18	-12	08	10
5. Conduct age 9	34	27	31	-54	-	36	54	21	29	66	32	23	29
6. Emotional abuse	10	33	31	-26	47	-	63	48	44	29	34	35	42
7. Physical abuse	29	25	39	-34	69	44	-	48	44	27	20	27	29
8. Sexual abuse	06	11	35	-29	43	57	41	-	55	21	29	19	18
9. Degree of CSA	27	21	34	-38	52	65	55	74	-	25	23	26	19
10. Conduct at 17	22	13	20	-21	63	39	36	17	20	-	37	25	22
11. Neurosis at 17	13	28	24	-10	39	38	25	30	30	40	-	31	30
12. Attachment	09	19	11	06	36	44	23	34	42	29	37	-	67
13. Family climate	11	19	14	-12	20	39	27	40	43	29	36	65	-

Note: Decimal points omitted. Correlations for girls below the diagonal, for boys above the diagonal. rs of .15 and above, p <.01. "Neurosis at 17" indicates correlations of scores on measure of emotional disorder.

Table 9   Multiple regression of predictors of prolonged child sexual abuse from previously collected data in 290 females

Variable	Correlation before m.r.	Partial correlation	Variance regression
Mother's years of education	.36	.36	13.0%
Chronic poverty (when child 6 & 9)	.30	.19	16.6%
Parent figure when child 6 and/or 9 not biological parent	.28	.20	20.7%
Separation from either/ both biological parents when child 6 or 9	.24	.13	24.8%
Child's vocabulary score at age 6	.22	.20	29.2%
Mother's Stress Score when child 6	.22	.12	30.8%
Child's functional/neuro-logical disability, age 6	.20	.04	31.1%

Note: Partial correlations of 0.15 and above significant at the 5% level or beyond.

Table 10   **Multiple regression analysis of variables predicting conduct disorders in 290 females at age 17**

Variable	Correlation before m.r.	Partial r after m.r.	Cumulative variance explained
Emotional abuse factor score	.39	.39	15.2%
Physical abuse factor score	.36	.19	20.4%
Negative family climate	.29	.14	23.1%
Weak attachment to parent(s)	.29	.08	24.5%
CNS problem/difficult temperament	.22	.17	27.1%
IQ/Achievement	-.21	.04	27.6%
Sexual abuse factor score (who abused, how, duration)	.20	.07	28.8%
Chronic poverty	.20	.08	29.9%

Note: Variables entered step-wise based on their original correlation with Emotional Disorders. First order and partial correlations of 0.15 and above are significant at the 1% level or beyond. Multiple correlation of above items with conduct disorder score, 0.55, p <.001.

Table 11 Multiple regression analysis of variables predicting emotional disorders in 290 females at age 17

Variable	Correlation before m.r.	Partial r after m.r.	Cumulative variance explained
Emotional abuse factor score	.38	.38	14.4%
Weak attachment to parent(s)	.37	.10	16.1%
Negative family climate	.36	.09	17.2%
Sexual abuse factor score (who abused, how, duration)	.30	.19	19.4%
Maternal stress	.28	.02	19.6%
Physical abuse factor score	.25	.01	19.6%
Chronic poverty	.24	.10	20.5%

Note: Variables entered step-wise based on their original correlation with Emotional Disorders. Correlations of 0.15 and above are significant at the 1% level or beyond. Multiple correlation of above items with emotional disorder score .46, $p < .001$.

Table 12 Multiple regression analysis of variables predicting conduct disorders in 275 males at age 17

Variable	Correlation before m.r.	Partial r after m.r.	Cumulative variance explained
Emotional abuse factor score	.29	.29	8.4%
Physical abuse factor score	.27	.13	11.2%
Weak attachment to parent(s)	.25	.16	14.5%
Sexual abuse factor score (who abused, how, duration)	.25	.19	18.1%
Negative family climate	.22	.05	19.2%
CNS impairment/difficult temperament	.21	.18	22.1%
Chronic poverty	.20	.03	22.3%
IQ/achievement	-.18	-.01	22.3%
Maternal stress	.16	.01	22.2%

Note: Variables entered step-wise on the basis of their original correlation with Conduct Disorders. Correlations of 0.15 and above are significant at the 1% level or beyond. Multiple correlation of above items with conduct disorder score. 0.47 P<.001.

Table 13   **Multiple regression analysis of variables predicting emotional disorders in 275 males at age 17**

Variable	Correlation before m.r.	Partial r after m.r.	Cumulative variance explained
Emotional abuse factor score	.34	.34	11.6%
Weak attachment to parent(s)	.31	.20	16.2%
Negative family climate	.30	.08	17.4%
Sexual abuse factor score (who abused, how, duration)	.23	.16	19.5%
Physical abuse factor score	.20	.01	19.4%

Note: Variables entered step-wise based on their original correlation with Emotional Disorders. Correlations of 0.15 and above are significant at the 1% level or beyond. Multiple correlation of above items with emotional disorder score, 0.44, p<.001.

Table 14   **Multiple regression of predictors of prolonged child sexual abuse from previously collected data in 290 females**

Variable	Correlation before regression	Partial correlation	Cumulative variance explained
Mother's years of education	-.36	-.36	13.0%
Chronic poverty (when child 6 & 9)	.30	.19	16.6%
Parent figure when child 6 and/or 9 not biological parent	.28	.20	20.0%
Separation from either/both biological parents when child 6 or 9	.24	.13	22.8%
Child's vocabulary score at age 6	-.22	-.20	24.4%
Mother's Stress Score when child 6	.22	.12	26.8%
Child's functional/neurological disability, age 6	.20	.04	27.0%

Note: Partial correlations of 0.15 and above significant at the 1% level or beyond.

**Table 15 Risk factors up to child's ninth year predicting a history of
child sexual abuse**

Risk factor	Proportion with prolonged sexual abuse
Mother did not complete high school: 34 cases at risk	20.6%
Chronic poverty: 23 cases at risk	17.4%
Father figure not biological father: 43 cases at risk	16.3%
Vocabulary score at age 6 in lowest quintile: 58 cases at risk	17.2%
None of the above risk factors: 508 cases	3.9%
One of the above risk factors: 35 cases	17.1%
Two of the above risk factors: 15 cases	26.7%
Three or four of the above risk factors: 7 cases	42.9%

Note: Eta (a non-linear measure of association derived from analysis of variance
of the nominal category of sexual abuse across the four ordinally scored risk
categories: none, one, two, three or four) 0.49, $p < .001$. Since risk factors have
an overlapping incidence, several cases fall into more than one risk category.

Table 16 Comparison of self-esteem levels by sexual abuse before and during presumed normal adolescent identity problems

	CSA ended before age 11 N=23	CSA began or continued at ages 11, 12, 13 N=12	No CSA, equal levels of emotional or physical abuse N=35
SE in poorest quintile at age 9	39.1%	33.3%	40.0%
SE in poorest quintile at age 13	26.1%	50.0%	48.6%
SE in poorest quintile at age 17	30.4%	58.3%	34.3%

Note: 'CSA' indicates Child Sexual Abuse. 'SE' indicates self-esteem. 'Poorest quintile' indicates the 20 per cent of scores indicating the poorest self-esteem for the whole cohort of 565 subjects.

Significance: Chi-squared, 4 d.f., 4.67, not significant.

5 Long-term Evaluation of Group Counselling for Women with a History of Child Sexual Abuse: Focus on Depression, Self-esteem, Suicidal Behaviours and Social Support

CHRISTOPHER BAGLEY AND LORETTA YOUNG

Introduction

A number of studies (reviewed in Bagley and King, 1990) suggest that rates of suicidal behaviour (suicidal ideation, deliberate self-injury, and attempted suicide) have an elevated incidence in women who were sexually abused in childhood. Since these earlier studies using clinical or specialized samples, a number of well-conducted epidemiological studies have established suicidal behaviour as a *major* long-term sequel of child sexual abuse. This emerged for example, in a New Zealand study (Mullen et al, 1993) of a random sample of 2,250 adult women which found that 13 percent had experienced sexual abuse in childhood. The very high levels of suicidal behaviour associated with prior sexual abuse "were out of all proportion to the level of measured psychopathology". (p. 728) Suicidal behaviour as a specific sequel of child sexual abuse was the focus of the Dutch research by Van Egmond et al. (1993). In a random sample of 1,054 adult women aged 20 to 40, those who recalled sexual abuse had an attempted suicide rate of 14 percent, compared with 4 percent in matched controls. In a further study by Van Egmond et al. (1993) of 158 women admitted to an emergency department following a suicide attempt 79 (50 percent) had experienced sexual abuse in childhood. These 79 women had been abused by a total of 148 different males, and for most of the women the sexual abuse had been prolonged. The women who had been sexually abused in childhood had on average made four prior suicide attempts, compared with two prior attempts in the non-abused.

A Canadian study which surveyed 2,112 high school students (Bagley, Bolitho and Bertrand, 1995) also confirmed prior sexual abuse as a key marker for suicidal ideation. The 53 girls who reported "frequent unwanted sexual assaults" had frequent suicidal thoughts in 13.2 percent of cases, a rate five times higher than in the non-sexually assaulted. In a Canadian study which randomly sampled 750 women aged 18 to 27, from the community 31 per cent of those who had been victims of prolonged sexual abuse had made a suicidal gesture in their lifetime, compared with 4 per cent of women without such a history.

It is not certain that sexual abuse has a direct, causal relationship with later suicidal behaviours, since co-occurring family dysfunction, parental loss, physical and emotional abuse may have some causal significance, or interact with sexual abuse in determining pathways to suicidal behaviours. However, in work using regression analyses we have found that sexual abuse in childhood remains a significant predictor (explaining about five per cent of variance in measures of suicidality) when the effects of emotional abuse, physical abuse and parental separations were controlled for (Bagley, 1995; Bagley and Ramsay, 1997).

One reason why suicidal behaviours may have such an elevated incidence in 'survivors' of child sexual abuse is the fact that the abuse has imposed on the victims a sense of bodily shame, so that there is a converging syndrome in such adults of self-injurious behaviours, eating disorders which distort body image, and poisoning of the body through the ingestion of drugs and alcohol. An argument for this syndrome convergence is made by Bagley (1995), and supportive evidence comes from a number of studies (Andrews, 1997). McCauley et al. (1997) refer to these multiple symptoms as the "unhealed wounds" of child sexual abuse.

Group Work with Women who have Survived Sexual Abuse

The pioneering work of Forward and Buck (1981) demonstrated that social work therapists can have a key role as leaders of group therapy for individuals who experienced (and "survived") child sexual abuse. Forward and Buck's work was focussed on adolescents, and most studies available address group work with teen survivors. A number of studies have shown that group treatment models with adolescents can reduce social isolation, reduce guilt, give feelings of empowerment, give social skills training (e.g. role-playing court appearances), enhance self-esteem, and enable members to engage in therapeutic arts projects. Usually the reported gains are based on uncontrolled designs with follow-up studies (e.g. Furniss et al., 1988). However, a few studies have used control groups in group work with adolescents. Rust and Troupe (1991) identified impairment of self-esteem (which can be an antecedent of suicidal feelings) as a consistent sequel of child sexual abuse. The authors evaluated a therapeutic programme which involved counselling and group work with 25 girls aged 9 to 18 (mean 12.5 years). Control subjects were 25 non-abused girls, matched for age, IQ, and income level (measured by participation in a free lunch programme). At pre-test abused girls had dramatically poorer self-esteem. Group work focussed on lifting the burden of blame, and giving advice and reassurance around difficult tasks (e.g. giving evidence in court). Other activities involved artistic and creative expression, and social activities and excursions which enhanced peer-bonding. About 80 per cent of sessions "involved the slow, arduous task of building self-esteem through continuous encouragement, support, and praise" (p. 425). Post-test measures of self-esteem for the CSA group and controls after six months indicated highly significant gains for the treatment group, in comparison with controls.

In Verleur et al's (1986) study the subjects of the experiment were 30 adolescents aged 13 to 17: a six-month group treatment programme was offered to 15 of the 30 girls. The group was female-led, and focussed in weekly meetings on discussions of abuse issues, self-esteem improvement, and knowledge and appropriate understanding and use of sexuality. At the beginning and end of the treatment period, group members and controls completed the Coopersmith Self-Esteem Inventory. The experimental group showed significant gains in self-esteem levels. Although self-esteem levels also increased in the controls, their gain was only about half that demonstrated by the treatment group.

Group work is now a preferred treatment option for adult women whose psychological problems (including suicidality) reflect childhood abuses and social work therapists are particularly suitable for leading such groups. Evaluations of such adult groups suggest that some, but not all women make significant gains on standardized measures following participation. For example, Alexander et al. (1989) randomly assigned 65 women who had been sexually abused in childhood to one of three conditions: a 10-week interpersonal transaction (IT) group; a 10-week process group; or a wait-list control group. All women completed the test battery at the end of group treatment, and again after six months. Results indicated that all women in treatment groups, regardless of type of group and individual therapist showed significant reductions on measures of depression, psychological symptoms, and irrational fears, and improvement in social adjustments. These significant gains were not found in the wait-list controls. These gains were generally maintained after 6 months.

However, the gains in mental health were relative, and many women needed further therapy and support even after group participation. In addition some women benefited considerably, and some not at all. Follette et al. (1991) examined factors which predicted failure to make gains in interpersonal adjustment, following group therapy. The strongest predictors of poorer outcome were fewer years of education, combination of physical and sexual abuse, and higher initial scores on the mental health measures, abuse type (intercourse), and current marital status (poorer outcome for married women). In discussing these findings, the authors suggest that the most severely damaged women are those who dropped out of school early, which might account for the association between fewer years of education, and lack of response to group therapy.

In the most recently available study of group work intervention by social work therapists, Richter et al. (1997) allocated 115 female survivors of sexual abuse directly to groups, or to wait-listed control groups. Survivors who completed the group work intervention were significantly less depressed, and had significantly improved self-esteem than their wait-listed counterparts. Gains were maintained at follow-up six months later. Richter et al. (1997) in their literature review located some fifty studies which had used group work techniques with sexual abuse survivors; but few of these studies had used any kind of controlled design, or had used standardized before-and-after measures. de Jong and Gorey (1996) in a review study located seven publications which described some kind of controlled comparison in group work with sexual abuse survivors. They conclude that about three quarters of participants in such groups make positive gains in affect and self-esteem, gains which can be made from groups running 15 weeks or less.

Background of the Present Study

The study reported here was developed in the context of a longitudinal study of a cohort of 500 at-risk children and 500 controls, studied from birth to age 17 as part of a study of the interaction of risk factors and later stressors influencing

146

the development of conduct disorder (Bagley, 1988). Mothers of children in the cohort completed a number of measures of mental health, and childhood development measures (Bagley, 1988 and 1992).

In studying factors which led to the development of suicidal behaviours in mothers of the cohort, Bagley and Young (1990) developed a model based on the work of Brown et al. (1986), which proposed that for some (but not all) victims of incestuous child sexual abuse the following sequence of events occurs: because of sexual victimization, the child's self-esteem is diminished, as well as her capacity to relate to others and to cope with later stress. Other factors which often accompany sexual abuse, such as emotional and physical abuse and separation from a parent, usually compound these problems. The victim brings into adulthood a particularly vulnerable ego and chronically impaired self-esteem. Poor self-esteem is not by itself directly linked to depression and suicidal behaviour, but makes the victim much more vulnerable to stress. When stressors do occur, social support can prevent the onset of serious depression. But former sexual abuse victims, besides having chronically impaired self-esteem, also often lack the social skills which enable them to have stable support figures, and they are particularly prone to develop serious depression in the face of stress.

A considerable amount of personality and mental health data were collected for mothers, including details of abuse, physical, emotional and sexual, occurring in the mother's childhood, using previously standardized measures (Bagley and Ramsay, 1986; Bagley, 1989 and 1990). Standardized measures of depression (the Centre for Epidemiological Studies in Depression scale - Radloff, 1977) and self-esteem (the Coopersmith Adult Scale - Bagley, 1989) were completed at the outset of the experiment in group therapy.

In the data sweep which took place a year before Time 1 (commencement of experimental group therapy) twenty four per cent of the adult women studied reported serious sexual abuse (at least unwanted, manual contact with the child's genital area, up to the age of 16). Eighty percent of women who had experienced sexual abuse in childhood, who *currently* had chronically impaired self-esteem, and who had faced significant stress in their lives in the previous year, had current symptoms of serious, clinical depression (Bagley and Young, 1990; Bagley and Ramsay, 1997). Similar results were found at the second stage of the follow-up. Low self-esteem reflecting childhood abuse which combined with social isolation and current stressors, was a potent combination in predicting the onset of serious depression in the longitudinal study, prior to entry into experimental group therapy.

The longitudinal design employed was able to demonstrate the chronic nature of vulnerability, and the non-chronic (but often intermittent) nature of depression in many women with a history of childhood abuse. Brown's model combining the factors of vulnerability (reflecting child abuse and family disruption), current low self-esteem, and lack of social supports to buffer depression-provoking stress was strongly supported.

The group therapy was conducted by an experienced MSW-level social worker and focussed on (1) how mothers who had experienced abuse in childhood coped with their own mothering tasks; (2) the influence of "negative" voices from childhood on current functioning, using group work to improve self-esteem (employing Firestone's "voice therapy" model), which aimed through therapist and group support to exorcize these voices from the past; (3) attempting to increase interpersonal warmth and empathy as a means of increasing acceptance of the self, using a method described by Wildra and Amidon, 1987; (4) reducing social isolation in various ways, including networking mothers with one another; and with a befriender, a volunteer mother of the same age, living in the same neighbourhood. It is acknowledged that using multimodal, eclectic group therapy in this way makes it difficult to isolate which part of the therapy (or which therapist) is responsible for any positive change.

Evaluation used the "wait-list" control group method in the following way. Women who had a history of sexual abuse, who were above the cut-off point for "clinical depression" on the Radloff CESD scale for screening depressive illness (Barnes and Prosen, 1984) were referred for psychiatric consultation, since we were advised at that time that social work therapists should defer to psychiatric expertise for such women - this was in fact one of the conditions imposed on us by the university ethics of research committee. Thirty four of the 620 women who were retained in the longitudinal study and who were judged to be seriously depressed were referred to psychiatrists, and were not offered enrolment in group therapy. Those who declined included three women who were currently receiving treatment for drug or alcohol addiction. Because of the original method of sampling in the birth cohort (including women from economically poor backgrounds, and those who consumed drugs or alcohol in pregnancy) the sample is biased towards women of lower SES (Bagley, 1992).

Forty additional women were selected, who had (a) a history of child sexual abuse; (b) currently, low self-esteem - Coopermsith score in lowest quintile; (c) showed some signs of depression, with CESD scores in the highest two quintiles, when the very depressed women were excluded. These forty women were offered group counselling, and 34 agreed to participate: they were randomly assigned to either a group which met weekly for one hour over 15 sessions, or to a wait-list control group. Each group contained eight or nine women, and there were no drop-outs, although the group leader did give parallel individual support to five women who missed group sessions in the early stages. In all groups, which met in the setting of a Children's Hospital, there was complete attendance after the fifth session, apart from absence due to domestic or medical (non-psychiatric) emergencies. Unlike the study of Richter et al. (1997), the majority of the women offered counselling came from blue-collar backgrounds, and only three had education beyond high school.

Measures of depression and self-esteem (now employing the Tennessee Self-Concept Scale - Fitts, 1965, since women were very familiar with the short Coopersmith measure) were completed prior to commencement of group sessions, and six months later at Time 2. A sociometric instrument was added, asking respondents to nominate all "good friends whom they could turn to at a time of stress". At Time 1 (prior to any group therapy for all 34 women) and at Time 2 (6 months after enrolment in therapy for the first group of women, and immediately prior to entry into groups for the wait-list controls prior to entry into therapy) the CESD, Tennessee and Sociometric measures were completed.

At Time 3, six months after the initial group had ended therapy, and immediately after the wait-list controls ended therapy, the instruments were completed once more. The first report of this study (Bagley and Young, 1990) indicated that the initial therapy group showed statistically significant, decreased levels of depression, significant increases in self-esteem, and a significantly increased number of individuals nominated as "good friends who I could turn to at a time of stress", in comparison with the controls. Following 15 weeks in therapy, at Time 2 (12 months after the commencement of the research) the wait-list controls also made statistically significant gains in all areas.

The Present Research

The purpose of this chapter is to examine, three years after the original experiment was completed (i.e. at Time 4), whether gains made by women in therapy were maintained; what the mental health status of the very depressed women referred to psychiatrists was; and what was the continued status of a comparison group of women matched for age, ethnicity and SES who had not experienced any kind of childhood abuse, and were not depressed or suffering from impaired self-esteem at Time 1.

Measures: The measure of self-esteem used was the Coopersmith Adult Form (Bagley, 1989), which respondents had not completed in the past three years. The CESD Depression Inventory was used once again, as was the standardised measure of suicidal ideas and behaviour (Bagley and Ramsay, 1986), which measures in the past six months, suicidal thoughts, plans for suicide, and acts of deliberate self-harm. "Attempted suicide" is an event which is also measured separately, and involves an act of self-injury in which the person had the intention or desire to kill themselves.

Methods of Research: At Time 4, all mothers were interviewed in their homes, as part of the periodic data sweep in the longitudinal study of development of the children of the mothers. Interviewers were trained graduates in social work, education and nursing.

Results

Sample loss is an inevitable factor in a longitudinal study such as this, and we were only able to locate 29 of 34 women who had been in the group counselling programme in the follow-up at Time 4. At this time we were also able to interview 28 of the 34 women who were given psychiatric referral. One of the original 34 referred women had committed suicide two years after being seen by a psychiatrist. None of the 28 referred women whom we were able to contact had been enrolled in any form of group therapy. Those women we could not trace did not differ in any noticeable way from the women in the relevant groups, in terms of scores on standardized measures at Time 1, and abuse histories.

Table 1 indicates that gains in the social and psychological measures of the women enrolled in group counselling were generally maintained. Comparing results at Time 1 and Time 4 (six years later) indicates a significant increase in self-esteem (Sandler's t-test for matched pairs 2.78, p<.05>.01), a significant decrease in depression (t=2.59, p<.05>.01), and a significant decrease in recent suicidal ideas and behaviour (t=2.10, p <.05>.01). However, the very depressed women not enrolled in groups but referred to psychiatrists had failed to make any significant gains in terms of depression reduction, self-esteem elevation and lessening of suicidal ideas and behaviour. Their increment

150

in lifetime suicide attempts (28 per cent increase) was greater - but not significantly so - than the increase of 19 per cent in lifetime suicide attempts in those entered into group counselling. Two thirds of this increment in the group counselled women occurred in the wait-list control group, and some women spoke of their frustration at being offered help but not being able to enter the groups immediately. It should be noted that one of the depressed women referred for a psychiatric help killed herself, compared with none of women in group counselling. In the year prior to interview at Time 4 *none* of the women who had been in group counselling had many any kind of suicide attempt. In terms of social isolation, there was a significant reduction for the counselled group (t=3.12, p,<.01>.005) with no significant change in the depressed women who were not group counselled. By Time 4, the group counselled women resembled the non-abused women in terms of their psychological profiles. Nevertheless, some women made more psychological progress than others.

An exploration of what factors predict positive change in profiles of depression, self-esteem and suicidality in the abused women is presented in Table 2 (for correlational analysis, incremental change in the direction of better mental health has been averaged across these three measures). A range of factors was examined, including those identified in Follette et al's (1991) study (years of education; severity of sexual abuse; initially very poor mental health; marital status, as well as a number of additional factors). Only two factors emerged with any significance in our own study: the first was the *combination* of sexual abuse with emotional abuse, using the measures described by Bagley and Ramsay (1986). This finding supports that of McGee, Wolfe and Wolfson (1997) who found that it was combinations of emotional and sexual abuse (of all abuse types and combinations) that had the worst impact on adolescent mental health.

The second factor associated with less favourable outcomes following group (and psychiatric) treatment was lack of maternal support for the respondent when, as a child, she revealed within-family sexual abuse. Often (in the seven cases where lack of support occurred) this took the form of actually blaming the victim for the abuse: a case history illustrating this is given in Bagley and Ramsay (1997). These two factors (combinations of emotional and sexual abuse; and blaming by mother) also explained some of the failure of women to make mental health gains when referred to psychiatrists, and when the two groups are combined, the two factors - combinations of abuse, and mother's failure to support - are statistically significant predictors of failure to make mental health gains.

151

The degree to which linking the women in group therapy to both women who had similar childhood histories as a mutual support, and to a "befriender" in the community is demonstrated by answers to the questions: "In the past two years have you had any kind of stress or crisis in your life?" and "When facing this crisis, did you seek advice or help from a friend or relative in your community?" Of the group-counselled women 25 per cent had faced such a crisis, compared with 31 per cent of the depressed women referred for psychiatric help. *All* of the group-counselled women had sought advice and help from someone in their community, compared with only three of the nine depressed women referred to psychiatrists. In the 57 control subjects 14 per cent had faced significant stress, and five of these eight women had sought help from a significant other person (mostly their marital partner). An interesting finding was that a quarter (7/28) of the women in the group therapy had moved from what they had previously described as marital or partner relationships in which violence, abuse or domination featured. Only one of the depressed women referred to a psychiatrist had ended such a relationship. While these proportions experiencing stress and seeking help are too small to permit significance testing, the trends are suggestive and deserve further replication with larger samples.

Discussion

Our finding that women with a history of child sexual abuse are more socially isolated, and have poorer social support networks has been confirmed by Gibson and Hartshorne (1996) who found that "victims of sexual abuse were found to be more lonely and less likely to utilize their social support system than the controls" (p. 1087). Reducing such social isolation is one of the factors on which group therapy for this vulnerable group should focus. One of the difficulties in replicating group work with such populations is that their multiple needs (relating to social isolation, higher levels of depression, and poor self-esteem) mean that groups may have to address a number of these issues in each group session. What determines the level and type of group interaction is the level of psychological impairment which each particular group presents, and this may very quite markedly from one situation to another. Because social workers have to work in co-operation with other professionals (e.g. psychologists and psychiatrists) the kinds of population which they can access in terms of group work may vary between professional settings, countries, and types of research design. The present population, it should be remembered, was accessed by an epidemiological survey and not by self- or professional-referral.

It is noteworthy that Alexander et al. (1989) could not find any differences in outcome when groups following different models of counselling ran in parallel. It may be that women with a history of sexual abuse elicit, from sensitive women group leaders, a common type of response. The overriding needs of this client group for a reduction in feelings of guilt, shame and responsibility for the earlier abuse tend to dominate any group session, and any therapist must deal with these issues first. In our design, only when women were moving in the direction of guilt-reduction was the idea of mutual social support introduced, and so the group process employed may have to be modified to meet the needs of a clinically referred group.

Our failure to enrol the most depressed group of sexual abuse survivors in group therapy is salutary. Two-thirds (19/29) of the psychiatrically-referred women had been prescribed some kind of anti-depressant or tranquillizing medication (compared with 3/28 of the women in group therapy, medication prescribed at some time by their general practitioner). But past or present use of medication bore no relation to levels of depression and self-esteem measured at Time 4, six years after initial referral. One of these referred women, despite psychiatric treatment, had committed suicide. While of course there is no certainty, we do feel that had this woman been enrolled in one of the groups, with subsequent social support and befriending, she would not have killed herself. This conclusion supports an earlier observation (Bagley and King, 1990) that the methods traditionally employed by clinical psychiatrists are not particularly suited to the needs of abuse survivors. However, there is some recent evidence in change in values and methods with which psychiatrists and other physicians now approach the needs of abuse survivors (McCauley et al., 1997).

A feature of the statistical analysis of change in the present study is that it used Sandler's t-test for matched pairs, rather then Student's t-test for group means, and conventional analysis of variance models (Chambers, 1955). In our design each individual woman's score is compared with her own score on the same test at a later time. Most studies which examine change compare *group* means; this kind of statistical comparison could lead to inaccurate results, since means could be distorted by sub-groups of women with large gains, or by movements in a negative direction. This could lead either to failure to focus on subjects who were particularly suited for a particular kind of group, and/or to ignoring women for whom the group experience was particularly unsuccessful.

Ethical constraints (imposed by an ethics of research committee) forbad us from offering group counselling to very depressed women. In retrospect, this condition of the ethics committee was ill-considered. Another ethical problem we faced was that of allocating women to wait-list control groups. It is clear that some women were distressed in the hiatus period of several months, between being offered the prospect of therapy for a problem which had secretly troubled them for years, and the commencement of therapy. Several women became suicidal in this waiting period, and did receive individual counselling from the social worker. In a future design, if limited resources for therapy were available, we would offer such therapy to the selected group immediately.

The relative failure of some clients to benefit from group therapy is an important issue, not often addressed in research on group therapy. We could not replicate the factors identified by Follette et al. (1991), and they may have been dealing with a different kind of client group. However, the factors we did identify do accord with other research: the combination of different kinds of abuse has been identified as a factor associated with poor social and psychological adjustment in work with other populations (Bagley, 1996; McGee et al., 1997). The failure of a mother to support a young adolescent who reveals sexual abuse is also a known factor in poor long-term adjustments (Everson et al., 1980; Sirles and Franke, 1989; Heriot, 1996). Women with such problems should perhaps receive individual counselling before joining groups, since it possible for them either to be overwhelmed by the release of affect which inevitably occurs in such groups; or else they may dominate the group's early sessions with their expressions of distress. In our own groups, such women generally remained rather unforthcoming, supporting the idea that they had been unable to express feelings about particularly traumatic events: being both emotionally and sexually abused by parent figures, either simultaneously by one or more parent figure, or sequentially, including rejection for having been a victim.

Table 1 Long-term gains in self-esteem and reduction of depressive affect in women in group counselling

	Social Isolate		Self-Esteem Low		Depressed		Suicidal Behaviours		Attempted Suicide	
	T1	T4	T1	T4	T1	T4	T1	T4	T1	T4
Markedly depressed at Time 1 (N=28)	21%	14%	72%	64%	100%	61%	64%	64%	36%	46%
In group counselling (N=29)	17%	3%	52%	28%	69%	34%	45%	27%	21%	25%
Comparison group (N=60)	0%	0%	37%	38%	35%	37%	30%	33%	5%	5%

Note: T1 = Time 1, and T4 = Time 4, six years after Time 1. Original comparison group matched on a one-for-one basis with the group counselled and depressed non-counselled groups, with matches for age (within one year) and amount of education (within one year), and the selection criterion that none of the controls reported sexual, physical or emotional abuse in childhood (up to age 16). Of the original contrast group of 68, 60 were available for interview at all four data collection points.

Percent for self-esteem (Coopersmith scale), depression (CES-D scale) and Suicidal Behaviours Scale are those above the third quintile point (i.e. the 60% vs 40% split) for the entire sample when interviewed at Time 1 and 4, six years after Time 1. (Continued on next page.)

Percent attempting/completing suicide are lifetime prevalence rates, so will automatically stay the same, or increase. One women who was clinically depressed at Time 1, committed suicide three years later and is not included in the above table.

Chi-squared test comparing counselled women and control women at Time 4: no difference significant at the 5 percent level *except* life-time events of attempted suicide (Chi-squared, 1 d.f. 9.33, $p<.01>.001$). Depressed women at Time 4: all comparisons with both counselled women, and contrast group women significant at the 5 percent level or beyond.

Table 2   Predictors of failure to make gains following group/psychiatric therapy at follow-up three/ four years after therapy or referral

	Correlations in group counselled Ss (N=28)	Correlations in psychiatrically referred Ss (N=29)	Correlations in both groups (N=57)
Two+ kinds of childhood abuse (emotional/phys-ical/sexual)	-.21	-.42**	-.34*
Ss mother failed to support her after sexual abuse revealed	-.21	-.30*	-.23*

*p<.05. **p<.01.

Direction of scoring means that a negative correlation indicates that abuse combinations and mother's negative reaction predicts failure to make long-term gains.

PART III
ADOLESCENT OUTCOMES

6 The Youngest Profession - The Oldest Oppression: A Study of Sex Work

SUSAN McINTYRE

Introduction

This study of juvenile prostitution is based on a field study in the Canadian city of Calgary over the period of a year, during which time 50 sex trade workers (41 of them female) many of them under 18 were interviewed, based on snowball sampling at street level. The methodology of the study was framed within a grounded theory approach, using a feminist approach in the interpretation of research material and the construction of a typology of motivations and background factors for young sex trade workers. A fuller account of the background and findings of this study are contained in McIntrye (1994). A broad range of social and demographic questions were asked of respondents, and all but two of the interviews were taped. Notes were taken during all 50 interviews, and this allowed a constant review of the information given.

The following quotation describes the process that the researcher followed:

> At the beginning of the research, interviews usually consist of open-ended conversations during which respondents are allowed to talk with no imposed limitations of time. Often the researchers sit back while the respondents tell their stories. Later, when interviews and observations are directed by the emerging theory, he can ask direct questions bearing on his categories. These can be answered sufficiently and fairly quickly. Thus, the time of any one interview grows shorter as the number of interviews increases, because the researcher now questions many people in different positions and different groups, about the same topics. (Glaser and Strauss, 1967:76)

A year was spent immersed in the lifestyle and world of the sex trades, both the sex workers and professionals involved. This opportunity afforded this feminist researcher an insight and experience which was priceless in the development of this research.

> In sum, then, a feminist approach to research for a feminist methodology usually involves a focus of socially significant problems; feminist researchers typically become involved with the research subjects; they also aim to record the impact of the research on themselves. They disclaim any pretension to 'value free' research and set out to make explicit their own values. They also aim to evaluate the usefulness of their research; this usually means engaging in direct discussion with the 'user community' as opposed to the 'scholarly community'. (Gelsthorpe, 1990:94).

I found the use of Grounded Theory and a feminist methodology to be complementary. Grounded Theory allowed the opportunity for immersion into the sex workers' life while the feminist methodology insisted upon face to face interviews and recognised that this would have a direct impact upon the researcher.

Initial Findings

Many young persons gravitate to the street where their 'street family' looks after their needs and they feel wanted, nurtured, supported and protected initially. As one 14 year old woman so candidly stated, "You know you are eight years old, you need to be nurtured and you need to be cared for and nobody was doing that for me. I was doing that for everybody else". This young woman was able to articulate that she often took to the streets where she received attention and had her needs met. When asked whether they saw anything within their family which contributed to their involvement in sex works, the following summary was established. Some individuals did not see a history of abuse within their family contributing to their involvement in sex, while others described sexual abuse, and chaotic family life.

Anything Family Life Contributed to Your Sex Work

Response	# Respondents	% Respondents
No nothing did it myself	16	32%
Family chaos	13	26%
Drugs and alcohol	2	4%
Sexual abuse	11	22%
Deprivation	4	8%
Family member working as sex worker	3	6%
I don't know	1	2%
TOTAL	50	100%

The following represent a summary of some direct quotes in reference to family contributory factors into street work:

> When I was younger I didn't know it was bad when people tried to do things to you, so basically I never thought prostituting was ever bad. People do it to get paid for it, rather than to have people just take it. (Elaine)

> Yes. Them just not being there for me and listening to me. Them not teaching me the proper tools of how to deal with my emotions, no sex education at all. Because my mom hasn't dealt with her own sexual abuse, she liked it when I was seductive. She would buy me seductive clothes to wear because that was the thing, you know, to get yourself a rich man. So I think that they had a big part in it. (Tamara)

> Sometimes I really think that the sexual abuse, my father turning that love that I had for him into something sick and demented and me thinking, so that's all men really want, is to lie and to cross over and then deny it. Like, do something to me that is wrong, but it's sexual, like, is that the way to every man, is through sex. Sometimes I put that in my head so that I can put some of the blame on him, but I know ultimately it was my decision, but he introduced me to sex, I was a virgin. He introduced me to sex and I think that played a big part in it. (Samantha)

In the development of the interview schedule, it was established that benefit could be obtained in gaining insight into the background of abuse experienced by other family members. In looking at the generational transmission of abuse (McIntrye, 1983 and Finkelhor, 1979) it became apparent that an understanding of the cycle of abuse within families can often predict future family functioning if the cycle remains uninterrupted. The following is a summary of the thoughts of those interviewed on other family members' experiences with physical and sexual abuse. The vital finding from this question is that those interviewed identified a *background of abuse in other family members: 62% identified physical abuse and an overlapping 56% identified sexual abuse.*

In interviewing sex trade workers, the focus was on a history of sexual abuse which occurred *prior to their involvement in sex work.*

Violated Sexually Prior to Sex Trade Work

	Sexual abuse		No sexual abuse	
	# Respondents	% Respondents	# Respondents	% Respondents
Male	9	100%	0	0%
Female	32	78%	9	22%
TOTAL	41	82%	9	18%

The crucial finding here is that *82% of the total of sex trade workers interviewed had been sexually violated prior to sex trade work.* I attribute the elicitation of this high proportion of prior sexual abuse to three major factors. Firstly, the author is a trained clinician and is comfortable when discussing a history of abuse with clients. This level of ease was transferred into this research study. As professionals working with abuse victims we have only in the last decade become comfortable with asking this question of our clients (McIntrye, 1983). I would hypothesise that traditional research assistants are not comfortable with such questions and clients quickly pick up this level of discomfort. The second reason hypothesised for this response rate was the length of time that this author spent in the downtown of Calgary. The final reason is that the interviews took place in comfortable, safe surroundings away from the stroll area and in times outside of traditional sex trade work hours.

The following represents a breakdown of the age at the time that sexual abuse occurred.

162

Age At Time of Sexual Violation

Age of abuse	# Respondents	% Respondents
3-6 years	8	16%
7-11 years	20	40%
12-17 years	13	26%
Never abused	9	18%
TOTAL	50	100%

As we can see from this, the most sexual abuse (56%) occurred prior to the age of 12. When considering who were the individuals who sexually abused these children, the following was reported:

Who Sexually Violated You?

	Male # Resp. (%)	Female # Resp. (%)	Total # (%)
Family member	2 (22)	13 (32)	15 (30)
Community person and family member	2 (22)	6 (15)	7 (14)
Community person	3 (33)	11 (27)	14 (28)
Stranger	3 (33)	2 (5)	5 (10)
Not violated	0	9 (22)	9 (18)
TOTAL	9 (100)	41 (100)	50 (100)

Young men are more likely to be abused in the community by known individuals or strangers. Young women are more often abused by a family member, rarely by strangers.

Physical Abuse Violation

The following represents the definition used for physical abuse:

> A child is physically injured if there is substantial and observable injury to any part of the child's body as a result of a non-accidental incident.

Violated Physically Prior to Sex Work

	Physical abuse		No physical abuse	
	# Resp.	% Resp.	# Resp.	% Resp.
Male	5	55.6	4	44.4
Female	31	75.6	10	24.4
TOTAL	36	72.%	14	28.%

From the above table we can see that *nearly three quarters of sex workers had a history of physical abuse in their backgrounds prior to the commencement of sex work.*

Respondents were asked about intercourse, delivery of oral sex and the recipient of anal sex. These questions appeared in the later part of the interview when individuals were very comfortable and we had already discussed the issues of abuse and violence. The following represents a summary of the sexual experiences of this population which, in most situations, occurred prior to their induction into sex work.

First Experiences
Age of Fondling, Vaginal Intercourse, Oral and Anal Sex

Age	% Fondled	% Vaginal	% Oral	% Anal
3-6 years	34%	8%	4%	0%
7-11 years	36%	38%	30%	2%
12-15 years	28%	46%	44%	14%
16-18 years	2%	6%	22%	16%
Never	0%	2%	0%	66%
Can't remember	0%	0%	0%	2%
TOTAL	100.%	100.%	100.%	100.%

Who Fondled, Vaginal Intercourse, Oral and Anal Sex

	% Fondled	% Vaginal	% Oral	% Anal
Father	10%	8%	4%	0%
Stepfather	10%	6%	6%	0%
Granddad	8%	6%	6%	0%
Uncle	8%	2%	4%	0%
Foster mom	2%	2%	2%	0%
Husband	0%	0%	0%	2%
Peer	36%	60%	50%	6%
Stranger	10%	4%	2%	6%
Neighbour	12%	8%	0%	0%
Teacher	4%	0%	0%	0%
Other	0%	2%	20%	8%

When examining vaginal intercourse, 46% of occurrences happened while the child was 11 years of age or under. The experience of vaginal intercourse occurred with an adult family member in 24% of cases and when we consider this with additional categories of individuals, 36% of sex-workers' first experience with intercourse would be considered to be sexual abuse. It is worth noting that one young person had their first experience with vaginal intercourse while involved in sex work.

Examination of anal intercourse illustrates that 66% of those interviewed had no experience in this. Of the 34% who have experienced this, 16% were under the age of 16 and 16% were over the age of 16, and one individual could not remember at what age, nor was he prepared to say who with. Anal intercourse is not as common as I had originally thought. It is probable that this is a recent change given the high risk of this activity since the onset of the HIV and AIDS epidemic. This is also an activity that a small percentage of sex workers engage in most often in their personal life, or it was a forced activity. This is generally not a common sexual behaviour for this population nor one that they want to partake in.

Many young persons' first sexual activities occurred at younger than average ages. Not only did this occur at a young age, but it was also sexual abuse. The probability exists that early sexual abusive experiences are certainly one of the contributing factors leading to sex work.

Age of Running

Young persons who run from home and then end up in sex trade work often began their career of running at a very young age. James (1978:50) found that 11 per cent of young women prior to the age of 12 had run and that 15 per cent had run at age 12, and finally that 23 per cent had run at age 13. Weisberg (1985:170) found that males might begin running later, but they tend to be gone for longer.

When asked for this study, "At what age did you run at", the following was reported.

Age of First Run

Age of run	% Female resp.	% Male resp.	% All resp.
6-8 years	0	44.4	8
8-10 years	7.3	0	6
10-12 years	22.0	11.1	20
12-14 years	43.9	11.1	38
14-16 years	9.8	0	8
16-18 years	0	11.1	2
Above 18	2.4	2	2
Never ran away	14.6	22.2	16
TOTAL	50	100.%	100.%

What is important from this finding is that 34 per cent of those under the age of 12 years had run away from home at least once overnight. This is significantly higher than previous studies completed by James (1978). Over three quarters of sex workers had run away. Males tended to run away from home at an earlier age than females. As noted, males were more likely to be sexually abused in the community and this seems to correlate with the young age of running. In our culture, males tend to have a greater degree of community freedom to play at a younger age and this could again be seen as significant in experiencing running away at an earlier age.

Why They Ran

Some of the reasons given for running were:

> *My dad tried choking, strangling me and beating me. I was really young, 12. My dad tried to kill me. (Natasha)*

> *I was 12 when I ran away for the first time and it was because I started to drink alcohol and I became very rebellious and also I was being sexually assaulted by a bunch of guys in the Calgary Housing that I was living in. I couldn't handle it, so I ran away. (Jocelyn)*

167

I met this girl and we became friends and all that stuff and I was having family problems. I was sick and tired of what my step-dad was doing and she was having family problems. We were like 11 years old. At least 40 times, oh yeah. They used to find me and I'd run away four hours later. I just hated it. Most of the places I ran away from were group homes and stuff. (Amber)

Yeah, all the time. Every time they'd put me in a group home, I'd leave the next day or five minutes later. (Luke)

I was twelve and I was realising that I was gay ... and then I started telling people that I was gay and, of course, that caused a lot of turmoil or whatever in my family. Yeah, I got a ride and went to Vancouver. A year and two months. I kept in touch with my mother. So I kept in touch with her, like every three or four months I'd give her a phone call. (Matthew)

Pines (1981) found that 78 per cent of young people involved in sex work had begun as juveniles:

> Both male and female adolescent prostitutes become involved in prostitution at an early age. For adolescent girls, the average age for the initial act of prostitution is 14, and available data reveal the same mean age of entry into prostitution for adolescent males. (Weisberg, 1985:155)

The following table indicates that 76 per cent of workers began prostitution under the age of 16 and 86 per cent began under the age of 18 with a mean age being 14. These findings are consistent with the existing literature.

Age of First Prostitution "Date"

Age	# Respondents	% Respondents
10 years old	1	2%
11 years old	1	2%
12 years old	8	16%
13 years old	13	26%
14 years old	9	18%
15 years old	6	12%
16 years old	3	6%
17 years old	2	4%
18 and over	7	14%
TOTAL	50	100%

Worst Experience with A Client

Description of worst date	# resp.	% resp.
I was punched and hit	9	18%
Gun used - raped and robbed me	5	10%
Raped and robbed at knife-point	10	20%
Strangled	4	8%
Raped	5	10%
Robbed	4	8%
Handcuffed/tied and raped	4	8%
No bad dates	9	18%

As can be seen, 82 per cent have experienced "bad dates" while working in sex trades. Bad dates are more likely to be experienced and reported by females. The following are some of the experiences that sex workers have had with bad dates:

> He was super nice, real interested in things that were happening. Took me out, said he wanted a blow job, I said money first. He grabbed me by the hair and said "You fucking bitch, you'll do it now". He had big rings, so I didn't chance it. I just said, "You don't have to pay. I'll just give you a blow job, don't hurt me." I went to put on a condom and he said, "No, you can do

it without a condom" and I'm like, God, this is like not my night. I finished, he pulled a knife and robbed me. Get the fuck out or I'm going to stab you. (Elaine)

A date hit me with a crow-bar. Then I had a friend of my pimps put a coat hanger up me and ripped a one inch gouge in my cervix. One time a trick tried to rob and strangle me, and I pretended I was epileptic and was rolling my eyes, shaking and spitting all over him. He got freaked and let me go. (Katlyn)

He took me to his hotel room. Nothing really happened, and then he brought this gun out and he was putting it to my head and wanting me to give him a blow job while this gun was to my head. That was scary. (Jocelyn)

That was in Thunder Bay when I was raped. I was there for about a month and a half. I was with a date in his room and he decided to rape me. He never used a condom or nothing. (Sara)

Who Are You Most Connected To?

Who most connected to	# resp.	% resp.
Parental figure	7	14%
Peer	11	22%
Boyfriend/husband	8	16%
Sibling	2	4%
Sibling and parent	2	4%
My child	1	2%
Child and parental figure	1	2%
Sibling and significant other	2	4%
Sibling and outreach worker	1	2%
Jesus Christ	1	2%
Myself	12	24%

As can be seen many workers have connections and support sources; however, a great many feel that the only person they are connected to is themselves. When exploring their connections with themselves, workers most often stated that their experiences had taught them that they could not trust anyone.

170

In asking sex workers if they felt that they had grown up quickly, 92% stated that they had. They saw that the streets had been the catalyst for this growth and independence. There was also a common feeling that they had not been allowed to be children, prior to the street, in their own homes.

> *It was like I was growing up too quick when I was 13. I felt like I was 13 going on 20, but I was just learning and I knew I was in a big person's world. (Samantha)*

Sex work brought with it a sense of freedom allowing for new experiences with clothes, drugs and lifestyle. However, it brought with it a contradiction in the sense of danger and restriction of movement within the lifestyle which prevents and interrupts education, family and friend connections in the straight world. Well over half of those interviewed had, at one point, attained Child Welfare Status, and almost all had some form of contact with the Criminal Justice System. It is important to note that less than half of those interviewed had been charged with "Communicating for the Purpose". All those interviewed, except for one individual, have a specific plan to leave this work. Having this plan can be seen as a mechanism to ease the pain and frustration associated with sex work. This allows a sex worker a sense of relief in that they realise for themselves that this is only a temporary experience. Although this appears as a contradiction on the surface, it is an important feature in allowing a sex worker to continue this work knowing that it is not permanent.

Sex workers often experience negative feelings about themselves, and the activities they have been involved in. The end of an evening for a sex worker is often clouded with feelings of guilt and disgust, which often leads to drug/alcohol sedation. There is no doubt that the use of alcohol and drugs is a key feature in allowing a sex worker to cope with prostitution. It is a balancing act, in that excessive use while working leads to difficulties. However, some use is often important during working time to numb the pain; it is used as a way to cope with prostitution. Excessive use after working hours can also lead to difficulties in the physical and/or mental health arenas of one's life. Needing the opportunity for sedation allowing for numbness is important, yet it can become a health danger if used excessively during or after working hours.

The contradiction of control is another complexity faced by sex workers. They must feel that they are in control of their customers, that they control the activity, and the degree of intimacy. However, they know that at any point in time, this control can be taken away from them by a bad date. Although the issue of control is critical, sex workers live in constant fear that they will be assaulted and/or arrested, and lose their control. The continual fear that the next customer could be a bad date and/or a police officer is one a sex worker lives with daily.

The use of fantasies of harming dates is also another complexity of the working life. Sex workers use their fantasies to gain a sense of ultimate control, and humiliation over their dates. They envision control through visualising physical harm. Even when a sex worker's control has been taken away by a customer, they can still gain a sense of control over their customers through these fantasy visions of harm.

The constant level of fear and anxiety, and the street excitement is a built in contradiction to the work. Sex workers are always "living on the edge" of what could be next. This "living on the edge" is often seen as a terrifying, yet exhilarating part of the life style, another contradiction of this complex lifestyle.

Empirical and Theoretical Discourse: Some Overlap?

In reviewing the literature on prostitution, two trends become apparent. Most material has either an empirical format or a theoretical format. For example, the work done by Kate Millet (1971), although containing personal interviews, was very theoretical in origin and an empirical analysis was not a primary function of this work. A similar charge could be directed at the work done by Eileen McLeod (1982). In looking at the work done by Silbert and Pines (1981), and Kelly Weisberg (1985), a strong theme of empirical analysis exists, yet little theoretical material is developed.

The purpose of this chapter is to align the empirical findings from the *Youngest Profession* study within a theoretical framework. This will allow the development of a view of adolescent prostitution theoretically, yet which has within it an empirical base as its foundation.

Pathology of the Individual or Pathology of Society?

A great deal of the literature on prostitution focuses on the individual pathology, the illness of the prostitute. This sense of illness is most often seen as being "deviant". The individual is seen as being disturbed and it is this level of disturbance which results in the individual gravitating into sex work.

172

Personal pathology/deviance explanations isolate the phenomenon of adolescent prostitution in the individual. This view is limited in that it deflects awareness of the broader economic and social dimensions which impinge on a young person's decision to solicit on the street (eg. high youth unemployment, the absence of family support, and the necessity of meeting basic survival needs). (Mathews, 1984:7)

When we examine the literature by Silbert and Pines, (1981), Weisburg, (1985), and the Badgley Committee (Badgley, 1985), we see that this individual illness model is at the forefront. These are individuals that are in need of protection and assistance to leave this life. There is a strong focus on why they entered such an activity. What occurred in this young person's family life or social life that made them do this? No attention is directed towards the societal and/or cultural issues which play into this.

The alternative view to this individual pathological model is that which sees prostitution as an outcome of the functioning of society. Issues such as societal structure in the form of patriarchy, capitalism, the subordinate positioning of women and lack of economic opportunity play into the role and function of sex work. It is a global perspective which sees prostitution as a product of the structure of our society and sex work is a result of the issues within our culture. It is a macro perspective which sees prostitution as a pandemic symptom of our society. Writers such as Dworkin (1981), Brownmiller (1975), Smart (1981), Pateman (1990), Barry (1979), McIntosh (1976), MacKinnon (1990) and Shrage (1990) support this social and cultural ideological perspective.

> The demand by men for prostitutes in patriarchal capitalist society is bound up with a historically and culturally distinctive form of masculine individuality The structure of the relation between the sexes reaches into the unconscious early development of little boys and girls and out into the form of economic organisation in which the capacities of individuals, even women's bodies, become commodities to be alienated to the control and use of other. (Pateman, 1990:205)

My intention throughout the *Youngest Profession* study has been to look at the interweaving; the relationship between the individual and society in reference to prostitution. Yes, societal features as discussed in the feminist review play a major component in the existence of prostitution. Nevertheless, a reason exists as to why specific individuals are drawn to this activity of sex-work and why others choose not to. The opportunity exists for sex-work, yet specific individuals see this as a more befitting option for themselves than another. Giddens (1984) sees that the individual and society are mutually productive and function together. It is for this reason that Callero and Howard (1989:430) have stated that "to try and explain sexuality at the individual level is a little like the marine biologist trying to explain the behaviour and physiology of fish without the concept of water". It is my position that it is similar in trying to explain the concept of sex-work without the frame of reference of patriarchal culture.

The script can not be defined, learned, practised or expressed without society and its input:

> Prostitutes are the bearers of the structural oppression inherent in patriarchy's need to distinguish between "good girls" and "bad girls". (Hoigard and Finstad, 1992:183)

The Ideology of Demand and Supply

> It is an entrenched part of sexual ideology that men 'demand' sex and women 'supply' it and this ideology in turn helps to sustain the notion that prostitution is a 'natural' and universal relation. (Matthews, 1986:21)

Not only does this ideology help to maintain that prostitution is "natural and universal", it places women in the position to be the suppliers.

> *There's the type that are genuinely lonely and don't have any girlfriends and they need sex. They have their needs met, those are the easiest tricks in the world to do. Then there's the husbands that have little quirks and perversions that are either secret to their wife or repulsive to their wives so they seek out to satisfy their needs. There is a lot of them, an awful lot of them. Then there are the type that get all drunked up at stags, conventions or guys that come from the oil rigs, a gang type of an instinct. (Kathleen)*

If a male's sexual needs are not being satisfied, then it is his "rightful duty" to go to a prostitute or it "could result in a rape".

> One of the most pervasive myths which feed our distorted understanding of rape is the belief in the urgent sexual potency of men. Men are believed to have a virtually uncontrollable sexual desire, which once awakened, must find satisfaction regardless of the consequences. (Smart, 1985:65)

According to sex workers, reasons most often given by customers for purchasing the services of a sex worker is that their wives or girlfriends won't do it, they are bored, they need sex, they need something different.

Because men need a variety of sex. (Lucy)

Women are held responsible for making men have to resort to prostitutes so as to attain a variety of satisfaction.

A lot of men come down and get certain things that their wives won't give them. A lot of men are lonely, a lot of men just want to try it out, and I think a lot of men are addicted, are addicted to coming down and meeting somebody that they consider beautiful. (Samantha)

Non-sex workers have been unable to meet the sexual demands of their men so men have "no choice" but to seek out the sexual services of "other women".

Because they don't get enough or that frequent at home, something must be wrong at home. Sometimes they are just lonely. (Alexander)

From this we can clearly see a theme of the need to meet men's sexual desires because other women have failed to do so. This ideology clearly places the responsibility for the satisfaction of men's sexual needs on all women. This responsibility for sexual satisfaction is the responsibility of all women, not just his wife. Men require a variety of women for sexual encounters.

Sex work then becomes the responsibility of women. Sex work is the product of women who are not sex workers and have failed to meet "men's natural sexual needs".

Because their old ladies won't give it to them. I think it's more thrilling, but a lot of girls in prostitution are getting younger on the street, a lot of guys like that, younger girls. (Beth)

This places men in the position of being helpless due to a natural and pervasive sexual desire that they have no control over, and women, any woman, must assist in altering this innate need.

Typologies Which Influence the Entrance to and the Sustenance of Sex Work

A typology was developed in order to assist in understanding what influences an individual's entrance to, and sustenance in sex work. A total of six integrating types was developed after reviewing all contact with sex workers which had occurred over the years. These six basic types reflect the essential classifications observed and developed over time through interaction with sex workers, and assisted in the development of the interview schedule. The typology identified included the following:

Family of Origin	Separation and Attachment
Survival	Autonomy
Cycle of Abuse	Power and Control

It became obvious that what initially attracts an individual into sex work is not what usually influences them in maintaining them within this work. In other words, why an individual enters, stays or returns to sex work can change over time. I am therefore proposing that the above typology includes factors which "push" and "pull" (Lowman, 1987). These push and pull classifications are identified at an individual level and are essential as the individual interacts within the larger systems of society. These types of experience affect an individual's functioning within the larger society. It is the interweaving between the individual society that becomes the important (push and pull) interaction.

The larger macro theoretical explanation of patriarchy is important in understanding the production and maintenance of prostitution within our culture. Patriarchy is extremely useful in gaining an awareness of the global existence of prostitution. Nevertheless, it is of limited assistance in understanding the "push and pull" factors that an individual experiences while involved in and exiting prostitution. It is for this reason that I will focus on gaining an empirically based sense of how and why individuals move into and out of prostitution as opposed to a more global theoretical explanation such as patriarchy. There is no doubt that a gap exists in being able to bridge the individual typology to the more global explanation of patriarchy. A more specific empirical approach allows for and supports the development of defined intervention strategies, decreasing the time and/or eliminating youths' involvement in prostitution, and this is the central focus of my clinical work.

176

The types are analytically distinctive; nevertheless, they are not static, nor mutually exclusive. A sex worker can be affected by more than one type of action/motivation at any point in time; however, one will often be more pronounced at a specific time. At various points in time a sex worker can be under the influence of more than one type; nevertheless, one type will emerge as dominant due to the circumstances and needs of the sex worker. For example, an individual who is working from the family of origin type could begin the movement towards autonomy as they wish to gain identity separate from their family. When this occurs the individual's needs and desire for independence becomes greater and the typology of family of origin drifts into the background, even though this was the initial source of introduction into sex work. The typology can support and assist the understanding of the work life of an individual and could be conducive to understanding an individuals work life and assist in exploring alternatives to sex work. It is also important to note that not all six types will be experienced by any one sex worker. Some workers will have only encountered one type, where others have had experience and have been influenced by more than one of the six. The length of time an individual has been involved in sex work often correlates with movement through more than one distinct type.

Initial entrance into sex work most often occurs due to the typology of survival, family of origin, or cycle of abuse. This type is more structural and developmental in origin, and often sets the framework for entrance into prostitution. They are events which are structural in nature and have occurred such as abuse, family history or running away, and these events influence the entrance into sex work. Once into prostitution, types or categories such as autonomy, power and control, and separation and attachment can become influential as a result of sex work. In other words, they are a reaction to sex work, whereas the structural types result in sex work. It is important to also understand that once in sex work, the three structural types can still continue to influence and sustain sex work. Structural types only serve initially as proactive elements in entrance to prostitution; then all the types can become reactive, and assist in sustaining sex work.

During this study, both within the interviews and also during observation, it became apparent that individuals work for different reasons, and that over time these reasons can change. The experience of interacting with sex workers for a one year period allowed me the opportunity to chart and discuss with them the influences in their work life and style of work. These changes occurred subtly for some and were more drastic for others. Drastic changes were often the result of an actual specific single event which took place and was sometimes traumatic, such as a bad date. Subtle changes tended to occur over a period of time and regularly were influenced by adjustments and experiences to the work life or personal life alterations. This will become clearer in the following discussion which outlines the typologies, illustrated through quotes from interviews, and will then be further depicted by case examples.

After the completion of 50 interviews I was able to further develop the classifications within the typology; this was achieved through the close examination of all of the individual biographies. These biographies assisted in gaining clarity about the typology by understanding how individual experiences interplayed with larger social/societal experiences. What became critical to understand was the relationship and recognition of the individual biography within a societal framework. The classifications within the typology had the capability to review an individuals historical movements and patterns in sex work. The typology established that there was not a static or single causal explanatory phenomenon. The typology is able to demonstrate and explain that an individual's motivation into, sustenance, exit and re-entry in sex work can be articulated, analysed and explained by the various factors identified. The critical point being made is that a solitary explanation such as mental retardation (Glover, 1969), the need for money (McLeod, 1982), employment options and capitalist exploitation, or sexual vulnerability (Dworkin, 1981) have their value; nevertheless they are limited as single, all inclusive explanations. In contrast, the classifications in the typology developed in this study offer a composite, mobile and multifaceted explanation for sex work.

Descriptions of the Typology

Family of Origin

This type is focussed on the structural framework of the family, in that sex work is a natural progression within their family. This occurs as an intrinsic event within generations of one family. A history of sex work and/or street life is often a key element found in the family background of sex workers.

> *My sister and brother did it ... My mom, she never stopped me, never talked to me, never told me it was wrong, she condoned it, she would always borrow money from me. I took care of her. (Lace)*

178

Introduction and training for sex work and/or street life can exist within families.

> *I knew what my sister did, but I didn't understand it. Her man told her to turn me out. She'd been doing it since she was about 13. (Liz)*

This is why attention was paid during interviews to how an individual learned about prostitution, family abuse and family involvement in sex work and/or street life. It is important to also state that a family history in sex work legitimises, normalises sex work. The stigma often associated with sex work is non-existent as this is an established option available to family members.

> *My mom knew hookers and my dad used to play (was a pimp). (Lucy)*

The following illustrates the focus for the typology of family of origin:

- family history of street life as a sex worker, pimp, dealer or familiarity with a downtown lifestyle;
- options available to go to the street as you have a connection, understanding and familiarity with it;
- street life is within your personal repertoire as you are aware of it;
- the step into the street is not that far as you can access a route quickly and easily;
- the background of family does not need to be street active, it can still be close enough that you have some knowledge of street life;
- parents reinforce street life by using the money and the connection the young person has. They borrow money, drugs, and serve to connect them into the downtown scene;
- given the parental home and background, it seems like a reasonable generational progression for a young person to take.

From the quotes we can see how the role of the family of origin can be significant in an individual's move into sex work. The opportunity and knowledge base exists and in specific difficult situations the chance to access sex work as a viable alternative, as a problem solving mechanism, becomes a reality that some choose.

... my mom used to take me to the strolls and say don't you ever do this. I always thought she did this for a while ... I think my mom showing me prostitutes made me think it was glamorous and look at those clothes. (Katlyn)

The stigma of sex work is lessened. It is normalised through family experiences and this often disinhibits an individual's movement into sex work.

My mom used to tell me, if you're going to be a slut, you might as well sell it and not give it away ... but I heard my aunt was ... Like my mom kind of stuck in my head, "if you're going to do it, you might as well sell it. (Suzanne)

Survival

This type is concerned with the structural feature of survival, the key element being the economics of having basic needs met and achieved.

It is not a thing that people enjoy, but it is something they do to make their way in life. (Shelly)

The requirement to have these needs met is usually the result of runaway/ homeless youth who turns to the sex trades in order to obtain food, clothing, shelter, and protection.

I was broke and I had no money and I was starving and needed a place to stay. (Jackson)

During the interviews, a great deal of time was directed at inquiring about running away, the length of time of the run and offers of assistance made to runaway/homeless youth. Sex work offers the quickest form of employment for runaway/homeless youth who are under age, have limited if any employment background, and few cash oriented skills.

Yeah, when I was 15, met a live crowd and on my own ever since. I stayed at friends' houses and then I met my man. It was only like a matter of from May to end of August, three months before I met my man. For those three months I stayed a couple of months with my girlfriend in Edmonton, then I met my "man", stayed in a hotel for a couple of weeks, then I had my own apartment, full-time work. (Allison)

180

It should also be pointed out that adults who run into financial difficulty and are unable to obtain fiscally productive employment will also turn to sex work.

> *Got dropped off on the street and that was it. Was 23 when I had my first date. I needed the money. I owed $14,000 on a car. (Karen)*

Survival becomes the focus for individuals, where to sleep, how to pay for food, how to pay bills, how to buy clothes needed for this work, etc.

We can see how some individuals were runaways and felt that sex trade work was the only viable option available to them. Others experienced the financial pressure and needed to supplement their income and this often resulted in full time sex work. For some individuals sex work becomes an erratic solution to the need to problem solve financial and/or survival concerns.

> *For the first year I was living on the streets, prostitutes took care of me. I'd stay out on the stroll until 3 or 4 in the morning. When they were done with their date rooms, they'd give them to me, place to sleep. That's what got me so well into the girls' prostitution, which got me into running girls, running drugs, running guns, so on and so on, and I figured with all the illegal things I was doing, I might as well hustle and quit all the illegal things I'm doing. Crime doesn't pay. I'll never get locked up for hustling. ...There's the poem, Little Boy blew because he needed the money. (Luke)*

Cycle of Abuse

This type concerns individuals who are often placed or are placing themselves in high risk situations given their poor self image and/or lack of a sense of safety.

> *I just didn't have no opinion of myself and I just didn't care anymore. Like somebody could come up and shoot me and I would have laughed at them and said go ahead. I just didn't have any opinion at all of myself. (Amber)*

If a young person has been abused, and if this abuse has occurred in the home or community, their sense of safety is distorted:

> *My pimp raped me in Edmonton. Some guy by the name of John, he was a trick, a date, raped me in Thunder Bay. My step father in Kelowna, I was about seven, it was my first rape. I don't know if I could live a normal life after being raped three times, can't tell my friends. Well if I get raped again,*

181

you get used to it. You won't have a nervous breakdown or end up killing
yourself or something. (Sara)

They are unsure what it means to feel safe and how they know what is unsafe
given they were abused in what should have been a safe environment, they
internalise their own victimisations (Greer, 1975).

> The girls who have been mistreated, subjected to seduction turned into rape,
> often take the fault upon themselves. They think they must have made a
> mistake somewhere, that their bodies have provoked disgust, that they were
> too easy in their conversation. The internalisation of injury is what makes
> seduction-turned-into-rape such an insidiously harmful offence against
> women. What men have done is to exploit and so intensify the pathology of
> oppression. (Greer, 1975:388)

Often their self image is one that is cultivated and reinforced by abuse and this
can be achieved through sex work, as a sense of degradation, risk and pain is
continued. This is described very accurately by Marie, one of the sex workers
interviewed by Hoigard and Finstad (1992).

> It becomes a kind of revenge against myself, it has to do with destruction. It's
> when I feel the pain and nausea. (Hoigard and Finstad 1992:83)

Information about a history of drug use and self harming behaviours was key
in the interview schedule in obtaining material for the type involving a cycle of
abuse.

> Drug and alcohol use in prostitution was reported to be a consolation to many
> youth involved in prostitution and a way to help them cope with fear, violence
> and uncertainty of life on the street. (Canadian Child Welfare Association
> 1987:2-3)

This sense of chemical numbing allows for survival as so vividly described:

> *I was always loaded but at the end I knew that I shouldn't have gotten drunk*
> *cause I'd start fuck'n up, but I was lucky I never got jacked up. No-one ever*
> *took my money, nothing, except for tricks who wouldn't pay me or whatever.*
> *...I never worked a day straight. Anything I could get. When you take pills*
> *though, you don't know what they do. Only when I got home I'd take*
> *Halcyon or Valium.*

It is important to keep in mind that over three quarters of this population have a background of physical and/or sexual abuse. For some individuals their history of abuse is the major component which directed them towards sex work.

> *Growing up in my family was hard, there were a lot of hard times that I remember. I was sexually and physically abused by my step-father. I don't have good memories of growing up, just hard times. It's really hard to think about this, it makes me sad. Sometimes he would hit me so hard that I would have bruises for days. My pimps would hit me for not bringing in enough money to them, or they'd hit me cause I was fooling around too much on the streets. This happened for about two years. I was 13 to about 15 years old. (Shelly)*

For others, while earlier abuse has had some influence, other factors have a greater impact at this point in time.

> *Sometimes I really think that sexual abuse, my father turning the love hard so that I can put some of the blame on him, but I know ultimately it was my decision, but he introduced me to sex. I was a virgin. He introduced me to sex and I think that played a big part in it. (Samantha)*

Separation/Attachment

This type is sensitive to the individuals' need to belong or to be distant and unattached to anyone. The separation and attachment most often occurs in adolescents and often reflects the early experiences of youth.

If lack of resolution and/or disruption characterises the process of separation and overt patterns of attachment, a clinging type of response can manifest itself as pronounced distancing, due to failure to develop appropriate levels of attachments. During the interviewing, lines of inquiry which explored family involvement, support systems and connections, and regular customers were utilised. It became clear that those who did not like to have regular customers also had minimum contact with their family, support sources and other sex workers.

> *No. I don't have regulars. They are just too much hassle, they phone. I just don't like it. (Angel)*

Many of those interviewed had their needs for connection and worth through being attached to the street and the work they did.

> *Feel like I am somebody, makes me feel good about the way I look. (Rita)*

The street offers the opportunity for intimacy and connection for many sex workers. The street also offers the opportunity for solo, anonymous individuals to exist within an environment which is tolerant and supportive of distance and separation.

> *Relieved, lonely. Lonely because the night's over, because I'm alone. When I'm out there, there is a whole bunch of people and when I go home I'm just by myself. I really have no friends out. No one comes to visit. No, I wish somebody could look after me for once.   (Lace)*

The street is tolerant and supportive of fluctuations between wanting to belong and wanting no sense of attachment. It is often a more flexible and tolerant 'family' than their natural family.

Sex work supports and values lack of attachment with customers, and so for many this work is a suitable alternative. Nevertheless, one of the contradictions of sex work is how some workers gain a sense of attachment, a sense of worth from their customers. Many sex workers talk about how they enjoy the attention from customers and this meets their individual need for attention, that is somebody wanting them. Yet at the same time it meets their need for separation as it is a rule not to get close to your customers.

> *I felt that all these men were paying for me you know. Most of them were nice, I felt good about that, but I didn't really take a look at anything else. (Tamara)*

Autonomy

This type is concerned with independence in that the young persons need to grow up quickly and gain a sense of self. During interviews, attention towards a sense of independence, and what features and rewards sex work brought to them and denied them was pursued.

> *Yeah, I get to stay out all night, tell people no I don't think so, I had all the freedom I wanted, I could stay out all night. ...well actually I feel real*

confident on the stroll. I felt good looking and confident in the work I did and I could do it myself. (Alexandra)

When thinking of the term autonomy it became clear that for many sex workers this form is the quickest way for them to gain a sense of independence. Many sex workers have left situations to which they can not return and sex work is a way to gain that sense of autonomy and independence very quickly.

When you get out on the street and that you really notice like how street smart you get real quick, you grow up quick, like how people con you and stuff. Real smart. You realise that you can't run to your parents all the time and things like that. It's you life, you handle things basically. When you decide to pack up your clothes and go away from home and stuff like that, I didn't have to work (at home). My parents always gave me money, as soon as I left home, I didn't have to rely on them for money. (Annie)

We can see how the youth in care of the government, care which is time limited, can work in the sex trade as a bridging into adulthood. In many ways it gives them the opportunity to have their first chance at employment and independence (Sullivan, 1986).

Yeah, my mom and my sister, they never thought I could last in the real world. I said, you think I can't do it, just watch me. I lasted out there for 3 ½ months and I came home ... (Andrea)

Sex work often serves as the mechanism by which a young person can achieve a premature sense of autonomy and developmental leap into adulthood.

I was making all this money, I was shopping. I was paying off all my bills, I had a house. That is all in a matter of a couple of weeks. I had a house. That's just how it sort of happened and everything was getting really good. (Sandra)

A sense of independence or self sufficiency is often a major attraction and benefit of sex work, regardless of age. Many individuals discuss the sense of freedom they will obtain when they leave home. What is important to remember is that in the case of sex work, this is often a premature unplanned leaving home which occurs at a very young age. A sense of autonomy is achieved while on the street; however, many often feel their autonomy is compromised by the control they feel by their pimps and this contradiction is usually realised after months

185

on the street; nevertheless, this often varies over time given the pimp's role and level of control.

The following quote clearly identifies a distinct, and for this individual, a very attractive level of autonomy that can be gained through sex work. We can see how this sense of autonomy can play a role in attracting and sustaining individuals in sex work. Given previous life experiences the need and desire for autonomy is very pronounced and often occurs prematurely, and we can see how sex work assists in achieving this sense of personal freedom.

> *Because you have to be smart right away or you don't survive. A lot of people that you associate with are older, they were older than me. I had to take care of myself. ...Not only did I support myself, I supported him, plus he had a daughter with us too. I was a step-mother by the time I was sixteen and had her until I left him. (Allison)*

Power and Control

This type centres attention with regard to the powerlessness and lack of control many youth experience, and this can be further intensified by experiences of abuse. Sex work can provide an individual with a sense of control over their lives.

> *Yep, it taught me to be aggressive. (Suzanne)*

Sex workers have a great deal of control over customers as they will decide where to go, what to do and how much to pay.

> *Because when I get into a car, I'm like, okay buddy, this is the way it is, you don't like it you're beat. That's the way I am with everybody on the street. This is the way I am, this is the way I do things, if you don't like it, well fuck off. (Rachel)*

They have specific rules they expect a customer to follow. Men have the power to pay for these activities and at any point will just 'take' if they decide, and this is evidenced by the high number of bad dates experienced by sex workers.

Sex workers are often not in charge when they are not working and are somewhat reliant on the pimp, until they actually go to work that day, and then the sex worker is in charge.

Because when I'm on the street, it's me there. My man isn't there and if he wants to put on a skirt, fine, stand there and take control over me, but when I'm at work, I have to be in charge because it's my life on the line, nobody else's. (Samantha)

This impression of control over sexual interactions and the control they sense they have over men often is considered a bonus of the work.

I have a really bad attitude towards dates and I wonder why I'm out here. Most guys are just scum and I wonder if they are going to hurt me. ... When I'm on the stroll I look at license plates of the cars. I also look through the window at the faces and try to figure out what kind of a person the date is. If the guy looks too rough or too clean cut, there is no go with the guy. If the van or car has dark windows, there is no go either. I won't get in. I am very cautious on the streets. I need to keep safe so I can take care of my son. ...I am in charge. I never let a customer be in charge, I'm in control at all times and if I'm not in charge, I get out of the situation any way I can. (Shelly)

One young woman who is 15 years old told me how she worked. She would only do lays in car dates, and she hired a friend of hers to follow behind in his car and make sure she was safe. She did not want to be seen going anywhere in public with dates so car dates were all she was prepared to do. She always wore spandex pants and g-string and would only take down one pant leg. And this is what she told customers:

When it is time, I will light a cigarette and it takes me seven minutes to smoke it. I will put a condom on you and I put your penis inside me. You can not touch me and you have as long as it takes me to smoke this cigarette. If you come, wonderful, if not, your problem. (Michelle)

This level of dominance and direction is often essential for protection of those involved in sex work. This young woman felt that this was the only way she could do this work and be balanced, in a state of physical and mental equilibrium. Not all dates were prepared to allow this level of assertiveness and she often got out of cars, and had on one occasion had a very violent experience with a date who punched her and threw her out of the car after she finished her cigarette. In summary, this sex worker was so determined to attain the control and disassociate from the physical activity that she risked offending customers which could and did result in abuse. This was a chance this young woman was prepared to take in order to remain separated and in control of the activity.

187

Other ways for sex workers (both male and female) to gain a sense of control over their work is to rip dates off. When the opportunity presents itself, some sex workers will rob a date as this makes their work time shorter and can also assist in gaining encouragement from their pimps or friends.

Having regular dates is also another mechanism which assists workers in gaining control. Many workers like to have regulars as they feel it is safe and easy. Nevertheless, some sex workers do not like to have regulars as it allows a level of familiarity they are not prepared to enter into; the level of attachment is an invasion. To seek out and service regular customers can become an experience of contradiction for sex workers. Many sex workers want regulars, as it eases the job, yet for them often "familiarity breeds contempt". Sex workers who have regulars will often begin the process of "firing" them if a level of familiarity or closeness is breached. Caring about a trick and he knowing too much about you invades the level of control over work distance.

Is There a Cost to Sex Work?

Physical Issues

Sex work can take its physical toll on individuals working in this profession. As one male sex worker said to me, "I find I am exhausted at the end of an evening of work". He felt that it was part of his job to physically act interested and excited about his work. This young man said, "For a female sex trade worker, she can just moan and pretend, but for males, they have to look aroused, you must have some signs of an erection". This young man noted that even if he is giving a blow job to a customer, the customer will always take note of whether he is aroused or not. This young man has been hustling for close to ten years and believes his success stems from his ability to be "erect" while working. He believes that his ability to display sexual arousal with all customers is similar to an actor's ability to cry.

Sex workers spoke at length about the actual physical blisters that they get in their mouths from the continual movement of rubber, that is condoms.

> *I used to get rubber burns inside my cheeks, pretty weird shit. I could smell condoms all the fuck'n time. Condoms, all I could smell was fuck'n rubber. I swear that when I would take a leak I could smell rubber and I swear when I breathed I could smell rubber, I smoke and I was always drunk and I could still smell rubber. I used to carry mouthwash in my purse all the time. I*

could always smell rubber and I could always smell male sweat all the time.
It was disgusting. (Katlyn)

Another sex worker talked about her thoughts on condoms and her constant use of medication due to infections that she gained from her private life, not her work life.

> *One night I did 14 blow jobs and I had blisters ... A lot of times with blow*
> *jobs too you use a non-lubricating condom, you only had to spit on it, but*
> *if it's lubricated you get all this jelly stuff in your mouth. It's really quite*
> *gross. I would do a blow job and sit there and put your lipstick back on. It's*
> *disgusting once you think about it. All men that you sleep with you say*
> *"You're the first date I've had tonight", meanwhile you've had 8 or 9 other*
> *people. I would get raw on the inside of mouth and vagina. Your pimp goes*
> *out and black men don't wear rubbers right, your pimp goes out and screws*
> *everything in the bars and then you pick up everything. So you're constantly*
> *on Tetracycline. I never thought I could have kids. I had so much scar tissue*
> *from gonorrhoea. (Tamara)*

One woman talked at length about how she feels sex work has physically affected her own personal sex life. "Can you imagine, I come home after a night of doing 5-10 lays and my 'man' wants to make love to me." She went on to describe how the physical soreness from sex work prevents her from wanting to make love to her man. The blisters from vaginal and oral rubbing make it too uncomfortable. She was clear about saying: "I know the difference between my work and making love, trust me. I do, it's just the physical soreness from work stops me in my personal life. They sometimes cross over."

Fear and Sense of Danger

Sex workers talk about the continued level of fear and risk of violence that they live with. This is a critical component in understanding sex work. When they approach a customer on the street, immediately they must think "Is this a bad date; it is a cop?".

> *What's he going to do to me, stuff like that. Is he going to be a bad date, am*
> *I going to come back alive. You're always living on the edge, it's wild. You*
> *don't know what is going to happen and you're always, it's just weird. It's*
> *kind of like you're addicted to it because you never know what is going to*
> *happen. (Rachel)*

These thoughts enter an individual's mind every time they connect with a potential customer. This level of apprehension, once acquired, must always be present. Once a sex worker leaves with a date, this sense of danger, risk and anxiety continues until they return to the street on their own. The following comment dramatically demonstrates this point of fear, anxiety, almost excitement in the risk taking behaviour.

> *Yes, it's like playing Russian Roulette, because you don't know if you are going to get in a car and out of it. Or your pimp goes nuts and beats you and you get jacked up by some other "broads". AIDS, diseases, but not all think about it. Yes, I think that's part of it, part of the addiction. (Betty)*

This constant level of fear, risk and anxiety can be exhausting and invigorating at the same time. This level of fear and excitement is one of many contradictions presenting itself in sex work. This high risk behaviour in many ways becomes addictive, desired, one that the individual finds attractive and yet exhausting. Martin Plant (1992) in a book *Risk Takers* discusses the attraction, the addiction that youth have to risk taking and how this in many ways is a developmental feature of a youth gaining autonomy and a sense of individuation. A complex rationalisation process occurs as a youth enters into a risk behaviour.

> Young people, often at their physical peaks, typically view themselves as invulnerable. When tragedies happen to people, others often rationalise to reinforce the view that "it will never happen to me". This rationalisation is just as normal amongst drinkers, smokers, drug users as it is amongst racing car drivers or mountaineers. A notable feature of rationalisation has been identified by Davies. This is that when a person overcomes a risk, this is typically attributed to individual prowess, such as bravery or skill. If the risk ends in disappointment, even tragedy, this will frequently be ascribed by the protagonist to "bad luck" or to external factors. Others, however, may ascribe such accidents and failures to incompetence, poor judgement or other personal flaws. (Plant, 1992:114)

The risk for sex workers is immediate and constant. Sex workers are always vulnerable to assaults (customers and/or pimps) and criminal prosecutions. This is a high risk activity at all times and this is what makes the lifestyle rather unique. Research has shown that well over three quarters of sex workers have experienced a bad date which involved an assault. Sex workers realise that they are vulnerable and this level of vulnerability is always actively visible on the street. This level of risk/stress is always in existence in the life of a sex worker.

It can best be seen as a "living on the edge" lifestyle. The exhilaration that an individual attains through rock climbing is a time limited event, whereas a sex worker's lifestyle risk extends to the majority of time and is all encompassing.

In Calgary, prior to my field work there had been ten unsolved murders of sex workers in three years. This fear, anxiety and sense of risk has a reality base to it and sex workers, both male and female, fear for the violence that they could become victim to. Almost all sex workers in this sample had had, at a minimum, one bad date experience where they were robbed, battered, raped, violated with objects or a combination of these. It has been suggested (Hoigard and Finstad 1992:63) that this level of violence and fear becomes a normal part of the daily routine of sex workers. As discussed in the research findings, almost all individuals interviewed had experiences with abuse prior to sex work either in their home (parental or social services) and/or in the community. The experiences with abuse for this population is not abnormal; abuse becomes the norm, it is a customary experience for this group prior to and during sex work.

> It's possible that the women have been so exposed to violence that they become socialised to accept violence as a part of life. Besides, it is a question of the yardstick you use to measure. When life is otherwise characterised by degradation, humiliation, and insult, then perhaps violence doesn't appear as intolerable and extraordinary. Violence is uncomfortable, but not dramatic or unexpected. Life is not bed of roses, after all. (Hoigard and Finstad, 1992:63)

Gain and Pain

It is apparent from the study that this is a high risk work which takes its toll on the individual physically and mentally. The scars from sex work remain visible for many years. The following quote clearly summarises the position argued throughout this portion of the chapter, that being short term gain for long term pain.

> The impoverishment and destruction of the women's emotional lives makes it reasonable, in our eyes, to say that customers practice gross violence against prostitutes. The customers' physical violence against prostitutes is also massive, and it too, of course, creates anxiety among prostitutes. When prostitutes talk about the damages of prostitution, however, it is not the traditional violence they emphasise the most. Fractured jaws heal, split lips mend. Even anxiety dulls and fades. ...Regaining self-respect and recreating an emotional life is far more difficult. It is as hard as reconstruction of a hundred crown bill from ashes. (Hoigard and Finstad, 1992:115)

191

We can see from the findings of the present study how the above quote is reflective of the individual involved in sex work. What is also of relevance is how the role of prostitute is reflective of women's position within society. Even male sex workers are feminised to fit within a female mode. The role of woman as object and man as subject is predominant in our culture. Patriarchy is still the influence which suppresses and ensures that women remain in a subordinate position. Changes in legislation have clearly established that alterations in law have little or no effect on women's role. It often serves as an illusion, smoke and mirrors.

> For this reason, to abolish prostitution requires not legislative reform but a definite and radical change in the very basis of the definition of women. Such a change would need to occur throughout society, both on the level of structure and on the level of everyday life. In this sense the abolition of prostitution involves also the abolition of patriarchy. (Andrieu Sanz and Vasquez-Anton, 1989:79)

Concluding Comments

This chapter has reviewed the interweave between the individual and society. The issue of sexual scripts as designated by patriarchy and the ideology of male sexual needs as supply and demand has been outlined. The issue of woman's reputation being interpreted and limited by her sexual experiences and man's being furthered by his sexual experiences were seen as critical features within a patriarchal culture. Women's sexual script as the provider and males' need for penis feeding are central to the issue of prostitution and patriarchy.

Why specific individuals enter sex work and how they are able to do this work has become a major focus of this chapter. The typology explains what attracts and maintains an individual in sex work; this typology is not static in nature and alters over time for each individual. The typology will influence the strategies employed in being able to survive this type of work. Discussion of the physical and mental costs for this work suggest that sex work brings with it many contradictions, yet it can best be seen as "short term gain: long term pain".

7 Child and Adolescent Prostitution in Canada and The Philippines: Comparative Case Studies and Policy Proposals

CHRISTOPHER BAGLEY

Introduction

Through case histories and statistical accounts, this chapter examines work which informs the policy debate around child and adolescent prostitution. The information I draw on includes statistical findings from questionnaire studies of adolescent prostitution in America, Canada and The Philippines and personal observations from fieldwork in Calgary and Manila. I shall argue from a case study of Manila that this city has been unfairly cast as a centre of child prostitution; the situation seems to be worse in North America. This is illustrated by accounts of prostitution in Calgary, Canada.

North American Research Studies

Because of its complex and clandestine nature, it is difficult to undertake a random or unbiased survey of child and adolescent prostitution. While adolescent prostitutes (from about age 13) can be encountered on the streets, children younger than this can usually only be accessed through adult intermediaries who are highly suspicious of social workers, researchers and suspected police personnel. Most available evidence comes from retrospective studies - adult women recalling sexual exploitation when they were much younger; and observational studies of areas (which exist in every large city) where adolescent prostitutes parade. There is also a hidden face of prostitution - that involving young girls whose immaturity cannot be disguised, so that access is negotiated through intermediaries. Information from police following raids on back-street brothels where children and adolescents are entrapped is another source of data about these very young victims of the prostitution industry.

Earlier US studies of female adolescent prostitutes are summarized by Bagley and Thurston (1996a and b). Female adolescents in the sex trade are different in important respects from males. Adolescent women who become prostitutes experienced (in a number of studies) first coitus at average age of around 12 years (range five to 15 years); often this had involved a sexual assault by a close relative. These girls enter prostitution, on average, two years after first coitus. On the streets their physical and mental health is poor. Many have experienced physical assault, rape, abortion, STDs, drug and alcohol use after becoming sex trade workers. A high proportion have run from physically and sexually abusive homes, and had drifted into prostitution because of drug habits and the coercive activities of boyfriends, or pimps.

The San Francisco and Calgary Studies

The most comprehensive North American research on adolescent prostitution is that undertaken by Mimi Silbert and colleagues. Silbert and Pines (1981) examined the backgrounds of juvenile, adult, current and former female prostitutes working in San Francisco. Women were interviewed using a lengthy structured questionnaire, and trained women interviewers were matched with the respondents by ethnicity. Results indicated frequent histories of physical and sexual abuse in childhood, runaway behaviour in early adolescence, and extreme brutality and exploitation as an adolescent sex-trade worker.

In a Canadian replication using Silbert's questionnaire, Bagley and Young (1995) extended the American work through comparison with two control groups: women of similar ages to a sample of ex-prostitutes randomly selected from a community mental health survey; and women in the appropriate age range from the same community survey who experienced sexual abuse in childhood, but who had not entered prostitution. The study located 45 women over 18 who had left prostitution (in Calgary and Edmonton) during the previous two years. These women completed Silbert's questionnaire on childhood circumstances, as well as a number of mental health adjustment measures. The potential bias in the Calgary study is that it failed to interview women trapped in prostitution, and excluded those who died from drug overdose, suicide, murder and AIDS.

On indicators of childhood history, the Canadian ex-prostitutes were quite similar to Silbert's 200 US respondents: 53 per cent (58 per cent in US respondents) reported drinking problems in a parent; 40 per cent (38 per cent US) reported regular violence between adults in their home; 62 per cent (48 per cent US) had been physically abused as a child; 73 per cent (61 per cent US) had suffered sexual abuse in childhood. The average age at entry to prostitution was 15.4 years for the Canadian women, and 14.0 years in the US group. Ninety-four per cent of the Canadian group and 95 per cent of the US group felt extremely negative about themselves on entering prostitution; 70 per cent of the Canadian group and 62 per cent of the US group had been raped other than by a client, after entering prostitution. Most of these rapes took place when the women were under 18.

Comparison of the 33 ex-prostitutes in Calgary who recalled sexual abuse in childhood with 36 women in a similar age group from the community sample who had also experienced child sexual abuse, indicated that the abuse of the ex-prostitute (EX) group was significantly more prolonged and more severe than in the sexually abused community controls: 45 per cent of the EX group and 23 per cent of controls had been abused by different assailants on at least two different occasions; assailants were a biological father for 21 per cent of the EX, and four per cent of the control group. Seventy-three per cent of the EX, and 46 per cent of the control group were abused prior to age ten; 45 per cent of the EX and two per cent of the control group had been abused continuously for more than a year; 43 per cent of the EX and six per cent of controls had been abused on at least twenty separate occasions. Eighty per cent of the EX and 12 per cent of the sexually abused control group had experienced intercourse during the abuse; 30 per cent of the EX and five per cent of controls had experienced anal intercourse.

A number of questions were asked only of the ex-prostitutes, in order to investigate the possibility that sexual and other kinds of abuse had an influence on entry to prostitution: 40 per cent said that they entered prostitution as a direct result of prior sexual abuse. Eighty-two per cent had experienced sexual intercourse with a boyfriend (outside of child sexual abuse and prior to becoming a prostitute) by the time they were 15; 53 per cent had sex with at least six boys before entering prostitution, and 29 per cent had intercourse with more than 20 boys or men prior to entering prostitution. There was some evidence that this sexual promiscuity was a reaction to sexual abuse in the home. In addition, 31 per cent of the respondents had been raped as an adolescent, prior to entering prostitution, and separately from sexual abuse taking place in the home. Thirteen per cent started prostitution while they were aged 12 or 13. Three women had been used by family members as child prostitutes, beginning at the ages of eight, nine and eleven. All of these three women told horrifying tales of rape by parents, uncles, siblings and by paying clients, sometimes on a daily basis. Mothers of these three girls were also prostitutes, and two of their children were subjected to sadistic practices before, during or after being raped (see Bagley 1997, for analysis of this case study evidence on child prostitution).

The data suggest that the earlier the entry to prostitution, the more likely this was to be linked to sexual and other abuse in the home; 16 per cent began prostitution at the age of 18 or later, and none of these women had experienced sexual abuse as a child. Bagley and Young (1995) conclude following regression analysis of data and analysis of personal accounts of the ex-prostitutes, are that about 60 per cent of this sample entered prostitution as a direct or indirect result of child sexual abuse. A further 20 per cent entered prostitution as the indirect result of emotional or physical abuse. A major problem clearly involves the plight of runaway children and adolescents who are fleeing from abusive home situations. On the street the only means of survival are various forms of illegal activity, including theft, drug carrying and trading, and prostitution. For some, the entry to prostitution is a process of drift; but for the victims of the most severe sexual abuse, entry to prostitution as children and young adolescents can be through direct recruitment or coercion.

Another study of adolescent prostitution in Calgary by McIntyre (1995) provides supportive findings for the Bagley and Young (1995) study. McIntyre worked with prostitutes seeking services from the 'Exit' van (a mobile service unit for street hookers), and through these contacts obtained a snowball sample of fifty sex trade workers (including 41 females) aged 12 to 32. Eighty-four per cent had run from home before entering prostitution; 78 per cent of females and 100 per cent of males had been sexually abused prior to becoming a sex trade worker. Eighty-five per cent came from disrupted, broken or unstable families. Three quarters had begin sex trade work before age 16 (because of the method of sampling, it is unlikely that any young girls in 'trick pads' – a type of brothel – were interviewed). Three quarters of the women had been physically abused before leaving home; 80 per cent had not completed high school, and 53 per cent of the women had been charged with 'communicating for the purposes of sex'.

Sixty-two per cent of those interviewed had made a suicide attempt or act of deliberate self-harm; 82 per cent had been beaten up and/or robbed by customers. Drug use tended to follow rather than precede entry to prostitution, and was often used as an anaesthetic. Not surprisingly, these young people had very low self-esteem, and poor mental health. Being drunk or stoned made them more vulnerable to unprotected sex with customers, and rates of STD were high. Sex work detached the young adolescent from all other social institutions; the street and the pimp were now her exclusive family. The girl would take on a new name, a symbolic declaration that all previous life was left behind. Clients or Johns were regarded with contempt, and various ways were learned to end the sexual transaction as quickly as possible; in addition, girls learned to dissociate from the sex act, just as they had learned to dissociate themselves from the persona who was sexually abused as a child. One of her contacts led McIntyre to describe a single extended family in which 39 identified members were pimps or prostitutes, and children suffered routine physical and sexual abuse by parents and relatives before, during and after being sold as child prostitutes. During the period of McIntyre's fieldwork, ten female hookers were murdered in Calgary. McInnes (1995) a former vice detective and head of the Exit agency in Calgary calculated that within a decade of entering the sex trade, one in eight of the women who had not left prostitution voluntarily would be dead: from AIDS, drug overdose, suicide, or murder.

Calgary: Kid Sex Capital of North America?

In 1994 a mass circulation supermarket tabloid (*National Examiner*) carried a cover feature (Nelander, 1994) about 'child sex slaves' in Calgary, Alberta and carried a quotation from an unnamed official that Calgary was the child sex capital of North America. The headline 'Kidnapped Children' was followed by the sub-heading 'Innocent little girls are being tortured, starved and locked in filthy dungeons of despair'. The story continues: "Like cattle headed to the slaughterhouse, the frightened little girls are paraded naked – carrying bidding numbers – before pimps who shout out their offers and take their purchases back home for a nightmarish life as a child hooker ... They are tortured, beaten, starved and locked in filthy rooms where they're forced to have sex with up to 40 men a night in what cops call 'trick pads'. Cops say one hellhole in Calgary, Canada, was set up in a network of stark, barren rooms in the back of a pizza joint". Unlike most supermarket tabloid stories this account is, unfortunately, true (Toneguzzi, 1993). What is at issue however is whether Calgary is any different from other North American cities; the high ascertainment rate could be due to a vigorous vice squad. McIntyre (1995) estimates from a street-level study in Calgary that trick-pads (child brothels) have existed in Calgary since the early 1980s; Calgary may have been the first city in Canada where these child brothels became widespread.

Some of the runaways (or throwaways) are recruited in malls or at street level by pimps, and girls as young as 11 or 12 are sometimes held captive, abused, raped, given drugs and tortured until absolute obedience is obtained. Some girls are indeed sold to other pimps. The 'trick pad' rooms are usually furnished only with a mattress on the floor, and two boxes or bins, one containing fresh contraceptives, the other the discarded condoms. The girls (too young to be paraded on normal hookers' strolls) may have to service dozens of clients in one night. Disobedience brings burning with cigarettes or heated instruments, belting or whipping, or withholding of drugs or food.

The accounts of women in their late teens or early twenties confirm this reality that in a seemingly civilized society, 'girls between 11 and 15 are forced under death threats to work as sex slaves. Pimps are aggressively recruiting girls for trick pads at corner stores.' (Mofina, 1993). Mofina reports that up to October, 1993 police in Calgary had identified and rescued 109 young girls trapped in trick pad houses. An unknown number of girls continue to work in such places. Dolik (1993) quoted police sources in Calgary indicating that there were about 400 underage girls publicly working as street prostitutes, and at least that number working behind the scenes. The younger the girl involved in prostitution, the more likely it is that she is forced to work in a trick pad. Up to 1993, 11-year-olds were relatively unusual in such settings, but the majority contained many 12 and 13-year-olds. Potential clients are approached by pimps (or approach known pimps) in certain bars. Once the pimp or his agent is satisfied that the client is not an undercover cop, he will be driven to the trick pad. The fee to have intercourse with a girl of 11 or 12 is around $200 (street hookers charge about $100, or less). The fee to have sex with a 'virgin' is between $500 and $1,000. These are girls with little evidence of secondary sexual development, and they may be resold as 'virgins' 20 or 30 times. Once they are well known in one city, they may be sold to a pimp in another city and shipped to another Canadian Province. (One woman who had been treated this way told us that she was bound and gagged, and shipped in a car trunk for a 500-mile journey).

Dempster (1996) cited a police spokesperson in Calgary, suggesting that about 50 girls under 16 in Calgary go missing from home each month. The majority of these return home voluntarily after a brief period on the streets; but others are second and third time runners, and may never make contact with parents again. A Vice Squad detective indicated (in 1996) increased activities by pimps trying to recruit girls into prostitution, by hanging around malls and other places where young kids hang out (Dempster, 1996). Almost certainly, trick pads in Calgary continue to exist. The retired vice squad sergeant who is active at the street rescue level has persuaded ex-prostitutes to go on national US talk shows (Oprah etc.) warning parents and children about the dangers of juvenile prostitution (Sillars, 1995). Sillars describes the community initiative led by the former vice squad officer in Calgary – an 'Exit' van tours the strolls, offering free coffee and help to any hooker who cares to come into the van.

How accurate is the picture of Calgary as a centre of child and adolescent prostitution? Certainly, in this booming oil city (population 780,000) demand for prostitutes has always been high; but the extent of child prostitution (girls of 13 or younger) is still unclear, since much of it likely remains hidden. Various Canadian studies have indicated that the *average* age of entry to female prostitution (in all major cities) is around 15, meaning that a half of all street prostitutes enter the sex trade (not necessarily working directly on the street) before the age of 15, many as young as 13. I have an impression that police will tolerate adolescents who look like young women (i.e. are obviously not children) entering the street trade, but will intervene when the girl obviously looks like a child. The young teenagers on the strolls dress older, not younger, in order to both attract clients, and to avoid police investigation.

In addition, the finding of an average age of entry to prostitution should (according to McInnes, 1995) be revised downwards from the age of 15.5 (for the 1980s) to 13.5 (for the 1990s). This may reflect the trend for adolescents and older children in Canada and North America to have sex at younger ages (Bagley, 1997). My police informants in Calgary express anger and frustration that the problem of child and adolescent prostitution seems to be getting worse, and their legal remedies for combatting this wretched trade are often ineffective. Police have tended to ignore the boys' strolls in a different part of the city, since it appears that these boys (aged 12 to 17) are not controlled by pimps, and are working voluntarily on the streets.

Conceptual Problems in Research on 'Child Prostitution'

Joseph (1995) in a review of writing on child and adolescent prostitution in the Third World, implies that the publications on child prostitution she reviews are somehow accurate, and the product of scholarly enquiry. I would question this assumption for a number of reasons. First, the term 'child' is used very loosely (e.g. for any minor aged less than 18), and second, the studies are rarely the reflection of systematic social science or ethnographic research. Many studies often cited have not used reliable research methods in arriving at what are often no better than apocryphal accounts. In the literature on child prostitution writers frequently borrow from one another, and a statement by one author (based on a statement by a previous author) is quoted as if it were an objective fact, evidence beyond all reasonable doubt. Folk myths about child prostitution acquire the status of facts through retelling and quotation.

In reviewing the literature on juvenile prostitution we argue (Bagley and Young, 1995; Bagley and Thurston, 1996b) that a clear distinction should be made between child, and adolescent prostitution. Adolescent prostitutes (girls aged 13 and over) are sought because of their nubility and their newly acquired secondary sexual characteristics; the adolescent women involved usually emphasize their obvious sexuality. Child prostitutes (girls of around 12 or younger) in contrast, are taught to emphasize their innocence, and their lack of secondary sexual development. Furthermore, while the available research evidence suggests that adolescent prostitutes are numerous, child prostitutes in cities like Bombay and Manila are rare (or at least are well-hidden, and serve a clandestine market).

Joseph's (1995) writing on child prostitution in India and The Philippines draws on literature that is speculative and ill-researched, with writers quoting previous writers who cite previous writers, who cite what appear to be urban myths which are often expanded and elaborated in the retelling. The more horrific the tale, the more fascination it seems to hold, and the more the account is retold. In this chapter I have avoided reviewing what seem to me to be problematic studies alleging widespread child prostitution in Third World countries, with little basis in systematic evidence gathering. I am confident however that the evidence I have obtained through personal research in Bombay and Manila do present some valid findings.

The Philippines

A TV documentary shown in Britain (Carlton, 1995) featured an Irish priest who claimed to have discovered networks of child prostitution involving both boys and girls up to the age of 12, in the northern island of Luzon (which includes metropolitan Manila). The documentary claimed, quite falsely, that 'The Philippines is the sex capital of the world'. From extensive experience of Manila (and other northern cities in The Philippines) and of Calgary and other Canadian cities, I am certain that problems of child and adolescent prostitution are appreciably worse in Canada than in The Philippines.

The Philippines (especially the northern and central regions) is strongly Roman Catholic, and religious orders (Priests, Nuns and Brothers) have an extremely powerful role in socializing and controlling the activities of young people. The Philippines is also a country where, *par excellence*, personal lives and social activities are open to the scrutiny of others. Secrets are not kept; if children engage in illicit activity, everyone in the community soon knows. If a Western paedophile arrives, everyone knows who he is, and what he is looking for. He becomes fair game for elaborate confidence tricks in which the whole community (including police, who play an essential role) engage. The scam works like this: the paedophile is approached by a man offering a boy (or girl, according to the man's declared preference). The child is briefly viewed, and the man is told to come to a hotel room containing the child. Money changes hands, and the intermediary makes as if to leave. Then police burst in and arrest the paedophile. He is charged, but allowed to give all the money he is carrying as a supposed bribe, so that charges can be dropped. He leaves the country penniless and humiliated. There was of course no intention to allow the child to be touched sexually by the paedophile. This may be one reason why some Filipinos perpetuate the myth of the sexually available child when interviewed by foreign media. Sensational press and TV stories pull in more unsuspecting flies to the honey trap. Woe to the paedophile who sets foot in The Philippines!

While the sexual exploitation of children less than age 13 is probably atypical in The Philippines, there *is* a sex trade industry which features adolescents who are nubile, and of marriageable age in terms of Canon law. Many of these girls are from rural areas, and come to Manila with the sorrowful acquiescence of their family: these girls may become the sole breadwinner for a large family living in considerable poverty. Over a three-year period I made frequent trips from Hong Kong to Luzon in order to administer scholarship funds from a Canadian charity. Catholic nuns identified sex-trade workers who had done well in high school, and could complete an education which would allow them to return to their home province, and entering school or college.

At the time of this work, central Manila was lined with bars featuring girls who dance on stage and if selected by a customer would accompany him to his hotel. These bars were mostly frequented by tourists from Japan and Australia, with a smaller number from Europe and North America. Besides administering these research funds through the Catholic Sisters, a female researcher and I also conducted an ethnographic study in one of the largest of the bars (*Blue Hawaii*), in which about 100 bikini-clad or grass-skirted girls would perform elaborately choreographed routines on three separate stages, under the watchful eye of the *mama-san* who supervised the lives of these girls as thoroughly as the housemistress in a girls' public school.

The girls themselves lived in carefully supervised hostels, in which male visitors or 'followers' were not allowed. One of the stages in the bar was for the novice girls or 'virgins', as they were referred to by *mama-san*. Some girls remained virgins, earning their living as dancers. Others, at around the age of 14 or 15 were (if *mama-san* approved) allowed to go with customers. The client would pay two fees, one to *mama-san*, and one to the girl in his hotel room. Virtually all of the girls sent money home to their families and some lived quite ascetic lives. On Sunday mornings *mama-san* would lead her chattering crew crocodile fashion, to Mass. A few girls were overwhelmed with the amounts of money they acquired, and did follow the route of drug dependency. If this happened, they would be expelled by *mama-san* and their welfare became the responsibility of the Sisters. These Sisters would prevail on uneducated girls from abusive homes *not* to enter prostitution, on the grounds that they were too easily exploited.

Mama-san allowed a female Filipino researcher to interview 81 of the girls aged 14 to 19, actively engaged in prostitution, to be interviewed. The interview schedule included questions used in a study of sex trade workers in Calgary (Bagley and Young, 1995), but was administered in Tagalog by the researcher who had previously worked at *Blue Hawaii*, and who was now a student on one of the Canadian scholarships. I assumed that the degree to which girls would be frank about their families of origin would be similar in both cultures (Canada and The Philippines), although cultural factors would lead us to assume that if any bias exists, it would be in the direction of the Filipino girls being more honest.

The interviews with the Filipino adolescents (Table 1) indicated that they had entered prostitution on average, at the same age as the Calgary group with whom they were contrasted: this mean age of entry to prostitution was about 15 years (although many of the Filipino girls began working in the bar one or two years before becoming sexually active). Significantly fewer of the Filipino adolescents recalled sexual or physical abuse up to the age of 12. None had previously run from home, compared with 49 per cent in Canadian study who had run from home, temporarily or permanently, by the age of 12. The Canadian adolescents came from more disrupted homes, although the Filipino girls were four times more likely to have experienced death of a parent. Parents of the Filipinos were significantly less likely to have a drinking problem. Although 30 per cent of the Filipino adolescents (compared with 55 per cent of the Canadians) had experienced physical abuse (severe beatings monthly or more often), the Filipinos had experienced significantly more physical neglect than the Canadians. This was neglect (measured by an imposed 12-hour fast more than once a month) which for the Filipino girls reflected extreme poverty rather than wilful neglect. The Filipino girls were much less likely to have experienced intercourse during sexual abuse prior to entering prostitution, and their age at first intercourse was three years later than for the Canadian girls.

The most startling difference was the number of clients the two national groups had to serve in an average week. The Canadian group (who were older than the Filipino group when interviewed, and had already left prostitution) had when working served an average of about 56 clients a week, compared with the nine clients a week serviced by the Filipino girls. It should be borne in mind that our Canadian group were all women who had successfully left prostitution, and will have under-reported those permanently trapped in the nightmare world created by pimps and customers: thus these comparisons may have *underestimated* the amount of pathology in the lives of the Canadian women.

In The Philippines parents would sorrowfully part with their most physically attractive daughter. She would make the long journey by ferry or bus with an older sister or mother, who would tearfully hand over the child to *mama-san*. Most of the families of these girls lived in chronic, desperate poverty with no income at all other than the remittances of their teenaged daughter. This practice is not formally approved of by the dominant Roman Catholic church, but is implicitly tolerated. The conservative Bishops of The Philippines have forbidden the faithful to use contraceptives, and these are difficult to obtain through normal retail outlets. *Mama-san* did however supply these girls with condoms, and I have seen Catholic Sisters surreptitiously slip a packet of condoms to street girls (who are often also addicts, without the protection of a *mama-san*).

The formally diagnosed rate of HIV infection in The Philippines remains surprisingly low, the rate being a small fraction of the proportion of sexually active men and women in Thailand. This could reflect the fact that each prostitute (according to our study) in The Philippines has relatively few clients, compared with Thai and North American sex-trade workers. In 1995 only 98 new HIV cases were recorded by the Department of Health of the Republic of Philippines, making a cumulative total of 467 known cases of HIV/AIDS by April, 1995 since statistics began to be collected in 1984 (Morisky, 1995). The evidence suggests that health monitoring for HIV status is as well-developed in The Philippines as it is in Thailand (Tan, 1993); W.H.O. regional offices are maintained in both Manila and Bangkok. Tan (1990) describes the regular health checks available for the 65,000 registered 'hospitality women' in The

Philippines; social control mechanisms may prevent a girl from continuing to work after any STD is detected.

A paradox is the undeserved reputation which The Philippines has for child prostitution (as opposed to adolescent prostitution). The sex-industry in the northern Philippines is both highly regulated (by the Catholic Sisters working at street level) and ritualized. In many bars with dancing girls, a girl's encounter (and her loss of virginity) with her first client will be celebrated with a party, and the elevated earnings remitted home with pride. The careful monitoring of the sex-trade industry means that there is careful regulation of the age and type of young person allowed to enter. Prostitution is implicitly tolerated by the Catholic church because of the lack of economic alternatives, in a country in which so many people are desperately poor. Nevertheless, the amount of prostitution seems to be on the decline with the exodus in 1991 of American naval and airforce bases, and campaigns such as that by the Mayor of Manila which led to the closing of all the dancing-girl bars in Manila (including *Blue Hawaii*) in 1993. In the short-term the counter to the adolescent sex-trade industry in The Philippines is a support for Church authority and aid through specific developmental projects, financed by donor countries; and in the long-term, the development of alternative income and vocational opportunities for young people.

Conclusions

The statistical and case study evidence from North America on child and adolescent prostitution should leave us outraged at the cruel destruction of young lives. This sexual exploitation of young people should not be tolerated by a seemingly civilized society; to the extent that such exploitation of children occurs or is tacitly encouraged by lack of public policy, and the failure of police and social work action, our fine societies of the western world cannot be described as 'civilized'.

The first social policy question to be addressed is whether society should tolerate prostitution of *any* kind, let alone that which involves the exploitation of juveniles. Helen Reynolds (1986) in a wide-ranging review of 'the economics of prostitution' concludes that whatever legal controls are placed on the institution, prostitution will continue to thrive in one form or another. For example, controls on street soliciting may result in a form of communication for alternative services such as massage, or escorts. 'There are also some good things about prostitution, although those aspects rarely received the attention that the bad aspects do. The best thing about prostitution is that it allows a sexual outlet for some people who would otherwise be precluded from the type of sexual interaction they wish to have. For those whose social skills or current life situation does not allow them to engage in the sort of sexual activities that they would like, prostitution offers a choice of sex for hire on an impersonal basis ... If prostitutes are paid more money to engage in prostitution than in other kinds of work that they could and would do, then they are made better off by the existence of a market that allows them to earn money' (Reynolds, 1986, pp. 189-190).

Reynolds argues for the legalization of prostitution practised by adults (18 or over), with finite police resources being focused only on certain types of prostitution, particularly that involving juveniles. There is some sense in this proposal. In Calgary for example, despite the enormity of the problem the vice squad contains only half a dozen officers, who have to address the whole range of the problem including illegal soliciting by adult prostitutes, and the complaints of businesses and residence owners about prostitutes ruining their neighbourhoods. A regulated trade in which adult brothels are allowed, and call girls permitted to advertise freely would allow police to address the problem of juvenile prostitution.

Since 1988 it has been illegal in Canada for a man or woman to offer a person under 18 money or reward in return for sex. Thus customers of adolescent and child prostitutes could in theory be prosecuted. In practice this has not happened, and the only prosecutions of which I am aware concerned drug dealers who exchanged drugs for sex with minors. Police in Canada seem extremely reluctant to engage in 'sting' operations, which would involve a young person soliciting clients who would then be immediately arrested if they accept the proposition, knowing that the girl or boy was underage. McIntyre (1995) argues from her street level study that several adolescent hookers would be delighted to be the actors in these stings. Although pimps are occasionally caught and given long sentences it is the customers, the Johns who maintain the trade and it is these men whom criminal justice policy should address. One reason given by police for not acting in sting operations is that actions which drive underage prostitutes from the streets swell the numbers in the odious trick-pads, where girls can be confined and suffer horrendous maltreatment. The counter to this is that more vigorous efforts should be made to locate these institutions through the use of undercover agents (not necessarily policemen). In order to continue in business the trick-pads *have* to recruit paying clients, and herein lies their essential weakness. If clients can discover where these trick-pads are, so can police. All that is needed is greater political will, in allocating more resources in order to increase the ranks of the vice squad.

Several times in our research in Canada (Bagley and Young, 1995) we have come across worse case scenarios: for example, a girl of 10 or 11 complains to a teacher about sexual abuse at home. Child protection workers are informed. Father denies the abuse, and mother fails to support the child. She is removed into a group home, and recruited by older girls who are frequent runners, to take off from the group home into the down-town scene. For a few weeks life is full of parties, drink and drugs. But the girl is being set up by a pimp, and is soon enslaved by him through a combination of drug dependency and fear of further physical maltreatment. For a few weeks her virginity is sold several times. Then the burnings and beatings begin in earnest. She has to serve twenty men a night. She is sold and shipped to another city. By the age of 13 her spirit is entirely broken, and she is shifted from trick pad to street. By the age of 17 she is dead of a drug overdose; or has killed herself; or has been murdered. Human service options are quite clear, and again lack of funding and personnel inhibits satisfactory intervention. *All* runaways and abuse victims require effective, skilled and lengthy interventions offering psychological and social supports, and long term alternative residence if necessary.

The Manila case study shows how cultural traditions can greatly modify practices surrounding adolescent prostitution, and points to possible economic solutions to ending this sexual exploitation of adolescents. The implications of these and other case studies are that cultural regulation can effectively control the problem of child prostitution (even in The Philippines, where child prostitution despite western myths, rarely exists). Final conclusions point to three levels of control or regulation: child prostitution can never be tolerated by a civilized society; adolescent sexuality (in those say, 16 and over) should be tolerated, but only in relationships in which the younger person clearly has free choice, and is not overwhelmed by the structural power or wealth of the older person. We should tolerate and support older sex-trade workers, acting as independent, self-employed entrepreneurs, who could work independently of pimps. Government and people must face up to the problems inherent in the commercialization of sex, and produce humane solutions which protect the young, and promote healthy sexual exchange between adult strangers in ways which ensure that neither party is exploited.

Table 1   Comparison of family and abuse factors in the background of Filipino and Canadian sex trade workers

Variable	Calgary Sample (N=45)	Manila Sample (N=81)	Significance
Raised by:			
Mother and father	42.4%	60.5%	$p<0.05$
Mother alone	31.1%	28.4%	
Sibling	4.4%	1.2%	
Other relative	6.7%	9.9%	
Foster care/group home	15.5%	0.0%	
Death of parent	6.7%	25.9%	$p<0.01$
Step-father/cohabitee in home more then 6 months	42.2%	3.7%	$p<0.001$
Drinking problem of:			
Father/stepfather	44.4%	25.9%	$p<0.05$
Mother	13.3%	2.5%	$p<0.10$
Other household member	15.5%	16.0%	$p>0.10$
Physical neglect/extreme poverty (often hungry for 12 hours or more)	22.2%	50.0%	$p<0.01$
Had run from home for more than 24 hours	49.0%	0.0%	$p<0.001$
Physical abuse (excessive beating at least once a month)	55.5%	29.6%	$p<0.01$
Sexual abuse by an adult before entering prostitution	49.9%	9.9%	$p<0.001$

Table 1 (Continued)

Variable	Calgary Sample (N=45)	Manila Sample (N=81)	Significance
Sexual abuse before entering prostitution involved intercourse	26.6%	3.7%	$p<0.001$
Two+ assailants sexual abused her before entering prostitution	22.2%	3.7%	$p<0.01$
Mean age at 1st intercourse	11.4 yrs	14.8 yrs	$p<0.001$
Mean age at becoming a prostitute	15.4 yrs	15.2 yrs	$p>0.10$
Physical *and* sexual abuse	73.3%	34.6%	$p<0.001$
Maximum no. of clients ever in 1 week:			
100+	20.0%	0.0%	$p<0.001$
50-99	66.7%	3.7%	
25-49	11.1%	14.8%	
8-24	2.2%	60.5%	
<8	0.0%	22.2%	
Average number of clients per week when full-time	56.1	9.2	$p<0.001$

Statistical significance calculated by Chi-squared.

PART IV
SOCIAL WORK ISSUES

8   Child Protection and Children's Welfare: Complementary Priorities?

ELAINE SHARLAND

Introduction

A major debate has recently emerged in the United Kingdom, concerning the ways in which policies and practice in child protection are integrated with those surrounding family support and the promotion of children's welfare. Increasingly it is recognised that these dimensions of professional intervention may in theory complement each other, but that in practice they can operate in tension, to the detriment of each. This argument has been well put by both the Department of Health (DH), reviewing its own programme of commissioned research (DH, 1995) and by the Audit Commission (1994), examining the interface between health and social services for children in need.

Partly in response to such findings, local policy makers are now required to produce integrated Children's Services Plans (SSI, 1995). These must embrace child welfare and protection service provision, 'rebalancing' the two, and incorporating public, voluntary and independent sectors in so doing. At the same time, however, disagreement and uncertainty remain amongst policy makers and researchers as to whether and how far the tensions within and between children's services priorities may be resolved. These tensions exist both at the conceptual/epistemological levels, and at the levels of policy and structure (Hughes, 1996; Owen, 1996; Parton, 1996, 1997). Questions remain too around the extent to which partnership-based practice may be achieved within child protection (Platt and Shemmings, 1996; Thoburn, Lewis and Shemmings, 1995) and around the effectiveness of the criminal justice system in responding to child abuse (Davies et al, 1995; Wattam, 1997). These issues are amongst those currently under review by the Children's Services Strategy Group, in the process of revising and updating the Working Together Under the Children Act 1989 Guidance.

This chapter draws upon one of the 20 studies, commissioned mostly by the Department of Health, whose collective findings have now been widely disseminated in *'Child Protection: Messages from Research'* (DH, 1995). The discussion explores firstly the research and policy background to the study, and briefly describes its design. It moves on to explore several ways in which the dichotomies and dilemmas surrounding child protection and child welfare were articulated in the context of professional interventions in child sexual abuse. Finally, it considers these findings in relation to some of the messages elicited from the broader research programme, and to continuing debates around their policy and practice implications.

Background to the Study and Research Programme

The DH research initiatives to explore child protection services, and latterly family support services too, emerged from a context of high profile criticism, Public Inquiries and corresponding law and policy developments in the field of child care. Most significantly, of course, there was the radical reformulation of law in the Children Act, 1989, implemented in October 1991, along with accompanying Guidance and policy documents. Responding to research and lobby group critiques of childcare practice over a period of years (reviewed in DH, 1991a; Morgan and Righton, 1989) the Act heralded a tightening up and integration of legislation and policies in the area, with attempts to define needs and to identify duties in respect of children in need (Part III) and of children at risk of significant harm and in need of protection (Part V).

The DH research programme exploring child protection was initiated during the same period, in response particularly to events in Cleveland 1987, which cast doubt on the quality and effectiveness of services to children in this area. Most of the studies involved in the programme, including the project discussed here, spanned the period of early implementation of the Children Act and Working Together (1991) guidelines for inter-agency co-operation. The researchers came from a variety of backgrounds and disciplines. Their projects explored different but related aspects of the child protection system, from a range of conceptual, methodological and empirical bases. The relative merit of such a pluralistic - or pragmatic - approach have been argued in recent debate on the current state of social work research (Trinder, 1996; Little, 1998). The programme did, however, yield a composite, multi-faceted overview and critique of child protection services. Broadly disseminated, this is currently informing policy and practice development (DH, 1995).

Our own research project (Sharland et al, 1996), based in one urban/rural mixed county in the south of England, was originally commissioned as one of the more 'clinical' studies included in the Department of Health (DH) programme. It was to involve a more quantitative 'scientific' methodology than many others, and systematic emphasis on the relationship between intervention and outcome. As it evolved, its design increasingly incorporated a combination of methods and a more qualitative approach to exploration of process as well as outcomes. As it took shape, the study also became more (though not exclusively) oriented towards social work than medical practice; indeed the project team shifted in location from a child psychiatric to a social work research setting.

This shift was in many ways symptomatic of a convergence which occurred over time between the member studies of the programme. Having set out with related but rather different focuses of concern, as well as different methodological starting points, the projects emerged with a significant degree of consensus in their findings and in the messages to be drawn from them.

Design of the Study

The project had three principal aims: to look at the nature and pattern of professional interventions in cases referred for suspected child sexual abuse; to explore client and professional experiences of intervention; and to consider the relationship between early intervention practice and case outcomes.

The study was based on a community population of 147 families, involving 220 children. These constituted all of the referrals for suspected child sexual abuse made to police or social services in one local authority, over a 9 month period. Outline information on all cases, concerning case details, the history of intervention and decisions made, was collected one month after referral. From this survey base a smaller group, comprising 34 families and 41 children, was selected according to pre-defined criteria; this constituted the sample for an in-depth interview based study. Children, their primary parent and a key professional were interviewed at both 3 months and 12 months after initial referral to a child protection agency. Interviews were semi-structured, tape-recorded and analysed using quantitative and qualitative research techniques. The ethical, practical and methodological issues surrounding sample selection, access and confidentiality, were many. This chapter does not allow space to examine them, but they are fully explored elsewhere (Sharland et al, 1996).

Important to note at this stage is the fact that both the survey population and the interview sample were very mixed in profile. All were cases referred with concerns about sexual abuse but with, for example, varying degrees of certainty. By three months after referral, half of the cases in the interview study sample were thought certain to have been abused, a further third were considered definitely not abused; as for the rest, professionals were still uncertain. There was similar variation in the apparent source of abuse - just under half of the cases were thought to involve an abuser or suspect inside the family and household; the others involved individuals outside family or household, or, in two cases, suspects unknown. When considering both realistic goals for intervention, and actual outcomes achieved, the variation in case profiles was a very significant factor to be taken into account.

Several criteria, both facilitating and restricting, helped shape the way in which intervention process and outcomes were explored. Not least amongst these was the fact that the project involved a small scale, in-depth study, set in the context of a wider survey, with no experimental control. Exploration of the relationship between process and outcome was to a significant extent retrospective - by definition, cases could only be accessed following some professional intervention, since it was the very process of referral and investigation which defined them as 'cases' at all. Hence any 'before and after' intervention comparisons could only be made with the benefit of hindsight. Importantly too, these were times of turmoil and stress in the lives of all families concerned, but to varying degrees, in very varied circumstances and with varying resources for support. Thus there were significant limitations in how far particular outcomes could be taken to be the result of professional interventions alone, rather than the product of a complex web of factors, related and unrelated to suspected or actual sexual abuse.

Recognising these limitations, we chose to explore those dimensions of professional intervention, and those indicators of outcome, which seemed most appropriate, accessible, and meaningful in the context. We examined in most detail the early stages of intervention - referral, first professional contact with child and/or family, and the early investigative process. We did, however, give some attention to post-investigative 'follow-through' services too. Our focus was not merely on the occurrence, or not, of certain practices and procedures, but on the quality and style of practice, of professional relationships with children and parents, and of participants' perceptions of the intervention process.

When considering outcomes, it was important to concentrate on those outcomes which could reasonably be expected of the early stages of child protection intervention, rather than, for example, the more therapeutic outcomes which might be expected of longer term professional involvement. Amongst the outcomes explored, we included certain 'objective' measures, such as the achievement or not of effective child protection. Other outcome indicators tapped the quality of professional/client relationships achieved, and perceptions reached. These included the extent to which partnership-based working relationships were established between professionals and families, the degree to which parents and children felt that the intervention had been helpful, and the extent to which their perceived needs remained unmet.

The full findings of the study, in relation both to process and outcomes of professional intervention in child sexual abuse, are given elsewhere (Sharland et al, 1996). The present discussion concentrates on two central and related themes that emerged from the research and that resonate with the messages from other studies in the DH research programme. These are: the relationship between child protection and the broader promotion of children's welfare, and the interface between child protection, child welfare and the criminal justice process.

Child Protection, Children's Needs and the Promotion of Their Welfare

As described above, the survey population and the interview study sample comprised cases referred to agencies with *concerns* about sexual abuse. Hence it was predictable that a proportion would subsequently be filtered out of the child protection system, as evidence emerged to confirm that the children were not in need of protection. The principles of this filtering process are embodied in the Children Act legislation; details of its stages and procedures are set out in national child protection Guidance (DH, 1991). Thus local authorities have 'a duty to investigate when a child may be at risk of significant harm', and to decide appropriately whether they should 'take any action to promote or safeguard the child's welfare' (Children Act, s.47(1)). It may well be appropriate, in some cases, to conclude on the basis of informed enquiry that no further intervention is required. Equally, it may be the case that children are found not to be in need of protection, but 'unlikely to achieve or maintain ....a reasonable standard of health and development' and hence 'in need' of supportive professional intervention, to 'promote and safeguard (their) welfare' (s.17(1)).

While an effective and informed filtering process in child protection is recognized to be entirely appropriate, some studies in the DH programme have drawn attention to its present deficits. Gibbons and colleagues (1995) monitored the trajectories of all child protection referrals in eight local

215

authorities, finding that three-quarters were filtered out before reaching case conference, and that only 15 per cent were placed on the child protection register. As a result, they questioned whether it was appropriate for as many *'minnows'* to be caught up in the child protection net, recommending instead a more enquiry-based and family support oriented approach to intervention.

Our own small scale study similarly demonstrated the filtering process in action. Of the 41 children referred in the interview sample, 16 (39per cent) reached case conference, and 11 (27per cent) were in the end registered. Most importantly, we considered whether children and families had received any 'follow-through' services after early investigation. Our definition of follow-through services was broad, including assessment, support and/or therapeutic interventions. Our threshold was low - families who had had more than just one or two contacts with child protection professionals after investigation were deemed to have had 'significant' follow-through service. By 12 months after referral, we discovered that 15 families (44per cent) had indeed received significant follow-through, while 7 (21per cent) had had minimal service, and 11 (32per cent) none at all. Not surprisingly, case conferencing and registration appeared often to be the 'gateway to services'; follow-through interventions were more forthcoming for those who advanced through these formal procedures.

Our study pointed to deficits in the filtering process, less in relation to the appropriateness of an investigative response at all, than to the link, or gap, between child protection services and a broader response to children's needs. It was true that post-investigative support services were more likely to be forthcoming in cases where abuse was more certain, more severe and perpetrated by a household and family member. Nonetheless, we found that in the interview sample almost half (10) of the 21 children who had certainly been abused, received no follow-through services at all by 3 months after referral. Two-thirds (14) of the children certainly abused were not the subject of case conferences and almost as many (13) received no therapeutic intervention at all. On closer inspection, it became clear that the children least well supported were those who had been sexually abused by someone outside their family or household. In these cases, most commonly, there were no ongoing child protection concerns. Once the abuse had come to light, parents had shown themselves able and willing to protect their child from further violation. However troubled the child might be, however shocked and distressed their parents, their safety was not now considered to be threatened. In a professional culture which separated child protection from other childcare and support practices, and in a resource climate which prioritised risk over welfare, these children's welfare needs went largely unaddressed.

Children sexually abused by 'outsiders' were not the only group to have been poorly served by the child protection system. Some children who were not, in the end, thought to have been abused, but had been exposed nonetheless to the scrutiny of investigation, showed clear signs that they and their families had significant residual welfare needs. In certain cases these needs were directly the result of the investigation itself: these parents and/or children remained traumatised, their relationships and certainties disrupted by the casting of a shadow of doubt or suspicion of abuse. Others were simply experiencing welfare and relationship difficulties, unlikely to place the child at risk of significant harm, but likely to impair their welfare and development. Our findings were mirrored by those of Gibbons and colleagues (1995) who discovered that over 50 per cent of cases referred into the child protection system received no services beyond the child protection investigation, despite the presence of other child care concerns and need.

Both qualitative and quantitative indicators of outcome generated in our interview study suggested that children and parents were experiencing high levels of residual need following child protection interventions. According to several standardised measures, we found high and worrying levels of depression, post-traumatic stress and disturbed behaviour amongst the children, with no consistent evidence of improvement over time (Table 1).

Table 1 **Children's psychological and behavioural difficulties**

Depression (Kovacs CDI)	at 3 months	at 12 months
none	14 (42%)	13 (50%)
mild	11 (33%)	8 (31%)
significant	8 (24%)	5 (19%)
Total	33	26

Post traumatic stress	at 3 months	at 12 months
none	12 (36%)	6 (23%)
mild	12 (36%)	11 (42%)
severe	9 (28%)	9 (35%)
Total	33	26

Problem behaviour (Parental reports - Rutter)	pre-referral	at 12 months
none	16 (46%)	15 (48%)
mild	12 (34%)	10 (32%)
major	7 (20%)	6 (20%)
Total	35	31

* % = column percentage

Likewise, there was considerable evidence that parents were in poor psychological state measured by the GHQ at 3 months after referral, although they, unlike children, did appear to improve over time (Table 2).

Table 2   **Parents' psychological state (Goldberg GHO)**

Psychological difficulty	at 3 months	at 12 months
none	8 (29%)*	17 (65%)
some	8 (29%)	2 (8%)
high	12 (42%)	7 (27%)
Total	28	26

* % = column percentage

Evidence of residual disturbance gleaned from standardised instruments was supported by our qualitative discussions with parents and children. In 70 per cent of the cases interviewed, either the primary parent, or the child, or both spoke to us of the needs, difficulties or distress which remained with them at 3 months after referral. The level of need was not greatly reduced by 12 months.

Children's and parents' stories were by no means uniform, in respect either of their case histories or of the services they had received. Some, for instance, simply felt abandoned, having been offered no follow-through support services to help cope with the aftermath of disclosure, intervention, or other difficulties brought to light. Others - especially where the suspicion of abuse fell upon a family and household member - had in fact received substantial post-investigative professional attention, but none of it welcome, nor, in their view, appropriate to their needs. The latter mismatch may indeed be inherent in some child protection work - statutory interventions which are unwelcome or threatening are not easily perceived by those on the receiving end as helpful or appropriate. It is arguable that child protection services and personnel are not, by definition, those best placed to provide support in such cases. The problem remains, however, that considerable perceived welfare needs continued for a majority of parents and children, abused or not, and to a large extent these needs went unmet.

Children either described themselves, or were described by their parent, as experiencing a range of difficulties consequent upon early investigation and/or the discovery of abuse. Most significant was children's ongoing need for support and reassurance, that they were not to blame, not doubted, nor in some other way diminished. Some parents felt more able than others to provide this confirmation; some children were too protective of their parents' feelings to seek it:

219

I need someone to talk to. I need help and I just don't know who to share it with. (Child)

It's affected everything for her. Sometimes she likes talking to somebody else but me, trying not to upset me, I think that's what it is. (Mother)

He doesn't like talking to strangers, but he needs to ... He'll talk to me about everything except this. (Mother)

Children's continuing distress was frequently expressed in difficult and challenging behaviour - again not something with which parents could always cope:

She's got a lot of problems and I can't help her. She's playing up something terrible at school. It's to say: "Look, something's happened to me and nobody's taking any notice." I know why she's doing it, but I can't help. (Mother)

She could do with help, like counselling or something. Someone to talk problems out. She gives the impression of a very confused child. I'm sure there are problems behind it. (Mother)

The trauma of the investigation or discovery of abuse was exacerbated for some children by stigmatising or taunting responses from their peer group:

When he goes to school and gets called 'queer' and comes home crying, you feel terrible. I went round to the school and the teacher stopped the person who was doing it ... Kids really know how to hurt. (Mother).

Faced with this range and level of their children's needs, many parents were themselves suffering in the aftermath of either the discovery, or just the suspicion and investigation of their child's sexual abuse. The range of problems articulated by parents extended from difficulties and anxiety in trying to meet their child's needs, to struggling with their own feelings, and with the impact of recent events upon their own lives. In some cases, the senses of distress and powerlessness were overwhelming, and were confounded by the perception - accurate or not - that appropriate professional support would not be forthcoming:

Everything's piling on top of me. There's no-one there to help me. You can ask for help, but it tends to go against you. And anyway, I don't trust them (social workers).

A powerful component of parents' distress was often the sense of grief and loss, of their unsullied child, of their own identity as a caring, protective parent, and of trust in their relationships with significant others. One mother for instance, whose husband had, erroneously as it turned out, been suspected of and investigated for abuse of their daughter, described the painful and the lasting effects upon the marital relationship:

> *We still feel guilty... Like N* (child) *was playing with him, getting on his back, messing around with him. She'd got her nightie on and didn't have any knickers. I just looked at her and screamed for her to get off. He looked at me - I'll never forget the look on his face, as though he said 'You think I'm guilty.' It was awful. Just that split second you find yourself stopping doing things. You can't ever do the same.*

Another woman recognised that her daughter had been abused by a family member, but could accept neither the loss of innocence involved, nor what she saw as her daughter's complicity in the abuse. At the same time, she acknowledged sadly that this impaired her own ability to act as the supportive parent she would like to have been:

> *It's different now, it's changed. The barrier's there ... She's not my baby any more. I blame her as well ... I don't want to know. I know I have to, to be able to come to terms with it. But I don't want to. Until I come to terms with knowing what went on, I'm not going to be able to help myself or her. I know that.*

In this case, as in others, appropriate support was not forthcoming. Unusually here, however, the key social worker had pushed forward the case to a child protection conference, not because there were ongoing concerns for the girl's safety, but in the hope that the case conference might provide a gateway to support services. In the event, this hope was in vain; despite a promise of therapeutic intervention, none materialised. What was starkly illustrated too in this case was the often observed gap between parents' perceptions of their needs and their comprehension of, or demand for, services. Sufficiently poorly informed by professionals as to what a therapeutic intervention might be, this

221

parent was confused enough to wonder whether a brief doorstep visit by a social work team manager had in fact been *'the treatment'*.

The discovery, from our in-depth interviews, of so much perceived residual need amongst parents following investigations for suspected abuse of their children, has been echoed in other qualitative studies (Hooper, 1992; Cleaver and Freeman, 1995). This has a number of implications for practice. First of all, it may better inform professional judgement and decision-making about parents' ability or willingness to act to protect their child. Not infrequently, we observed that parents' shock and distress were underestimated or misinterpreted by professionals, and taken simply to indicate a lack of concern or responsiveness. As a result, valuable opportunities for working in partnership, enlisting a non-abusing parent's potential support and protectiveness towards their child, may have been lost - leaving the parent alienated and the child further adrift. More broadly, the discovery of considerable unmet psychological and emotional need amongst parents adds substance to the pattern of failure in service provision sketched by larger scale studies discussed above. It indicates that the organisational separation of child protection from child and family support services might be less than conducive to meeting the range of needs which may come to light through child protection referrals.

Significant as the polarisation of services might be, it is important to note too that a refocusing of children's services, towards integration, flexibility, and fluidity between child protection and family support, may indeed be necessary but will by no means be the sole guarantor of effective intervention. Our study explored many aspects of the process and outcomes of child protection intervention, suggesting several factors which may either facilitate or inhibit effective intervention. Other studies in the Department of Health research programme emerged with similar findings (DH, 1995).

Amongst the facilitators of good outcome, firstly, our research demonstrated that a range of professional practices may be considered helpful by both parents and children - regardless, or even in spite, of the fact that they occur as part of a formal child protection intervention. Helpful professional practices included: a sensitive, respectful and informed approach to clients, open and clear communication, and the ability to work in an empowering and enabling manner with parents while maintaining a child-centred focus. Moreover, where families perceived professionals to be acting in these ways, they were more likely to experience other positive outcomes: parents were more supportive and protective of their children, children were safer and parents and professionals achieved better shared understandings and working partnerships.

Of course it is not easy to ascribe a causal relationship here, but the link, and the significance to parents and children of the quality of professional practice, was striking. Hence, while there is certainly a case for reorganising children's services, structure and process alone are not sufficient. The quality of professional practice is central both to effective child protection and to effective child welfare intervention.

Secondly, and by way of qualification, we discovered that there were some case characteristics which almost by definition limited the possibilities for effective intervention. Throughout our qualitative examination of process and outcomes, we observed what can be described as a consistent core of families for whom even the best practice, and best integrated services might have little prospect of success. These were cases where parents found themselves the unwilling 'partners' in an investigation of abuse suspected within the family and household. These families were often fragile, hostile and threatened, with all too long histories of unhappy and unwelcome interactions with social service. Their stance towards intervention was perhaps best summed up by one woman, whose casefile occupied three filing cabinets in the local social services area office. As a child she had been frequently in care and on the wrong side of the law; her own children had been much abused in the past and she had fought off repeated attempts to remove them:

> I don't trust social workers. I never have done. They only use things against you. Anything you tell social workers they use it anyway against you. They're good at doing that ... I don't tell unless I have to.

The implications of this are significant. Case workers involved in child protection do need to develop resilience along with insight; they must not necessarily read poor outcomes as evidence of professional failure. However the interests of avoiding unwarranted demoralisation should not overshadow the objectives of providing as effective a service as possible. Central to this, we argue, is critical reflection upon the style and quality of interventions and their underpinning presuppositions, along with ongoing development of practice and integration of child welfare and child protection services.

The Interface Between Child Protection, Criminal Justice And Children's Welfare

One particular area of concern emerging from our study involves the questions of how far the criminal justice system is at present effective in responding to child abuse, offers justice to children and promotes their welfare interests. These issues have been the focus both of legislative, policy and practice changes during the last decade, and of more recent research-based critique of the effectiveness of such changes. These questions have been explored predominantly through looking at the effects upon child witnesses experiencing the processes of criminal investigation and prosecution. Our own findings address the same central questions, but from a different, though complementary perspective. Our attention has been drawn less to the impact upon children of *experiencing* the criminal justice process, than the impact of *failure to experience* the opportunity to do so.

During the last decade, legislative, policy and practice developments surrounding criminal proceedings in child abuse cases have embraced two primary objectives. Firstly, they have aimed at rendering the process more child-centred and victim-sensitive. Secondly, they have attempted to improve the potential of the process for producing good quality evidence as the basis for prosecution and conviction. A range of reforms has been directed towards these ends. Amongst these have been the dropping of the competency requirement that had formerly undermined the legitimacy of children's evidence, the avoidance of delay in hearings, the introduction of live video links and screens in court, and the relaxation of court protocols and formalities. Reforms in the direction of enabling children to give evidence while minimising the trauma attached, have culminated to date in the admission of children's evidence-in-chief on videotape. This development was approved by the Criminal Justice Act 1991 and supported by official Guidance in the Memorandum of Good Practice (Home Office, 1992). Further reform, indeed, is still being considered, with calls for the comprehensive adoption of pre-trial hearings, wherein children's evidence might be heard in its entirety, obviating the need for them to attend and be cross-examined in court at all.

The success and appropriateness of current practices regarding criminal prosecutions for child abuse, have recently come under critical scrutiny (Davies et al, 1995; Wattam, 1997). Where child abuse is concerned, it has been pointed out that the criminal justice process, concerned with prosecution, and the civil justice process, concerned with child protection, are framed and generally considered as entirely separate entities. However, as Wattam argues, while there is characteristically little recognition in policy or practice of the interface between the two systems, there has also been a tacit assumption that the interests of child protection and criminal justice are at least complementary, even mutual (Wattam, 1997). In fact, as Wattam reminds us, the Working Together Guidance advises that the decision to prosecute be made on the bases of three criteria: sufficient substantial evidence, the public interest and the interests of the 'child victim' (DH, 1991b). The child's best interests are certainly not prioritised above the other two criteria, nor indeed above the interests of other children who might in future need protection. There is an implicit assumption, however, that all of the factors favouring or disfavouring prosecution are complementary and compatible. Our own findings, and those of several other studies, suggest that this is not necessarily the case.

Recent reviews have shown that, allowing for wide variation, between 60 and 70 per cent of local authorities now conduct videotaped interviews in accordance with the Guidance set out in the Memorandum (SSI, 1994; SSI, 1994; Wattam, 1997). There are, however, several contra-indications as to the effectiveness of this practice. The first is that there has been no noticeable or sustained rise, as a result, in the number of prosecutions brought for child abuse. Most estimates before and after the implementation of the Memorandum suggest an ongoing prosecution rate of between just 5 and 10 per cent of referrals (Jones and Pickett, 1987; Wattam, 1992; Plotnikoff and Woolfson, 1995).

Secondly, despite the fact that evidence is now so frequently gathered on videotape in such a way as potentially to be admissible in court, there is nonetheless a very high rate of attrition from the criminal justice process. Mirroring the more general filtering out of children from the child protection system as a whole, it appears that a relatively small proportions of cases involving videotaped evidence is passed on to the Crown Prosecution Service (CPS), let alone brought to trial (Butler, 1993; SSI, 1994; Plotnikoff and Woolfson, 1995; Davies et al, 1995). Some studies have explored the reasons for attrition (Wattam, 1992; Plotnikoff and Woolfson, 1995). They note that, in addition to concerns about further trauma likely to the child, all of the following factors may influence professional decision-making against prosecution: the youth of the child witness, the relationship of suspect to victim, the lack of corroboration and, most importantly, the absence of an admission of guilt by the suspect. This being the case, Butler (1993), for instance, found that the average rate of submission to the CPS of video recorded interviews was just 24.5per cent, and the Social Services Inspectorate discovered that three-quarters of local authorities surveyed had had fewer than ten videos shown in court during 1993 (SSI, 1994).

Thirdly, even in those cases brought to trial with the use of videotaped evidence, the experience of the court process may indeed constitute further, system-generated abuse for child witnesses. Despite recent process improvements, the exposure to continuing delay, anxiety, intimidation and attempts in cross examination to discredit their evidence, may still conspire to create an averse experience for child witnesses (Wattam, 1992; Glaser, 1995). Worse still, the experience may be in vain. A fourth finding casting doubt upon the effectiveness and appropriateness of current practice in this area, is that the use of videotaped evidence in trials is not systematically more likely to achieve conviction (Davies et al, 1995). Judges and barristers continue to express doubts about the use and validity of videotaped evidence in chief, responding with skepticism and caution. There is concern too that the Memorandum itself may become the 'defence lawyer's charter', any deviation from its recommendations being held worthy of demolishing the prosecution case.

Thus considerable evidence emerges from recent research to suggest that the criminal justice process achieves neither protection nor justice for children, and indeed that children's welfare interests are not best served under the present system of criminalisation. Despite this, it is notable that recent discussion and initiatives towards shifting services in the direction of broader family support and promotion of children's welfare have not generally highlighted the question of the interface between child welfare and criminal justice. Our findings, and those of others cited above, suggest that there is a strong case for incorporating this dimension of practice into critical consideration of the needs of children referred into the child protection system.

Most authors are agreed that there is some, but in reality limited, scope for reform of the present criminal legal system. Current principles and practice, despite recent modifications, are fundamentally skewed in favour of the interests and rights of the defendant over those of the complainant, and give greater credence in general to the word of adults over children. The logical conclusion drawn from some of the studies cited is that the path of criminal investigation and prosecution in child abuse cases is best eschewed, since most frequently it fails either to open out, or to reach a desirable end point, prompting further trauma en route. Reviewers such as Glaser (1995) have suggested that there ought at very least to be rigorous pre-interview screening of cases, selecting as candidates for videotaped interview only those with a strong chance of proceeding to prosecution. The rest, it has been argued, ought never to be set upon the forensic route (Wattam, 1997).

Our study reaches similar conclusions, but proposes something of a shift in emphasis. We argue that while criminal investigation and/or prosecution may not commonly be either achieved or helpful, the personal and emotional consequences of non-prosecution must also be addressed by practitioners and policy makers. Our findings, based on child protection interventions made both before and after the implementation of the Memorandum (1992), suggest that the failure to prosecute child abuse cases may in itself be detrimental to children's welfare interests.

In three-quarters (24) of our original child sexual abuse referrals which implicated identified suspects, no police action or prosecution was proceeding after three months. In seven of these cases, police had never directly interviewed the suspect at all; in the rest, either the police or CPS decided relatively early not to take the matter further (Table 3). Most commonly, the authorities' reluctance to proceed rested on what they saw as the fragility and vulnerability either of the evidence or of the child, or both. In all, just five prosecutions occurred in the interview study sample, all of them involving 'outsider' abusers. Though the numbers are too small for inferences to be drawn, it is worth noting that only one quarter of the children who had certainly been abused saw their abuser brought to trial or convicted. Amongst the rest were five cases where the identified perpetrator was a household and family member, and five where the abuse had been severe and penetrative.

Table 3   Criminal investigation/proceedings by 3 months after referral

	'Insider abuse'	'Outsider abuse'
Prosectuion proceedings	0	5
Police action pending	2	1
Charges dropped	2	4
Police action, no charge	4	7
No police action	7	0
Total cases with identified suspect	15	17

In truth, most children's experience of the criminal justice system was that it let them down, often betraying the promise of justice which seemed to have been offered in the early stages of investigation. What we observed in this small scale study was the same 'filtering out' process as has now been identified

227

by larger scale research discussed above. Our findings confirmed that the criminal justice system in and of itself falls a long way short of offering protection to children.

More powerfully than in other studies, however, the qualitative material gathered alerted us to the trauma entailed for children not in experiencing investigation and prosecution, but in being denied these. This denial, it is argued, contributed significantly to the legacy of needs and distress with which many were left grappling unsupported. Children and parents often described to us the senses of disappointment, confusion, betrayal and fear that were consequent upon failure to prosecute. These were often compounded by the stark reality that the perpetrator remained living nearby and, to all intents and purposes, *'laughing'* having *'got away with it'*. One result, observed by parents and professionals, was that children were left needing both reassurance that they were believed and explanation about why, if they were 'right' and the abuser 'wrong', he had not been punished.

> *I think because the police haven't even interviewed him* (abuser) *yet, C* (child) *thinks, in a way, that they don't believe what he's saying.* (Mother)

> *A bit of an anti-climax maybe. A bit disappointed. I had to try and reassure V* (child) *that it wasn't because she wasn't believed ... I'd actually recommended that they could, both children, make very good witnesses ... But, I mean, I was disappointed they* (CPS) *didn't go forward. So what on earth could she* (child) *have thought?* (WPC)

Some children were left in need of reassurance that they were now safe; quite often this was not attainable. Justifiably, these children continued living in fear - sometimes of an abuser who remained at liberty and nearby, and sometimes of retribution. One fifteen year old girl, for example, whose alleged abuse police had decided was unlawful, but consensual, sexual intercourse, told us:

> *He said if I said a word of this to anyone he'll have so many people after me. I'm still worried. I've got a threat today off his girlfriend. She and her mate have threatened my sister... I got followed the other day by most of them. There was a gang of them near Pizza Hut and they just kept staring at me. I hid ... He lives over there* (points across the road).

Other children and young people became avoidant, not just of actual encounters, but of potential or imagined ones:

The last couple of days she's been walking the long way home, avoiding the flat, passing it at a distance. (Mother)

I worry, every time a motorbike goes past I think it's him. (Child)

In another striking case, a six year old girl had been severely abused by a non-resident family member, who continued to live locally:

Every time she sees a car like his, she's worried, she thinks it's him ... She's frightened he might come round in the car. If I'm not there M (child) *doesn't want to go out ... She may be alright, like J* (abuser) *not coming here, but it's in her little mind, it's getting to her.* (Mother)

This child suffered nightmares and enuresis as a result of her abuse. With psychiatric help, her symptoms abated for lengthy periods - only to be triggered again each time the she thought she spotted her abuser's car. Therapeutic intervention could not override the continuing damage wrought by the failure to prosecute and remove a perpetrator whose guilt was unquestionable to all the professionals involved. As the child's mother put it:

She's frightened of him still, terribly angry. I think she will only relax if he is put away.

The same point emerged from many of our interviews: whatever messages we give to children, that they are 'right to tell', and that 'it's not their fault', an unresponsive criminal justice system runs the risk of leaving them confused, disconfirmed and threatened. To make matters worse, professionals involved were frequently too disappointed with, or too inured to, this failure of response to address the issue directly with children or parents at all. The unhappy task of explaining to children that prosecution had not gone ahead, but that they were nonetheless believed and safe, all too often fell to parents, who themselves were disappointed and confused. One mother gave a poignant description of the double-bind in which she found herself:

My first reaction was relief that the children wouldn't have to appear in court because the only evidence was the child's testimony and he was denying it. How the child stands up to cross-questioning means they can't be sure of conviction. The children don't know charges have been dropped, just they don't have to appear in court. They're very relieved, but they asked if that means he's going free and I said "The police are taking care of it, don't worry".

229

Her plea, expressed by others too, was that here at least the professionals should provide a follow-through explanation:

> *I wish the police and social worker would call the family together to say why the case is not proceeding, not just phone up. I was left to explain to the children that it wasn't because they were not being believed.*

Our own reflections are somewhat more critical, and are made in the light of our broader observations about the quality of services to children and families. The failure of the criminal justice system to serve the best interests of children is one amongst several inadequacies in response to the welfare needs of children who experience child protection interventions. We must accept that radical, child-centred change in the criminal legal process is unlikely to come about. Likewise, we must acknowledge that child protection interventions may necessarily involve delicate and complex assessments of risk, with potentially serious and painful consequences. Within these parameters, it is argued, we do nonetheless as professionals have a responsibility to reflect upon, develop and refocus our child care and protection policies and practice. Refocusing must be in the direction of validating children's experiences, making appropriate commitments towards supporting their welfare, and honouring those commitments in providing services to meet their needs.

Concluding Discussion

The 'Messages' from the DH research programme, of which this study was a part, have been well broadcast and are being integrated into subsequent strategic planning of children's services. While the programme, like all good research initiatives, probably raised as many questions as it answered, its overall findings were remarkably coherent and the inferences drawn from them relatively clear. Child protection, narrowly defined, is fairly successfully achieved, but at the cost of children's broader welfare interests and needs:

> At the time the research was undertaken, the balance between (child protection and family support) services was unsatisfactory. The stress upon child protection investigations and not enquiries, and the failure to follow through interventions with much needed family support prevented professionals from meeting the needs of children and families. (DH, 1995, p.55)

230

Instead was proposed:

> A more balanced service for vulnerable children (which) would encourage professionals to take a wider view. There would be efforts to work alongside families rather than disempower them, to raise their self-esteem rather than reproach families, to promote family relationships where children have their needs met, rather than leave untreated families with an unsatisfactory parenting style. The focus would be on the overall needs of children rather than a narrow concentration on the alleged incident. (DH, 1995, p.55)

While policy makers and practitioners may be struggling in the present resource-starved climate with the implications of these recommendations, few dispute their validity. We do indeed need to 'get the balance right' in children's services. Amongst social work researchers and academics, however, there has recently been some lively debate about the implications of the 'Messages'. Indeed this discussion has provided a focus for articulating some of the key current theoretical and methodological debates around the nature of social work practice.

The most vocal critic has been Nigel Parton, arguing that amongst the DH research and recommendations:

> ... there are a number of conceptual and methodological problems and failure to thoroughly articulate and represent the tensions and complexities of child protection work ...   As a consequence..... attempts to shift the balance of policy and practice from narrowly defined child protection to family support for children in need may be far more difficult than the research suggests. (Parton, 1996, p.3)

Parton argues that while the DH account claims to recognise that child abuse is socially constructed, it fails to follow through the implications of this construction for child protection practice as a whole, and for the pivotal notion of 'risk'. If, he maintains, we do recognise the relativism of any distinction between risk and need, we must confront some complexities. There is no easy rule of thumb for social workers to distinguish between what is risky, requiring a child protection response, and what (or who) is needy, requiring support. Child care social workers must live with, acknowledge, even embrace uncertainty, while all the time being held to account for the responsibilities they carry and the decisions they make. Exhortations simply better to integrate protection and support services, or to adopt a more 'enquiry-based' and less 'investigative' approach, do not address the real tensions involved, but simply offer naive, unworkable solutions.

In response to Parton, a spirited defence has been mounted by some individuals involved in conceiving or conducting the DH research. Hughes accepts that 'a shift in balance between narrowly defined child protection and family support will be difficult', but sees the research as 'providing helpful insights for managers and practitioners who wish to make this shift.' (Hughes, 1996, p.115). In particular, he points out how well the programme focused on process and outcome to identify the sort of social work practice that is more and less effective. He is also more optimistic than Parton about the possibility of applying 'appropriate assessments and services to each case' (p.117), even though criteria for distinguishing high risk cases from others will always be contingent on subjective and evaluative interpretations. Owen (1996) takes issue with Parton at both the conceptual/methodological and the policy levels. She argues that 'abused children' and 'children in need' are not mutually exclusive categories, and that there is indeed no conceptual problem in understanding the relationship between risk and need. While administrative structures may separate the two, it is important that organisational and procedural factors do not dictate the philosophy and principles underpinning provision of children's services. It should and could be the case that:

> ... children in unsatisfactory environments can receive appropriate help from the same range of services, whether the focus is on risk or need. (Owen, 1996, p.257)

Owen argues that the while notion of 'abuse' is certainly socially constructed, this does not always and necessarily render it problematic. The construct of 'risk' itself tends to be problematic not in severe cases, where definitions of abuse are rarely disagreed, but precisely in those 'borderline' cases which are poised within the category of 'need', but on the edge of the sub-category 'abuse'. It is the overlap and relatedness of risk and need which must be addressed and catered for. In Owen's view, the problems of social construction per se need be neither disabling nor irresolvable for social work practice. Critical and reflective child care services which integrate child protection and family support both conceptually and in practice, are a desirable and, potentially, a realistic objective.

This author accepts the tensions highlighted by Parton, but shares, for the most part, the views put forward by Hughes and Owen. Our own research left us in no doubt that children and their families were in many cases left struggling with unresolved emotional, personal and relationship difficulties following child protection interventions. Most powerfully, it appeared that the procedurally driven divide between protection and support was in principle and in practice inappropriate and unhelpful. It was inadequate to the welfare needs of both abused and non-abused children and their families. The case for fluid, responsive and flexible services, capable of responding both to risk and need seems indisputable.

This is not, however, to suggest that social work decision-making in child care and child protection will be unproblematic, nor that they can ever be free of dilemmas, uncertainty and professional risk. Here it may be helpful in informing our thinking and practice to refer to recent discussions about the very nature of social work. Particularly useful is the work of White, who draws upon both hermeneutic and post-modernist theories, and focuses on the notion of 'reflexivity'. She argues the case that social work is a practical/moral activity; social work interventions in child care and protection as elsewhere, are based on 'sense making' activities, involving interpretative rather than rational/technical judgments (White, 1997, 1998). Practitioners are faced with multiple 'versions', which may make equally valid but competing claims to represent what is real or true. In response, social workers make contingent choices; individually or interactively they select and organise knowledge claims, guided, often unconsciously, by professional and cultural norms and presuppositions. Deciding what, for instance, represents good or poor parenting, what constitutes need and what risk, what is acceptable and what is unacceptable, is thus a practical/moral activity. That this is the case need by no means be seen as a problem, but it does need to be seen, acknowledged and reflexively critiqued. Social workers need to be alert not only to their values and theory bases, but to the fact that their formulations of the issues that confront them are interpretations, and as such are open to dispute. Knowledge acquisition may indeed be progressive, allowing social workers to prioritise between different versions or claims to authenticity. This progressive process, however, must become self-conscious and transparent. Moreover:

> ... epistemic reflexivity may only be achieved by social workers becoming aware of the dominant professional constructions influencing their practice. For example, within contemporary child-care services these pivot around notions of parental dangerousness and fragile childhoods. This does not mean that these constructions have to be rejected wholesale, simply that workers should be explicitly aware of the need to consider the consequences of their analyses and formulations ... (White, 1997, pp.748-9)

It is argued here that structural, organisational and procedural shifts towards integrating child protection and family support services are necessary but not sufficient. They will only be effective if accompanied by a shift in the culture of professional interpretation and reflexive practice. If policy makers and practitioners succeed in recognising the relatedness of risk and need, the contingency of their decision-making and the potential ambivalences between child protection, children's welfare and the interests of social justice, there is strong potential for improving our services to children and families.

Acknowledgements: Grateful thanks are due to the members of the research team, Hilary Seal and Margaret Croucher. Acknowledgement is also due to the Project Directors, David Jones and Jane Aldgate.

9 Mothers' Involvement in Child Sexual Abuse Investigations and Support: Community Care or Child Protection?

SHIRLEY JACKSON AND GRAHAM TUSON

Introduction

This study explores some of the common issues of partnership, user and carer empowerment, and the role of the professional which underlie recent policy and practice reforms in both adult and children's services.

An unintended consequence of reforming children's services and community care at the same time is that many departments have set up separate planning processes and some are reorganising into children and adult divisions, rather than following the explicit recommendation of the proposal that "....the full range of social services authority functions should continue to form a coherent whole". (Smale and Tuson et al, 1994 p.4).

This paper contributes to understanding how professionals can best go about building on normal care in the community in partnership with service-users, and citizens generally, through consideration of the specific experience of non-abusing parents, predominantly mothers, in the process of investigation, assessment and longer term responses to sexually abused children.

We discuss the nature of partnership in the light of recent research, including our own survey of self-help groups for mothers of sexually abused children, and argue that professional intervention should always be sensitive to, and build upon, the normal systems of care and control in the community, and not seek to replace them. In particular, we argue a need to see the non-abusing parent as the central person in any "package of care" - as effectively a "care manager", and that the professional social worker should remain in an essentially "marginal" (Smale and Tuson, 1993) position -involved enough to facilitate any necessary changes, and access to resources, in partnership with others, but not so involved that it becomes impossible to leave. It is argued that more effective partnerships than those which typically occur between professionals and non-abusing parents is both possible and desirable.

Centrality of the Non-abusing Parent

Recent research shows that in the vast majority of cases, abused children, including sexually abused children continue to live with the non abusing parent, usually the mother (Cleaver and Freeman, 1995, Farmer and Owen, 1995). For example, in their detailed follow up study of 120 case conference decisions Farmer and Owen concluded that: "By the end of the study most of the sexually abused children were living with non-abusing parent." (DH, 1995 p 63). This is consistent with the wider research picture of children and families being drawn into the child protection process, where it has been identified that "Nearly all (96%) of these children remain at home and the majority of those separated are swiftly reunited" (DH, 1995 p 39).

Although there is not a strong body of research specifically focused on the experience of the non-abusing parent in cases of child sexual abuse, it is clear from this contextual research that their role is central to the ongoing care and control of children in the community. Clearly, the non-abusing parent is one of the 3.7 million "care managers", *not* employed by social services departments or other professional agencies. (Smale, Tuson et al, 1994 p.1).

Partnership

The details of what parents in our study and the wider research found helpful in their relationships with professionals will be explored later. As previous studies have shown (Marsh and Fisher, 1992; Jackson and Morris, 1994), it is important to have some shared perception of the meaning of the concept of partnership, although this is becoming increasingly complex as our understanding of different levels and degrees of partnership develops. For example Thoburn et al, (1995) adapted Arnstein's "ladder" of consumer involvement using such distinguishing categories as partnership, participation, involvement, consultation, keeping fully informed.

Whereas Thoburn et al, (1995) found that "partnership", as they define it, was only achieved in 3 per cent of cases in their study, using the full range of categories of partnership they found that approximately half of the respondents felt that they had been involved in the proceedings . This finding is echoed in the study by Sharland et al (1995).

An increasingly used definition is provided by the Family Rights Group, namely that: "the essence of partnership is sharing. It is marked by respect for one another, role divisions, rights to information, accountability, competence, and value accorded to individual input. In short, each partner is seen as having something to contribute, power is shared, decisions are made jointly and roles are not only respected but also backed by legal and moral rights."

Why Partnership?

Recent studies have shown that working in partnership with parents produces better outcomes for the child:

"The quality and extent of partnership between professionals and families are major factors affecting the progress of cases and outcomes for children ... But partnership varies in quality and extent. In a quarter of cases it was not achieved despite auspicious circumstances..Agency policy and procedures or social work practice, or both together, account for much of this failure" (DH, 1995 p 47).

Sharland et al (1995) studied how the various stakeholders involved perceived the process and outcome of child sexual abuse investigations. A conclusion of the related study was that:

> There was persuasive evidence that the style of professional behaviour in the early stage of an investigation did have an effect on case outcome, and that the establishment of a working partnership between primary carers and professionals, focusing on the needs and welfare of the child, was an important sign that the intervention had served its purpose. (DH 1995 p.81)

Thoburn et al (1995) underline the important features of partnership: All family members stressed the importance of being cared about as people. They could understand the professional had a job to do and that procedures were necessary, but they strongly objected to workers in whatever profession who did not appear to listen, did not show warmth or concern or who did things only by the book. (DH, 1995 p.87).

Professional Support for the Non-abusing Parent

Recent research clearly indicates serious deficits in the quantity and nature of professional support to networks of informal care centred on the non-abusing parent. Sharland et al (1995) noted that post-investigation support was not evenly distributed and was particularly unavailable to families where the abuse was perpetrated by someone outside the family. These researchers also concluded that there was no direct connection between need and service provided and fairly random forces seemed to be at work in determining the consistency and continuity of service.

Farmer and Owen (1995) in their study of decision-making and outcomes noted that in half of their sample where the perpetrator had left the household, it was assumed the mothers could cope and cases were soon closed. In many of these cases difficulties then worsened. They conclude that the primary needs of the carer were reasonably met in only one third of the cases.

Why Not More Research Into Normal Care and the Role of the Non-abusing Parent?

Despite the studies previously discussed, research specifically into the role and experience of the non-abusing parent, and their partnership with professionals, is limited. There are many reasons for this, but the three main ones we identify are to do with firstly, the approach to intervention in cases of suspected child abuse; the problem of "targeting" only the "most needy" and false assumptions about the centrality of the professional in the networks of care and control. In respect of the first of these, Gough, for example, concludes:

"Since the whole concept of child abuse was largely based on parental responsibility for the distress of their children ... the service response was likely to be concerned with perceptions of the adequacy of the parents as carers. Yet child abuse research and sometimes child protection services were artificially separated from other research and practice concerning the support of children and families..". (Gough, 1993 p35).

The evidence is that of the large numbers of children who are the subject of child protection investigations, only a quarter proceed to child protection conference (Gibbons et al 1995), but less is known about the degree to which services are subsequently offered to the 75 per cent of children who leave the child protection system at this stage. Even less appears to be known about access to services by "children in need" who are not subject to child protection investigations.

Another related problem is the often unresolved tension between pressures to undertake the "downstream" work of targeting the "most needy", e.g. children subject explicitly to allegations of child sexual abuse, and the "up-stream" work required to prevent children and families falling into the river of difficulties which then results in their later becoming the target of crisis intervention. The clear tendency has been to focus resources heavily on the downstream work, and thus inevitably fail to provide sufficient "preventive", upstream, help, and also to tackle the consequences of "rescue". The low profile, or non existence of such up-stream work in practice, in which by definition the non-abusing parent would be centrally involved, will contribute to this being under-researched. This tendency has been clearly identified in both the Audit Commission report, *Seen and not Heard* and the Children Act Report, 1993.

The third major factor appears to be that the normal role of the non-abusing parent as a protector and educator of her children is most obvious in the everyday, routine, front-line interventions which characterise the bulk of child protection involvements, but which have simply not been the target of much academic research. For example, in his recent survey of research on professional responses to child abuse, (Gough, 1993), it is concluded that, taking the research field as a whole there is "... a relative lack of reference to routine child protection services." (Gough, 1993 p284). The research emphasis has been on the "treatment" activities of special projects and clinical teams, rather than on the lower profile experience of locally based social work and interdisciplinary teams, who deal with the bulk of investigations and assessments. Consequently, the relatively limited study of non-abusing parents has to be seen as symptomatic of this larger research deficit.

Some of the implicit practice and policy assumptions of the last decade have tended implicitly to overemphasise the importance of the role of professionals in directly providing forms of care, protection and control in the community. The fact is that for the vast majority of people, social work and social service agencies are peripheral to their lives because they manage a whole range of difficulties and conflicts for themselves without involving professional agencies. For example in their study of family support and prevention Gibbons et al conclude:

> The evidence suggested that the support of family, friends and neighbours, and the use of day care provision, might have been as or more important than the

help received from social services or from organised community groups. (Gibbons, et al, 1990 p. 149)

Professionals often fail to recognise their own marginality, and hence fail to recognise and support the capacities of people in the community, such as the non-abusing parent, to undertake normal caring and social control functions. For example, a recent prevalence study (Kelly, Regan and Burton 1991) based on a sample of 1200 young people, concluded that:

About one half of those who had experienced abuse told someone about the abuse at the time. The person they told was most likely to be a female friend or relative...Only 5 percent of incidents were ever reported to any agency. Of 1051 incidents only 10 resulted in any form of prosecution. (Kelly, Regan and Burton 1991, p 20)

Obviously, this can be read as a "scandalous" under-reporting of sexual abuse, and an under provision of professional help and control, which to some extent might be true, but it can also be read as evidence that many people use their existing social resources, and that it should be the proper role of professionals to identify and build upon such resources, rather than trying to replace them, which apart from not being what people want, may actually serve unwittingly to undermine them.

Our Study: Perceptions of Partnership and Parental Involvement

The purpose of this study was to gain some insight into issues affecting the inclusion or otherwise of non-abusing parents in the investigation process and the support of their children, from the viewpoint of parents who had been through the "system".

Methodology

For the purposes of this initial study, it was decided to contact already established support groups. Research into sensitive subjects is not a neutral, no cost activity and it was recognised that we would have insufficient resources to give adequate support to a random sample of interviewees. We used an already established national list and took the first three groups to respond positively to our request. Coincidentally, these groups were geographically disparate and therefore gave a national cross section. They were all situated in predominantly white areas and there were no black respondents. There was a mixture of women whose children's abuse had been investigated pre and post Children Act 1989. However, the majority had been investigated post Children Act 1989.

Semi-structured group interviews were undertaken by a female interviewer. The gender of the interviewer was considered important because of the history of "mother-blaming" in many explanations and models of intervention in child sexual abuse. (Hooper, 1992). Whilst this study was not initiated from an explicitly feminist perspective, feminist explanations of child sexual abuse have guided the focus and development of the study. Two out of three groups were for women only (mother's and in one case a grandmother), one group was specifically non gender specific and called a non abusing carers group. There were only women present at the interview and therefore the vast majority of opinion is from mother's whose children have been sexually abused by a man. This reflects the prevailing norm (Hooper, 1992). Thirty women's views were elicited in total.

Experience of Initial Contact

Based on previous experience it was assumed that most mothers would be told of the abuse by a professional. However, about 80 per cent of the respondents had been told about the abuse by their children and they had then involved the professionals, usually police and\or social services. This is significant in the light of the complex procedures developed both nationally (DH, 1991) and locally to inform parents sensitively. In fact, it is the parents, usually the mother, who inform the professionals. This is consistent with the findings outlined previously that it is children, their friends and their relatives who, through their own informal relationships do the bulk of the "child protection" work in the community, not the professionals (Hooper, 1991). As with assessing the needs of elderly people, for example, the main implication of this is that we need to consider carefully how in subsequent interventions professionals work in partnership in with all those people who are already involved providing care and control. The task is to expand and support the existing network of care, rather than deliberately or "accidentally" take over.

Whilst many of the women interviewed had felt a continuing inclusion in the investigation process, some had not. The most debilitating experience was of professionals taking over and the mother then feeling out of control. For one woman, her daughter had told an aunt, who had been visited by the joint investigation team, prior to informing the mother. The professionals insisted on

241

informing the mother themselves but the aunt disagreed and had to break the news to the mother over the telephone to avoid her first contact being with the police and social worker on her door step. This mother reported that she was very pleased she had learnt of the incident from her sister and not the authorities and felt angry that they had not listened to her sister.

Models of Investigation and Assessment

Investigation is essentially an assessment task, and it is clear from the reaction of some of the mothers in our study, and the problems reported repeatedly in abuse enquiries, that there continues to be confusion about the nature, practice and purposes of such assessments. A recent analysis of different "models" of assessment being used in "care management" (Smale and Tuson, 1994) is relevant here. Three models are identified - the Questioning Model; the Exchange Model; and the Procedural Model. It is argued that the Exchange Model of assessment is necessary if assessments are to be carried out in ways which are more likely to empower service users. The other two models which are widely used, albeit implicitly, provide efficient ways of meeting the organisations needs, and assessing eligibility for services or policing interventions, but do not empower users. It appears that the reaction of some mothers in our study is a response to the disempowerment involved in a "questioning model" or "procedural" approach to assessment.

This clearly has implications for the training of investigators. We have seen that working in partnership produces better outcomes in the protection of children, and most mothers do not know of the abuse. The preoccupation with identifying the abuser and whether or not there was collusion by the mother leads to a questioning approach which is the antithesis of partnership because it is based entirely on the agenda and purposes of the investigator, rather than on that of the mother. Our study has shown that this can be counterproductive.

Positive Partnership

Given their previous experiences and recent research evidence (Thoburn, Lewis, and Shemmings, 1995; Sharland, Jones et al, 1995), it was surprising to the authors how many of the respondents felt they had been included in the whole process of investigation. Many had very positive experiences of working with social workers on the joint process of conviction of the perpetrator and the

242

support and rehabilitation of the child. Fewer had positive experiences of working in partnership with the police, often feeling that they were not kept adequately informed of the course of the police investigations.

However, there seemed to be a clear divergence between those who had very positive working relationships with their social workers and those who seemed to have had very poor experiences. Those who felt they had been included cited the following ingredients to a successful working partnership. They were kept informed at all stages, the worker was always available, both on the telephone and in person. One mother said,

> *It's just important to have somebody whose on the end of a telephone. We found that we could ring them up anytime.*

They had regular contact, often weekly over along period. They also valued people who respected their opinion. One woman talking about the videoed interview said,

> *Yes, they respected my opinion on what I thought my child needed - i.e. time or encouragement and when she was ready to speak, "Do you think R would like to sit and relax for a while?"*

Another important feature was that they should give the impression to the child that they believed her/him. All of these features helped make the mother and child feel protected.

In contrast, one mother's experience describes the insecurity felt by many who had bad experiences.

> *I thought "Thank God, someone is going to talk to the kids, but they could not decide what to say, amongst themselves and I was left trying to explain to the kids what they were saying. They couldn't relate to kids and I felt worse and more alone afterwards.*

Other things which alienated mothers were not being kept informed, doing it by the book only, tunnel vision, having made their minds up early on and refusing to reconsider any aspect of the investigation. One mother said,

> *They put things in boxes and would not listen.*

Another mother complained

243

They seemed to be looking down their noses like this could not happen to them, but it could happen to anyone.

These responses are consistent with the earlier analysis of different assessment models, and the possible effects of the "questioning" and "procedural" models. "Doing it by the book" and "making up their minds early on" are good, vernacular, descriptions of these models. Also these mother's comments reflect similar accounts in other literature (Jackson,1994; Cleaver and Freeman, 1995; Farmer and Owen, 1995).

Professional Skills

Sharland et al (1995) report that:

> Wherever good relationships were encountered, the key elements generally had more to do with professional style than any particular action, so parents who felt they were listened to and, where possible, involved in the investigative process, were most likely to have positive feelings about the process. (DH, 1995 p.80)

Given the positive experiences of many of our respondents, clearly many social workers are employing the necessary skills and attitudes for working effectively in partnership with non abusing parents. However, some are continuing to exclude mothers from the process and this needs to be improved. During the course of our study, it seemed that there were two distinct groups emerging.

* One group seemed articulate, capable, generally coping reasonably well with parenting.

* The other group were the less articulate, seemingly more confused and needy group of mothers, who had not coped well with parenting generally and the specific difficulties the sexual abuse had brought.

Ironically, the latter group seemed to get a reduced and poorer service, with less evidence of working in partnership. What is going on here? Are they more difficult to work with and therefore partnership skills and attitudes are more easily stretched? Are they disbelieved more readily and therefore excluded at an early stage? Does the enormity of the task overwhelm workers and lead to early closure of the case once protection has been secured? This phenomenon has

244

been noted elsewhere (Farmer and Owen, 1995; Sharland et al, 1995). Sharland concluded that:

> No direct connection was found between the amount of support families received and what parents said they needed, nor were the needs and wishes which parents declared linked to the conclusiveness of the evidence that a child had been abused, to the gravity of the case or to the whereabouts of the perpetrators. The impression of fairly random forces were at work was similar when the researchers considered the consistency and continuity of service provision. (DH 1995, p.80)

But are these simply random forces or something more systematic? Conjecture could produce numerous options, but it would seem that more rigorous research of the forces at work in decision making at this stage is warranted.

Failure to Prosecute

One of the overriding concerns and sources of anxiety and distress for mothers focused on the prosecution processes for abusers. Some were told initially to try to stay friendly with the neighbours who were responsible and felt this soured further working relationships with the police. In many cases they had contacted the professionals because they thought they would be able to secure a conviction. They were not discouraged in this belief, despite the overwhelming evidence of low conviction rate. They felt that this should be better explained to both them and the child at the outset. The mothers were so upset about the low conviction rates, it is hard to see how this could be done sensitively and not add insult to their vulnerable position. However, there were clear areas for improvement in practice. One woman had only found out about the conviction of her ex-partner through the local newspaper. She and her daughter were still waiting to give evidence! Another woman was misinformed about the progress of the case and four months time was wasted, before the abuser was arrested. The inadequacy of waiting facilities at court caused some very distressing scenes. Plea bargaining and lack of conviction meant that many children felt that they had not been believed. The problems of failure to prosecute and the deep sense of betrayal by some children has been further documented in other studies (Sharland et al, 1995; Hallett and Birchall, 1995).

Care for the Carers

In the vast majority of cases the main work of supporting sexually abused children falls to the mother (Hooper, 1991). Whilst a number of mothers had good social work support with the processes of child protection, fewer spoke of good support for their and their children's responses. For most, such support was either lacking, or came later in the process. One woman said that the social services immediately after the first visit got her some help from a family centre. She started counselling straight away. This was not the experience of most respondents. Very few were offered counselling for themselves as mothers. Monck et al (1995) found that the mothers of sexually abused children who were given some therapy for themselves showed more of an improvement than their children. The likely knock-on effects of such therapy in the recovery of the children has also been alluded to. One mother in our study summed up the importance of support for her:

> *The mother has to be the rod of iron for the children and has to hold her feelings back to deal with the child. A social worker for the mum is the ideal so that mum knows there is someone there to support her.*

Some mothers felt that they had good social work support with the ongoing problems related to the abuse:

> *I do not know how I would have coped without the social worker as I did not have any support of her father or my family.*

Many had social workers for the first year, until the court case and found their regular support invaluable. Some felt that they did not need a social worker after a while but appreciated the opportunity even if they did not use it. The message seems to be of choice and respect for a mother to know when help will be useful. Others complained that social workers never came to see them after the initial investigation and if they did, made unhelpful remarks. One woman commented that a social worker had said:

> *"What do you expect, J was abused, she can't help how she is". But it was me that had to cope with the six children on my own.*

Recent studies have shown there can be a significant lack of adequate support for mothers in these situations. Farmer and Owen, for example, reported that:

In a third group (21%) the children were protected without any progress having been made. Most of these were cases of sexual abuse. Often the alleged abuser was out of the household, the mother was relied on to protect the child and the case had been speedily closed ... However, in only 30 % of cases were the needs of the primary carer reasonably well met. (DH, 1995 p 64).

They also found that scant attention was made to adequate protection and support plans at child protection conferences:

In over a third of the protection plans formulated at the first case conferences important aspects of the child's future protection were overlooked. The pre-occupation with risk meant there was simply too little time - nine minutes on average - to consider the needs of the family or what should be done. (DH, 1995 p.62)

This is significantly inadequate practice given the link between offering support to mothers and the likely greater protection for the child, but is to be expected given the huge emphasis in recent years on "downstream" crisis intervention, and the absence of models of practice which synthesise these two levels of intervention through the development of wide-ranging partnership with people in the community. All the time that professionals think they are central to care and control in the community, they will inevitable fail to meet the need, because there will never be sufficient resources, and they will simultaneously fail to develop community based resources.

Practice Implications

A conclusion of recent research is that:

The stress upon child protection investigations and not enquiries, and the failure to follow through interventions with much needed family support prevented professionals from meeting the needs of children and families. (1995, p.55).

Should findings such as this lead us to consider different ways of dealing with the needs of these children and their families? Many of the recent research studies and government publications (DH, 1995: Audit Commission, 1994; DH, 1994) lead us to question the wisdom of the present preoccupation with assessment of risk and lead us to a greater assessment of these children as children in need under s.17 Children Act 1989. Too many families struggling in difficult circumstances get prematurely defined as potential child protection cases rather than as families with children in need, leading to inadequate protection plans and few offers of appropriate services. The Department of Health research summary suggests adoption of a new emphasis in intervening. They conclude that:

> An approach that encourages a perspective on cases as *children in need in circumstances where there may be a protection problem* is more likely to lead to a wider range of services being used to ensure the child's safety and recovery. (1995, p.48)

Mothers in our study generally reported inadequate therapy or counselling for their children. It was either non existent, only offered too late in the process i.e. after the trial or involved therapists unskilled in communicating with children. This meant that few of their children had received adequate therapy in their eyes. This ties in with findings by (Farmer and Owen, 1995) that for about a half of the children in their study who had received no counselling, they had adjusted markedly less well and that for many of the children where social work support had also ended prematurely, their difficulties and those of their mothers deepened.

Support Groups, Self Help and Building on Strengths in the Community

Most women felt that the best support for them had been from their group. The following three comments sum up the value they place on the group:

(a)   *I found that helped more because it was mums who had been through the same situation. The counselling did me good but also the mums who had been through it.*

(b)   *You get all the problems with the children and you think you can't ring them up (SSD) for this but you can talk to the mums and even if you can't do anything about it, you've talked to the group and got it off your chest.*

(c)   *If we can't get through to one we can get through to another. It might only be a little thing. It might not be to do with the abuse, but with us being in the abuse group, we find that we are all good friends. But we are not friends that go to each other's houses and have cups of tea and coffee, but we're friends in the group.*

All the groups visited were well supported by social workers which was appreciated by the members. They were all however lamentably short of funds and always likely targets for financial cuts. Given the huge resource outlay with most child protection systems and support, these groups seemed to provide inexpensive and valuable services to the mothers and consequently to their children and should be encouraged and supported as much as possible.

Information and Empowerment

Most mothers felt that they had very little information about child sexual abuse, before, during and after the investigation. They felt that information, both verbal and written, would have been helpful at all stages. One mother said:

> *You know when you first find out, you can't take these things in. You get told things and it just goes from your mind, so you have to be told again or it has to be wrote down on a piece of paper. You can't remember what people are saying to you.*

Many women with hindsight said that they had noticed behavioural problems in their children months and years before the abuse came to light. In some cases they had sought professional help, but not realised the cause. They thought that some knowledge about possible signs of sexual abuse should be more available. In terms of prior knowledge, they felt it would be useful to have explanatory leaflets in public places. Very few of the women had been given any information either verbal or written on the likely effects of the sexual abuse. Many had questions still unanswered and were often unsure whether to attribute subsequent difficulties with the child to the abuse or not, whether to deal with it as they normally would or adopt different responses etc. All thought it would be very helpful to have a written guide for mothers on the likely effects of child's sexual abuse. Such a guide is being produced by one of the authors at the time of writing. They also felt that they needed help on how to cope with different situations such as how to protect but not overprotect the child, how to prepare the child and a new partner for the special needs of that child, how to cope with neighbours and friends lack of understanding. Whilst many felt that the group helped them enormously, they would have benefitted from on-going informative support from outside agencies.

Conclusions

The two major policy initiatives of recent years, the Children Act and the Community Care Act, have been widely, and unhelpfully, treated as separate and distinct developments, although this was not the original policy intention. However, it is significant that the implications of much recent research into the workings of the Children Act foregrounds the need for the same kinds of community based, collaborative and preventative work that has characterised both the best intentions and best practice in developing "Community Care". For example, it has been asserted that:

> A more balanced service for vulnerable children would encourage professionals to take a wider view. There would be efforts to work alongside families rather than disempower them, to raise their self-esteem rather than reproach families, to promote family relationships where children have needs met, rather than leave untreated families with an unsatisfactory parenting style. The focus would be on the overall needs of children rather than a narrow concentration on the alleged incident. (1995 p. 55)

That conclusion seems very similar in its implications to the following:

> A major fault in implementing the current reforms may prove to be a failure to build on people's normal capacity to care by overlooking the fact that carers and cared for can be given more support and choice by encouraging the involvement of a wider section of the community. There is a need to put in resources at times of crisis but these will not account for long-term care. This can only be provided by changes in patterns of care over time; by long-term development work, by directing professional time, expertise and energy at developing people's resources in the community; not just to target the "most needy", but also those social situations where care is absent. (Smale et al, 1994 p.6)

Whilst many non-abusing carers value the service offered during and post investigations into child sexual abuse, they clearly need to be the "nodal" points of networks of care; these networks themselves need to be expanded, supported and better resourced. Professionals need to be educated, trained and supported to work more effectively in partnership, and this means that service-users, such as non-abusing parents, should become equal partners in the training and development of professionals, at both basic and post-qualifying levels. The changes in professional culture and expectations required to develop better partnership around child sexual abuse, and which build on the strengths of individuals, families and communities, are essentially the same as those required for effective partnership practice with all service users.

Acknowledgements: We would like to acknowledge the help provided by the University of Southampton Small Grant Fund, and to acknowledge the interests and cooperation of several "mothers groups" in different parts of the country.

PART V
OFFENDER ISSUES

10 Men and Women who Kill, and Men who Abuse Children: A Study of the Psychiatric-Child Abuse Interface

COLIN PRITCHARD AND JULIA STROUD

Introduction

In their study of men in Scottish prisons who had committed sex crimes involving children, Waterhouse and colleagues (1994) identified a group who had committed brutal crimes of violence against adults and children, often involving sexual assault and violation. These men appeared, in reflection of their own brutal childhoods, to be involved in a series of attacks on conventional society and its morality which involved the most brutal and unforgivable of crimes, the sexual murder or rape of a child. But the motivation of these men did not appear to be overtly sexual: their crimes were those of violations of a morality which had betrayed their own childhoods, and they were as likely to murder a child as they were to rape an adult.

These men might be classified by the psychiatric definition of 'sexual sadists' (Gratzer and Bradford, 1995). Since a number of British researchers (Grubin, 1994) have identified a group of men (including men who have murdered) who fall into this diagnostic category, one of the purposes of this overview and study is to identify the characteristics of two populations: men and women who kill children, for whatever motive; and men and women who sexually assault children. We wish to explore the overlap between these two populations, with the frame of reference of social work and social psychiatry, drawing conclusions for policy and action with regard to dangerous offenders.

255

The Abuse of Children

Some three decades ago Kempe at al's (1962) work on the 'battered child syndrome' began the process of raising public and professional awareness of child abuse (Greenland, 1987). In emphasising the ubiquitous nature of physical abuse, however, Kempe (1962) and with a few notable exceptions (Bagley 1985, 1997; Bagley and Thurston 1996a; Pritchard 1991 and 1995), most subsequent commentators have overlooked the psychiatric dimension. Since Kempe's seminal work the dominant perspectives in child abuse have been defined mainly, if not solely, by child care (i.e. paediatric and social work) professionals (Greenland, 1987; Noyes, 1991) and the original oversight has been perpetuated. Moreover, the practical effect of the child abuse enquiries of the 1980s was to emphasise legalism and the administrative procedures associated with child protection, rather than analysis of the multi-dimensional nature of abuse.

The lack of focus upon parental mental health in child care and child abuse work has continued in spite of the fact that clinical research has demonstrated a frequent association (eg Quinton and Rutter, 1984; Bagley, 1995; Hawton et al., 1985; Huxley et al., 1987; Andrew et al., 1991; Pritchard 1991 and 1992; Famularo et al., 1992 and 1994; Sheppard 1994). To illustrate this point, Hawton et al., (1985) identified a well documented risk of abuse, in 29.8 per cent of mothers who attempted suicide. In spite of such evidence, there has been little attempt in practice to make connections between child care/abuse and mental health issues (Sheppard, 1994). Recently there have been indications that a greater emphasis is to be placed upon family support in child care/protection practice (Audit Commission, 1994; Brindle, 1995). It is suggested however that a knowledge of the relevant mental health factors is essential if accurate assessments are to be made and appropriate support offered, so that family support and child protection can indeed deliver a continuum of services of different types for the complex needs of individual cases (Davies and Little, 1995).

The focus upon physical abuse in this discussion reflects the fact that studies on child homicide in psychiatric literature and on psychosocial stress in child care and social policy literature afford a good delineation of the issues (Egeland et al., 1980). In parenthesis however, it should be noted that Bagley's research (see chapter in this volume) makes a strong case that the factor which subsequently is associated with long-term psycho-social damage to the child happens where 'emotional' abuse occurs in the presence of either physical or sexual abuse - indeed Bagley's work seemed to show this is the key to

256

psychological damage, the betrayal, abuse and exploitation of the relationship, irrespective of the child's previous vulnerability (Bagley 1997, Bagley and Thurston 1996a).

In comparison, analysis of parental mental health in relation to sexual abuse and neglect is less well advanced (Ethier et al., 1995). In the current environment of concern over the violence committed by mentally ill persons, it could be suggested that a discussion of the relevant issues will only serve to increase the stigma experienced by both mentally ill individuals and parents who harm their children. Well-informed persons, however, are aware that the current concern does not relate to any actual increase in violence by mentally disordered persons (Home Office, 1994) and that the majority of parents with a mental health problem to not harm their children (Pritchard, 1991). The interim report (Appleby et al., 1997) of the National Confidential Enquiry into adult homicides and its association with mental illness showed that whilst the mentally ill do have proportionately higher rates of violence, it is predominately first against themselves, then against their families, and relatively rarely against strangers. Indeed in 1996 there were only 28 such deaths (Appleby et al., 1997). Nonetheless, this piece of evidence hardly seems to dent the stereotypical media image. In order to further improve preventive strategies, there must be discussion and analysis of the issues surrounding the mentally disordered parent who may abuse or kill their child.

This chapter is in two parts: first a review of the research literature on child homicide by various assailants; and then an interim report of a decade of child homicide in a Southern English county, together with analysis of sex crimes against children.

Part I: Intra-Familial Homicide

It is generally accepted that most killers of children are found within their families, predominately their parents (Sommander and Rammer 1991). Child homicide is a multi-faceted phenomenon with complex, intricate and heterogeneous causes (Barker and Morgan 1992; Bagley 1985; Bagley and Thurston 1996 a and b; Bourget and Bradford, 1986 and 1990; Bourget and Labelle, 1992 a and b). While there has been immense public and professional concern about child homicide over the last two decades, this concern has focused predominantly upon deaths due to the child abuse-neglect syndrome (Greenland, 1987; Bourget and Bradford, 1990; Noyes, 1991). Indeed, child homicide has been equated with, and is almost synonymous with fatal child abuse. Much professional knowledge about the issue relies upon this child abuse literature (Jason, 1983). Thus, although child homicide is a heterogeneous phenomenon the professional response to it might be described as discrete with the responsibility for child protection becoming the major preoccupation of the paediatric and social services (Greenland, 1987; Brockington and Cox-Roper, 1988; Noyes, 1991).

Indeed Munro (1998) exploring the 'knowledge base for social work' in child protection had no psychiatric reference at all! And even Parton's (1996) review of child welfare, in a three page bibliography had only one mention of psychiatry, even though Foucault (often cited by social knowledge theorists in the psychiatric field) had many mentions. Scott (1998) shows that the situation (the neglect of mental health concepts by 'child abuse' workers) is the same in Australia; but at least she acknowledges the classic work of Hallet and Stevenson (1980), which showed that effective intervention relies upon inter-disciplinary cooperation.

One dimension of child homicide that has received much less professional attention (Famularo et al., 1992) is the fact that research findings indicate a significant incidence of psychiatric diagnoses among persons who kill children (Resnick, 1969, 1970: Scott, 1973a and 1973b; d'Orban, 1979, 1990; Korbin, 1986; Bourget and Bradford, 1990: Bourget and Labelle, 1992; Pritchard, 1992). In a study of 89 women remanded in Holloway Prison and charged with the killing of their child(ren), d'Orban (1979) found that 16 per cent had a psychotic illness, 21 per cent had reactive depression and 43 per cent had a personality disorder. In fact, d'Orban found only 16 per cent (i.e. 14 women) who had no psychiatric abnormality at the time of committing the offence. Similarly, Somander and Rammer (1991) studying all 79 cases of child homicide in Sweden 1971-1980 found only 10 out of 47 perpetrators were not mentally disordered when examined by a psychiatrist after the crime.

In the light of such findings, it appears apposite to examine what is known about mental disorder in relation to child homicide, which most child protection literature sees as the extreme consequences of child abuse (Kempe and Kempe 1978, Greenland 1987), leading to a focus in this discussion upon the diagnosis of major psychiatric disorders in perpetrators of child homicide. Since some writers have made a distinction between child abuse-neglect deaths and other forms of child killing (Greenland, 1987) it is important to be clear that all child homicides are being considered. The trouble with Greenland and a number of child-protection experts is that they often lacked systematic evidence about an extreme behaviour which is statistically very rare. They could not overcome the difficulty of obtaining a large enough sample to do any proper analysis, though we hope to demonstrate an approach in Part II which goes some way to resolving this difficulty (Cox and Pritchard, 1995).

Of course, the characteristics of child abuse-neglect may be present as well as a diagnosable mental disorder (Bagley and Thurston 1996a). However, referring to preventive measures in relation to homicide, Bourget and Labelle (1992) state that 'a multi-dimensional phenomenon requires a multi-dimensional approach' (ibid, p.670). We will argue that to deal with the risk of the extreme of 'child abuse', focusing upon the mental disorder dimension *rather* than upon the child abuse-neglect syndrome, will better assist identifying situations where children are at a higher risk of suffering serious physical harm. Moreover, since child care/protection and psychiatric professionals are working in a climate of great public alarm and anxiety over both child homicide, and the perceived dangerousness of mentally disordered persons, it seems essential that there is accurate knowledge of *both* issues.

The term mental disorder used in this discussion means diagnosable mental illness and personality disorders, including psychopathic (dissocial) personality disorder. The term is employed since it is the generic term used in the Mental Health Act, 1983. Mental illness and psychopathic disorders are both specific categories of mental disorder to which the Act applies (s1(2)(a)). Issues relating to mental impairment or learning disability, are not examined in this review, though we note that the presence of drinking problems or drug dependency often exacerbate problems of behavioural control brought on by mental illness and/or personality disorder. It is also possible that mental illness occurring in an individual chronic personality disorder (Pritchard et al., 1993) is one of the causal factors leading to violence against self and others.

Since mental disorder has long been viewed negatively, and is often stigmatised (Miles, 1987; Fernando, 1988), it may be considered controversial to examine the association between mental disorder and child killing. Practitioners however, will be aware that there are infrequent occasions when in acute and severe crises, a mentally disordered person may pose a risk to another person's safety (Bean, 1986). Mental disorder and child homicide do warrant the highest level of professional attention, not only in respect of children's safety, but also 'morally' in terms of preventing the 'abusive trauma' that perpetrators often themselves experienced as children.

To kill a child, especially one's own child is 'unthinkable', and such assailants are ostracised from their family and community forever (Bluglass, 1988; Fraser, 1988). This shocked response is *normal*, for there is a danger that we in the child protection field forget how relatively rare active abuse is in the total population. It is in every respect *abnormal*, yet we slide on a slippery slope when in attempting to understand the individual assailant, we are as non-judgemental as possible. Most of us feel 'hate' on occasions towards those we love; but we should remember that the vast majority do not assault others, and we are in error when we begin to assume that such behaviour is actually more frequent than it is.

The number of 'abnormal' murders (i.e. manslaughter due to diminished responsibility, infanticide, suspect insane, suspect committed suicide) has not increased dramatically, but has remained relatively constant (Bowden, 1990; d'Orban, 1990), whilst from the early 1990s the overall murder rate in the UK has declined slightly and in a number of Western World countries (WHO 1997). Thus the mounting public concern over mental disorder and violence, which has led to new legal powers (i.e. the mental Health (Patients In The Community) Act 1995), does not relate to actual increases. Indeed, the interim report of the enquiry into homicide and suicide by psychiatrically disturbed people in 1996 found that out of the 500 'homicides' in the UK, there were 100 'diminished' responsibility verdicts, the vast majority of which involved members of their family.

With respect to 'normal' and 'abnormal' homicide and gender Wilczynski and Morris (1993) showed that whilst 'normal' homicide was almost exclusively a male province, a significant proportion of 'abnormal' homicides were committed by women (d'Orban, 1990), with children of the family forming the largest group of victims at between 46 per cent (Morris and Blom-Cooper, 1964) and 44 per cent (d'Orban, 1990) - again underlining the importance of the child protection-psychiatric interface.

The Number of Children Killed and Age Groups Most at Risk

Violent deaths of children are rare events (Greenland, 1987; Bourget and Bradford, 1990), and exact rates of child homicide are subject to debate. Pritchard (1992), using WHO Annual Statistics (1991), found there had been a 'substantial' reduction in children's homicide in England and Wales. He concluded that all children's homicides (0-14 years) fell by 56 per cent in England and Wales and 24 per cent in Scotland between 1973 (total = 117) and 1994 (total = 56), and led the world in the reduction of child homicide over the past twenty years. Creighton of the NSPCC (1993),and Americans Lindsey and Trocme (1994) in their different ways expressed dissatisfaction with these general findings, and Creighton (1993) and Wilczynski and Morris (1993) also urged caution, suggesting that homicide statistics are likely to be an underestimate because of *inter-alia,* misclassification of deaths and accidental and legal difficulties in proving some 'suspicious' deaths as homicides.

However, Pritchard (1993, 1996) answered the critics two ways. First international comparisons over time are measuring like with like, and therefore one can use mortality statistics with a degree of confidence because any assumed 'under-estimating' is consistent across countries over time. And, crucially the 'undetermined' deaths have been found to be proportionately consistent over time, and whilst it is possible to miss a few cases, it smacks of special pleading to suggest that are many such cases. Moreover, when the Office of Population Censuses and Surveys (OPCS) data are used, combining both homicide figures and 'undetermined' deaths, a 35 per cent reduction in children's violent death rates is still found, which still put England and Wales at the head of the Western World 'league table' of reductions in child murders (Pritchard 1996). The latest figures available (for 1994: WHO 1997) found 52 child homicide (victims aged 0-14) in the whole of the UK, including Northern Ireland - a rate of 4.6 per million. Of course, the real point for consideration is that the violent death of any child is one death too many.

Babies aged under one year are the age group most at risk of death by homicide (WHO 1997). The increased risk to infants under one year of age is also supported by research. In d'Orban's (1979) study 44 per cent of the victims were aged under one year and, of a total of 109 victims, 36 were under 6 months. While this is the period of post-partum disorders, it must be noted that only a quarter of these 36 babies were the victims of mentally ill mothers. The two major groups responsible were 'battering' mothers (i.e. deaths that fitted the child abuse-neglect syndrome) and 'neonaticides' (i.e. killing of an unwanted baby within 24 hours of birth by the mother, who was not mentally ill - Resnick 1969 and 1970). In general, d'Orban (1979) found that 'battering mothers' when they did kill, tended to kill young children: 89 per cent of the victims of battering mothers in his study were aged under 3 years. Resnick (1969) also concluded that the victims of women who were suffering from acute mental illness at the time of the offence were more evenly distributed between the age groups. This was also the case in respect of the victims of 'retaliating' women (aggression towards spouse displaced upon a child). Similarly, d'Orban (1979) found that the mentally ill and 'retaliating' groups of women were the groups likely to have multiple victims. Recently reported cases have also illustrated this. For example, in 1993 Tracey Evans, who had a history of mental illness for which she had received in-patient treatment, was sent to a Regional Secure Unit after drowning her two young school-age sons in the bath at their home (Brindle, 1993) and in January 1994 Sharon Dalson was detained in Rampton after strangling her son (aged 6) and suffocating her daughter (aged 5) while experiencing delusions (Ivory, 1994).

The Extent and Nature of Psychiatric Studies of Child Murders

Child murder has received only 'sporadic' attention in psychiatric literature (Jason, 1983); Bourget and Bradford (1990) likewise report that 'only a few authors' (ibid, p.233) have reported on child homicide from a psychiatric perspective. Most reports must perforce focus upon a small number of cases (d'Orban, 1979). Research in the earlier part of this century describes larger series of cases admitted to Broadmoor (Hopwood, 1927) and to Holloway (Morton, 1934): these studies, however, are of historical rather than practical usefulness given the substantial changes and advances in the understanding of psychiatric disorders, psychosocial issues and changes in social conditions (d'Orban, 1979). There are relatively few research studies of larger samples reported in contemporary literature, reflecting the fact that child homicide is an infrequent occurrence. The most noteworthy recent studies of larger samples would appear to be:

1.   Resnick (1969): 131 filicides (88 maternal, 43 paternal) identified from world literature on child homicide 1751-1967.
2.   Scott (1973a): a classification of filicide applied to 46 paternal and 39 maternal filicides in Morris and Blom-Cooper's 1964 study of 764 persons indicted for murder in England and Wales 1957 -1962.
3.   D'Orban (1979): 89 women charged with killing their child(ren) and psychiatrically examined on remand in Holloway.
4.   Bourget and Bradford (1986 and 1990): 13 parents (4 male, 9 female) charged with killing their child(ren) and referred to a Canadian forensic psychiatric Service for assessment before trial.
5.   Falkov (1996) explored 100 cases of parental filicide: 32 were clearly psychiatrically disturbed; for another 23 there was insufficient evidence to confirm a diagnosis but there was ongoing contact with the psychiatric services. Interestingly he highlighted difficulty in getting comprehensive information so the 55 per cent with psychiatric links is probably an underestimate. However bearing in mind the prevalence rate of mentally disordered people in the community of 'parental' age - the confirmed 32 means the mentally ill were over represented by a factor of more than thirty times.

Resnick's (1969) study of the world literature on child homicide might be considered a seminal work, in that this study appears to have re-kindled interest in understanding child homicide from a psychiatric perspective. D'Orban's (1979) study is referred to extensively in this discussion as being the most recent of the larger studies, in light of the clear diagnostic criteria and methodology employed. Bourget and Bradford's (1990) study is similarly clear, although their sample size is small. Somander and Rammer (1991) have made a most valuable and useful examination of all child homicides in Sweden 1971-1980; however, the main focus in their study was identifying intra and extra-familial homicides and the psychiatric diagnosis of the perpetrators was not the primary focus.

It should be noted that all the research studies identified above relate to filicide, i.e. the killing of a child by its parent(s). There is consensus in all studies that child homicide is committed by parents in most instances (West, 1965; Harder, 1967; Resnick, 1969; Rodenburg, 1971; Scott 1973a; d'Orban, 1979; Bourget and Bradford, 1990; Somander and Rammer, 1991; Bourget and Labelle, 1992). Jason (1983) appears to be one of the few researchers suggesting that child homicide is not predominantly intra-familial: Jason examined the FBI statistics on child homicide 1976-1979 and found two patterns of child homicide. With children aged 0-3 years the homicide was intra familial, but with children over 12 years the homicides were extra familial and involved guns or criminal acts. Jason felt these latter homicides indicated children being unsupervised in a violent adult environment.

It has already been seen that a significant proportion of 'abnormal' homicides are committed by women. In line with this a higher incidence of maternal filicide is reported in a number of studies (Harder, 1967; Resnick, 1969; Rodenburg, 1971; d'Orban, 1979; Jason 1983; Bourget and Bradford, 1990; Falkov 1996). However, the data on filicide is contradictory (Bourget and Bradford, 1990), and earlier studies have found a higher incidence of paternal filicide (Adelson, 1961; Scott, 1973a; Somander and Rammer, 1991). The changes of course may be a reflection on the changing life-styles of females: as they begin to live more like men, they die [and kill] like men (Pritchard 1996). Using the Home Office Criminal Statistics (1990), Wilczynski and Morris (1993) found that 395 parents were suspected of filicide between 1982-9 and that 44 per cent were mothers. However, where the victim was under the age of one, mothers made up almost a half (47 per cent). Given these conflicting research findings it appears reasonable to conclude that child homicide by a father is in general as likely to occur as that by a mother (Grunfeld and Steen, 1984). This is atypical, when considering the general pattern of violence which is usually inflicted by males. Somander and Rammer (1991) emphasise that extra-familial child homicide outside of the USA is rare: in their sample of 77 child homicides, 65 were intra-familial and 12 extra-familial. Of these 12 extra-familial murders, in only 3 cases were the perpetrators complete strangers to the child-victims: in the other 9 cases the assailants were acquainted with the children, being for example, an uncle or former boyfriend of the victim's mother. There is consensus that when the perpetrator is a stranger to the child the dominating motive for the homicide is associated with a sexual assault upon the chid (Harder, 1967; Grunfeld and Steen, 1984; Wallace, 1986; Somander and Rammer, 1991).

The Falkov Report (1996), the largest and most thorough of its kind, summarizes much of what was previously known, clearly indicating a major degree of psychiatric disorder amongst intra-family assailants. Falkov also complains about what he saw as an overly unidimensional approach by 'child protection' workers, who despite the obvious benefits of 'Working Together' (DHSS 1984), had clearly not done so (Falkov, 1997). This leads to Falkov's (1998) criticism that: 'The failure of child agencies to routinely consider adult mental health implications for children - the fact that substantial psychiatric morbidity was found highlights the need for more work in this area - parents with severe personality dysfunction are clearly relevant to child protection considerations, [and], protecting children and supporting parents with mental health problems will require active collaboration between child and adult services.' This states our position exactly.

Classification of Child Homicides

A major focus in the major research studies identified is the classification of different types of child homicide. While classification by motive has advanced understanding of child homicide (Bourget and Labelle, 1992), it appears that confusion can also result (Scott 1973a). For example, the classification 'altruistic' (Resnick, 1969) covers both the mercy-killing of a severely handicapped and dying child by its parent(s) and the killing of a child by a depressed and suicidal parent who believes that he/she is saving the child from a cruel world. It can, moreover, be difficult to assign one case to a specific group: for example, in d'Orban's sample, 12 subjects classified as 'battering mothers' also had a mental illness (reactive depression). 'Accidental' filicide appears a particularly misleading category and Somander and Rammer (1991) suggest that 'fatal child abuse' is a more appropriate classification to indicate 'disciplinary measures to eliminate disturbing behaviour of a child without the intention to kill' (ibid, p.53).

It appears that on balance classifications are not particularly useful in practice where the focus is on prevention and identification of high-risk situations, as opposed to a retrospective analysis of motive or impulse. It is proposed that it is, in fact, helpful for practitioners - medical, nursing, and social work - to have knowledge and understanding of the psychopathology associated with child homicide. Such knowledge may alert practitioners to symptoms in their patients/clients which may potentially post a risk to a child's safety.

The Psychiatric Diagnoses Associated with Child Homicide

The following major mental disorders are identified as being associated with child homicide: puerperal mental illness, depression, schizophrenia, and personality disorders, including psychopathy (Resnick, 1969; Rodenburg, 1971; Scott, 1973a, 1973b; d'Orban, 1979: Bourget and Bradford, 1990; Bourget and Labelle, 1992, Falkov 1996).

An obvious difficulty in attempting comparisons in order to identify significant trends is the use of different diagnostic criteria by the researchers. Resnick (1969) does not identify which criteria he uses and his findings should be treated with some caution since his study is based upon filicides reported in World Literature 1751-1967. The studies of d'Orban (1979) and Bourget and Bradford (1990) are to be preferred since the International Classification of Diseases (WHO 1974), and the American DSMIII-R criteria respectively are employed.

In general, different studies identify a different incidence of each disorder. For example, schizophrenia is considered a significant diagnostic category by West (1965), Resnick (1969) and Myers (1970). Conversely however, d'Orban (1979) reports only four cases and Bourget and Bradford (1990) none. Likewise in a number of studies major depression with psychotic features was the most common diagnosis, particularly for maternal perpetrators (West, 1965; Harder, 1967; Resnick, 1969; Rodenburg, 1971; Scott, 1973a). Nevertheless, both d'Orban (1979) and Bourget and Bradford (1990) find personality disorders more prevalent. It should be noted that in the more recent studies, no diagnoses of Munchausen Syndrome by Proxy (factitious disorder) were made. While it may be difficult to identify clear patterns and trends from the available research data, there is consensus that there is a significant incidence of mental disorder among perpetrators, and Meadows (1996) has argued that the Munchausen syndrome is often missed and is probably more frequent than is appreciated.

Although personality disorder is the leading diagnosis for 'battering' mothers in d'Orban's (1979) sample (17 of 36), reactive depression was also a diagnosis (12 of 36) in this group. Falkov (1997) is especially wary of the combination of personality disorder in the presence of depression. It seems reasonable to conclude from this literature that the mental disorders identified were indeed present at the time of the offence.

The Role of Stress

It is important to note that research studies also identify that the perpetrators of child murder experience significant levels of psycho-social stress. Bourget and Bradford (1990) concluded in respect of their Canadian sample that exposure to a variety of psycho-social stress prior to the offence was often a major factor, and identified the following: family stress, marital separation or stress, unwanted or difficult pregnancies/deliveries, disabled chid and serious financial problems. Likewise, d'Orban (1979) concluded in respect of his sample that 'Most women in the study were subject to multiple adversity'. (ibid, p.563) d'Orban found that 71 per cent of his subjects experienced severe marital discord, 32 per cent housing problems and 30 per cent financial difficulties. Lack of social supports in the face of severe stress may also be a precipitating factor in maternal child abuse (Seagull, 1987).

The stress factors identified by d'Orban (1979) and by Bourget and Bradford (1990) are of the same tenor as the major on-going difficulties identified by British researchers - Brown and Harris (1978), Brown (1987), Brown et al., (1987), Brown et al., 1990, and Andrews et al., (1990), as being of aetiological significance in depression. These include financial, housing and marital problems, loss of a mother, three or more children at home, and lack of a supportive spouse. It seems important to link Brown and Harris' (1978) findings to those on the psycho-social stress experienced by persons who kill children. It seems likely that stressors of various kinds are important in both the development of suicidal depression, and of child murder. The simplest model is that in which long-term stressors from childhood result in diminished self-esteem and the ability to elicit social supports; current stressors cause extreme depression in vulnerable women, who in turn neglect, injure and on rare occasions kill their children. The evidence for this general model appears to be strengthened by the findings of Hawton and Roberts (1981) and Hawton et al. (1985) who studied the association between attempted suicide in mothers and abuse (or risk of it) to children. Well-documented evidence of serious child abuse in 29.8 per cent of mothers who were referred to a general hospital following a suicide attempt was found. Likewise, Pritchard (1991) assessed data on 60 families who were on an 'At Risk' register and found high levels of psycho-social stress, with two-fifths of mothers experiencing 'some form of depression'. The child protection- psychiatric interface was markedly present in studies of the caseloads of the Social Service and Probation departments (Pritchard et al. 1992; Hudson et al. 1993; Stewart and Stewart 1993; Cox and Pritchard 1995).

In summary therefore we conclude that, concerning the killing of a child, the evidence points to a strong mental disorder element in female assailants, and in this sense such women have a different dynamic from the 'ordinary' 'child-neglecting-abusing' family, in which the dynamic of psychiatric illness assumes prominence. Social work assessment and referral of mentally ill mothers could assist in preventing further tragedies. However, we would stress the mere presence of a mental disorder in not an automatic reason to remove a child, since rapid and effective out-patient treatments and home care supports are effective for many types of psychiatric illness. Falkov (1997) suggests and we concur, that every option should be considered for the most worrying categories, psychopathic/sociopathic personality disorders, and the paranoid type of schizophrenias.

The above review has laid out the situation as we see it and we can now test out the strength or weakness of our emphasis upon the child protection-psychiatric interface in a study, which analyses a decade of child homicides in an English county, based upon an analysis of police records. The study sought to examine whether there are any identifiable characteristics of child homicide assailants which would assist in determining risk levels and prevention of the extreme consequence of child abuse. Our review of all child homicides also provides the opportunity to consider extra-familial assailants, 'stranger murders'.

Part II: Extra-Family 'Stranger' Child Murders

This study emerged from the practical difficulties found when trying to evaluate the outcomes of men referred to a control and management project for Child Sex Abusers (CSAOs) (Pritchard and Cox, 1997).

Response to Child Sex Abuse   Child sexual abuse offenders (CSAOs), the vast majority of whom are men, arouse extreme reactions (Barker and Morgan, 1992; Beech et al., 1996). This was reflected in the Criminal Justice Act 1991 with its powers to consider the need to protect potential victims rather than considering the immediate offence and grants powers to Judges to give enhanced sentences. Such powerful responses reflect the reaction of both 'public' and 'professionals', which have implications for practice: how *does* the individual practitioner reach people whom the culture believes are 'beyond the pale'? Irrespective of techniques, all types of human-service intervention do better when the client is engaged in a positive rapport, eliciting mutual trust (Ford et al., 1997). Furthermore those working with this client group have an ethical imperative to seek to rehabilitate and reintegrate such offenders back into their families and society if at all possible. This makes risk assessment very important, as efforts to balance natural justice may clash with concerns for potential vulnerable victims (Dominelli, 1991; Cox and Pritchard, 1995), creating particular pressures upon the community services.

The aetiological theories of why child molesters are so orientated, are complex and range from the purely psychological to the bio-physiological, including the idea that they themselves are the end product of a cycle of abuse. Thus much CSA (since the fixated offenders with many victims are those most likely to have been sexually abused themselves) reflect society's 'failure' to protect them in *their* childhood (Bagley and Thurston, 1996b; Bagley, 1997). However since these issues are discussed in other chapters, all we wish to highlight is the double-bind situation that front-line staff can often find themselves in when trying to determine between different vulnerabilities and types of victim status.

Criminality   It is generally assumed that CSAOs are a fairly well defined deviant group, with the debate centring around seeking a 'typology', with efforts to separate out the intra- and extra-familial sex offenders. However, non-family abusers have been found to be more often involved in other types of crime (Simon et al., 1992), and as emerged in our own research 'convicted' CSAOs are actually more criminal than the average offender in that they often have more convictions for a wider range of non-sexual offences than non-sex offenders *in addition* to their sex offences (Cox and Pritchard, 1995). In the public mind the CSAO is associated with violence against children, and it is the child who is sexually assaulted in brutal fashion by a stranger or non-familial abuser who epitomizes the nightmares of parents and society.

The research reported here addresses this anxiety since it explores the life-time criminal convictions of 118 male child molesters, paying particular attention to violent offences. We concentrated entirely upon criminological aspects in order to contribute to the debate about assessment and management of risk. We also report here for the first time a study which examined all those who murdered children over the decade 1986-95 in an English county, in order to identify from amongst 'special categories' the backgrounds of the assailants.

We postulated four such categories of child murderer, which could have overlapped, but in effect did not do so. These are:

(1)   those with previous convictions for non-sexual violence;
(2)   the mentally disordered;
(3)   the child-neglecting-abusing parents;
(4)   and the child sex abuser.

Brief Methodology Child Sex Abuse [CSA] was defined by a *conviction* for any of the following criminal acts which involve a minor (a person up to the age of 16): Gross Indecency; Indecent Assault; Buggery; Rape or Attempted Rape; Incest; Under-Age Sexual Intercourse; Indecent Exposure; and Pornography Involving Minors. All included in the final sample had at least one other conviction in the first four categories, the other convictions being in addition to these first four, especially Gross Indecency and Indecent Assault. An important implication is that the sample excludes those child abusers whose behaviour remains either undetected or unconvicted, and whilst the sample can not be comprehensive, it is based upon very tight definitions.

The First Sample The sample was drawn from a two year cohort of Sex Offenders, which included 137 men aged between 17 and 73 years who had been sexually involved with children, and were referred to two control and management programmes in the community. To avoid false positives we excluded any client who at that time had either no previous or current conviction (19 men), so the final sample consisted of 118 men with at least one sex abuse conviction against children. The men were referred mainly by the Probation Service, or the S.S.D., and it was clear that the vast majority of clients attending such programmes had an element of compulsion in their referral. However referral itself did not guarantee acceptance on the programme, as some were considered unsuitable for treatment either because of perceived risk or lack of commitment. The group does then hold some biases, and is also probably not representative of 'un-detected' offenders, who are probably more socially competent than those who enter into the statutory agency networks (Bagley 1997; Cox and Pritchard 1997).

How representative is this sample of CSAOs in the system? Based upon an examination of records of all known sex offenders in the county for 1986-95, over the ten years 20 per cent of these men had offences against adults only, similar to our 19 per cent. There was also a match in respect to female offenders, as our sample contained only one women (1 per cent), whilst over the decade there were only seven other female sex offenders (1.5 per cent). The one female in the group was excluded from this analysis. Thus it is reasonable to assert that the two year cohort is representative of men known to be involved in the sexual abuse of children. Consequently the sample can serve as a marker for the special category of 'child sex abusers' when we come to look at the child homicide assailants.

Data Information was drawn from the life-time convictions of the men, and only *convictions*, either for sex or other indictable offences, were counted, thus excluding 'taken-into-consideration' offences; hence the figures err on the conservative side.

Indictable-and-Sex [IS] versus Sex Only Offenders [SO] The cohort fell naturally into two groups; those who also had other types of indictable convictions, designated the Indictable-and-Sex (IS) group, of which there were 75, i.e. 64 per cent of the sample; and those with only a sex crime i.e. the Sex-Only (SO) group, consisting of 43 men, 36 per cent of the sample.

Cautions Until this study is replicated, this paper should be considered as an interim report, although we know of no other work on child molesters' *life-time* convictions, and despite its sensitivity and a degree of incompleteness, nonetheless we thought it right to make these early findings accessible to practitioners.

Findings

Age The Indictable and Sex (IS) group were much younger than the Sex Only (SO) group, 55 per cent versus 23 per cent being forty and less, indeed, 31 per cent of the IS were aged 30 and under, compared to 14 per cent of the SOs. Conversely 42 per cent of the SOs were aged 51+ compared with only 15 per cent of the ISS.

Age at First Conviction for Indictable Offence Whilst 71 per cent of the ISs had been convicted by the age of 25, only 12 per cent of the SOs were so young when first convicted of a sexual offence. Of practical significance is that 58 per cent of the SOs had their *first* convictions after the age of 41, compared to 15 per cent of the ISs. This shows that apart from their sexual proclivities, the IS were much less socially competent than the SO group, who probably avoided detection more effectively.

Relationship to Victim Only 9 per cent of the ISs were fathers of the victim, compared to 26 per cent amongst the SOs; and 77 per cent of the ISs were not related to their sexual victims, whereas 51 per cent of SOs had a family link. In total, 67 per cent of the sample were *not* related to their victims.

Targets of Perpetrators and Their Sexual Convictions There were no significant differences with respect to gender of the offender's targets, between the IS and SO groups, so we report on the whole sample. Whilst some men abused only girls (48 per cent), and some exclusively boys (27 per cent), others targeted both genders. One in five (21 per cent) also had a sexual conviction against adults (16 per cent of the SOs and 24 per cent of the ISs).

There were no marked differences between the two groups, so again we report upon the total sample of 118 men in Table 1.

Table 1   All types of sexual offences by perpetrators and numbers of convictions: sex only (SO) and indictable plus sexual offences (IS) compared by most serious type of offence

Type of Offence	SO: Total offenders 43	SO: Number of offences	IS: Total offenders 75	IS: Number of offences
Indecent Assault	39 men 91%	161 offences	67 men 89%	224 offences
Gross Indecency	11 men 26%	26 offences	23 men 31%	46 offences
Buggery	5 men 12%	11 offences	16 men 21%	28 offences
Rape and Attempted Rape	3 men 7%	5 offences	12 men 16%	15 offences
Indecent Exposure	4 men 9%	6 offences	2 men 3%	17 offences
Incest	4 men 9%	11 offences	5 men 7%	13 offences
Unlawful Sexual Intercourse	3 men 7%	3 offences	7 men 9%	10 offences
Total Number of Offences		223		353
Other Offence Not Used for Classification: Making Obscene Film with Minors	1 2%	1	0	0

Ninety percent of the men had convictions for indecent assault, and almost a third, 29 per cent for gross indecency. The numbers of victims are not known, although there is some evidence from police files that their victims exceed their conviction rate by as many as 20 or 30 times (this involves some men in 'sex ring' type crimes- see Bagley, 1997 for definitions).

Virtually every man had more than one *kind* of sexual offence, an average of 1.76 for the IS group, and 1.60 convictions for the SOs. However, the Sex Only group had a higher average *number* of sex convictions - 5.19 each compared with 4.71 for the IS group, which may be because the SOs were on average older, and have had more time to accumulate convictions. Of particular concern were the fifteen men (13 per cent) who had convictions for rape and attempted rape, who had twenty such convictions.

Table 2 lists the range of Other Indicatable Convictions: for 75 IS men, the catalogue is stark.

Table 2   **Non-sexual violence and other indictable convictions in the sexual and other indictable offences group**

Offence	I and S MEN n = 75	Number of Convictions
Actual Bodily Harm	20 (27%)	43
Grievous Bodily Harm	6 (8%)	9
Wounding	1 (1%)	1
Abduction	6 (8%)	6
Possession or Use of Offensive Weapon	11 (15%)	11
Total of men with convictions for violence	*35 47%*	*70*
All violent offences (as defined above) by the violent men	*150 offences*	*2.0 each*
Burglary	29 (39%)	104
Theft, Fraud and Handling	56 (75%)	260
Robbery	5 (7%)	7
Criminal Damage	25 (33%)	59
Other: Obscene Phone Calls, Cruelty to Animals, Child Neglect, Immoral Earnings, Arson	13 (17%)	22
Total of 'Other Indictable' Offences	*152*	*522*
Other Minor Offences - Breach of Peace	15 (23%)	22
Taking and Driving Away	24 (32%)	60

Of the 75 IS men, eleven men (15 per cent) had convictions for Possession of an Offensive Weapon, including firearms. In parenthesis, two SO men had current legal firearms certificates. It was not possible to judge the seriousness of these offences when for example in one case the weapon was a pen knife, whereas in others it was an axe or a shotgun.

In terms of Actual and/or Grievous Bodily Harm, 35 of the IS group (47 per cent) had convictions for violence against the person, averaging two violent crimes each. Placed in the context of the whole sample, 30 per cent of CSAOs had convictions for extreme, non-sexual violence. The IS men had an average of 6.83 'other indictable' property convictions each (theft, burglary etc) being responsible for 512 convictions.

Theft was the most frequent offence in 75 per cent, followed by burglary, in 39 per cent. With respect to criminal damage, again we could not judge seriousness, which ranged from a broken window, to fire-wrecking someone's car.

In summary, the 75 IS men had an average of 6.83 convictions each, in addition to their 4.7 sex convictions (including offences against both minors and adults) each. Thus in one sense, the IS group were more broadly criminal than sexual offenders. Their sexual aggression seemed part of a more general syndrome of dishonesty and criminal acquisition. They were violent generally, violent in the course of theft, violent in sexuality, and stole virtue as well.

The 11 men involved with weapons backgrounds are of special interest, as they had the worst criminal profile of all. They averaged 2.6 convictions for violence against the person; 5.9 sex convictions; and 10.3 other indictable each. Extrapolating these men from the rest of the IS group, they had 45 per cent of all violent convictions, having four times the average rate of the IS group, a ratio of 4.06:1. The ratio for other indictable offences was 1.61:1, and, 1.31:1 for sex convictions. Their violence was a particular feature of their criminality in addition to their sexual abuse.

One intriguing finding was that 23 per cent of the sample had a least one 'not guilty' verdict or 'case withdrawn' decision after being brought to court charged with a sex offence. With respect to non-sex charges, only 15 per cent of men had such outcomes: thus it was somewhat easier to successfully defend a sexual rather than a non-sex charge. Using the above findings as preliminary evidence for the extent of CSA amongst this county's population, we turn to reviewing all child murders in the county in the period 1986-1995.

Sample Two: Identifying Child Homicide Assailants

In a county with more than 600,000 population over the decade there were eight children (up to age 15) murdered, six by parents and two by non-family strangers. Thus there were seven assailants aged between 17 to 39. Of the Parental Murderers, one was a 'neglecting' parent, on the 'At Risk of Abuse' register, one other had convictions for violence against the person, and the remaining three including one parent who killed two children. All were mentally disordered. Two of these mentally ill murderers were women.

Whilst the rather high proportion (60 per cent) of mentally disordered assailants fits our early discussion, the base numbers are very small. The point is that, predominately we know that the murderers fall into three clear, discrete groups: a man or woman in a partner/living-together relationship which has gone wrong; a woman who is mentally ill and suffers extreme stress; and those deaths occurring during criminal activity. If therefore one adopts an epidemiological approach, based upon the size of the potential cohort, the intra-family child murder rate for the county becomes 3.56 per million [pm]; and the 'Stranger' murder is 1.98 pm. While this is a very, very small rate, a different picture comes into focus when we define a more precise population at risk. Based upon the known incidence and prevalence of mental disorder in the general population, of the three Mentally Disordered Parent Assailants, this group killed at a frequency of 154 pm, i.e. more than fifty times the notional rate in the 'ordinary' or 'normal' parent.

Based upon the numbers of men aged between 17-39 with convictions for violence, the rate becomes 206 pm. And, based upon the numbers of known 'neglecting/abuse' parents, i.e. those on the SSD books, the 'neglecting' parent's rate becomes 274 pm, which in clinical and epidemiological terms has both significance and relevance.

However, what of the 'Stranger' murders? Both the two male assailants had prior convictions for child sex abuse, both men belonged to the IS type, and one also had convictions for violence. It is known from police records that there was a total of 439 men with convictions for a sex offence against a child in the ten years, which of course includes our two year sample of 118 men.

Based upon this, we can calculate that the Child Sex Abuser murder rate becomes 4,556 pm; but since they were both of the Indictable and Sex Offender type, this rate would more accurately be said to be 12,903 pm which has both significance and meaning. If our 'estimates' of the frequency of child homicide are broadly accurate, then this implies that the CSA with violence murderer's frequency was 50 times greater than that of the 'neglecting' parent; and more than 80 times that of the 'mentally disordered parent.

We must reiterate that these findings are an interim report, and the study needs replication in other areas; but research on a range of 'community services' clients in the county in question has invariably matched national research in terms of the service users' psycho-social characteristics (Pritchard et al., 1992; Pritchard and Clooney, 1994; Cox and Pritchard, 1995; Akehurst

276

et al., 1995). Consequently we have a degree of confidence that the patterns we have found are what our theoretical knowledge would expect, and will probably be similar to other CSAOs in Britain.

In summary therefore despite the small numbers involved, we found as would be expected, the majority were killed by parents, a majority of whom were mentally disordered. Proportionately however it was the CSAO with other serious convictions who presents an even more serious risk.

Pulling the two parts of the study together, what tentative conclusions can we draw?

Discussion

The Mental Health Dimension There appear to be two major patterns in child homicide, first the more frequent group of assailants, the mentally disordered; and secondly the group who are less frequent but who have a higher rate in terms of the population at risk, the men who were previously categorized as Child Sex Abuse offenders with other indictable or/and violent convictions.

We first consider those serious assaults directly associated with acute mental illness, i.e. puerperal psychosis, depression, schizophrenia. The nature and quality of the symptoms of the illness (e.g. delusional beliefs) are usually the origin of the severe assaults. If delusions are present, it is essential to determine whether the child is involved in the delusional system: practitioners, therefore, must ask about the 'unthinkable' and 'unaskable' to assess the threat of violence/homicide (Prins, 1981 and 1991). Serious, often repeated, assaults may also be directly associated with dissocial (psychopathic) personality (Falkov, 1997; Stroud, 1998). The assault relates to the perpetrator's 'callous unconcern' for others, a low threshold for frustration and discharge of aggression and an inability to feel remorse (ICD-10: WHO, 1992). Morris Beckford, the stepfather of Jasmine Beckford, who was found guilty of her homicide, might be considered to have facets of dissocial personality. The persistent nature of the violence he committed were evidenced by the 'multiple scars ... consistent with repeated episodes of physical abuse' from which Jasmine ultimately died (Blom-Cooper, 1985).

Secondly, assaults may be associated with a combination of factors, i.e. personality disorder, depression and severe environmental and psycho-social stress. There is no deliberate intent to kill, and the assault occurs when a crisis precipitates a loss of control in a severely stressed individual. This type of assault equates with the 'child abuse syndrome' (Justice et al., 1985). It is important that future research investigates this interactive process further.

Professional knowledge of and responsibility for child protection are important issues arising from a review of child homicide and mental disorder. The introduction of internal markets in social services has fragmented services (Hollows and Wonnacott, 1994) and has led to the introduction of non-cooperating, specialist child care and adult teams.

Practically, therefore, social workers undertaking child care and child protection work may not have adequate knowledge about mental disorder and may not be able to recognise situations or risk. Indeed, while research has long identified an association between parental mental health and problems in child care (Hawton and Roberts, 1981; Isaac et al., 1986; Pritchard, 1992; Sheppard, 1993), the ability of social workers to identify specific mental illness appears no greater than chance (Huxley et al., 1987). It seems essential that the connections between child care and mental disorder are both recognised and taken account of in practice. Sheppard (1993), reviewing maternal depression and child care, makes the case for 'a mental health child care worker' in light of the indirect, but formidable evidence of the association.

While Social Service Departments are the lead authorities responsible for child protection (Home Office, DoH et al., 1991) a mistaken view has evolved that child protection is solely - or at best mainly - the province of Social Services (Noyes, 1991). In fact, both the National Health Service Act 1977 and Section 27 of the Children Act 1989 provide that health authorities must assist Social Services with the safe care of children. The importance of psychiatrists and general practitioners being alert to chid protection issues is illustrated by research. Resnick (1969) found 40 per cent of filicidal parents were seen by a psychiatrist or other physician shortly before the crime. d'Orban (1979) reported that at the time of the offence 60 per cent of his sample were in contact, in order of frequency, with a general practitioner, psychiatrist, social worker and health visitor. Bourget and Bradford (1990) likewise established that a significant number of homicidal parents came to the attention of psychiatrists before the tragedy, which is an obvious current hiatus for which both 'sides' ie Social Service and Psychiatry are equally responsible (Stroud, 1998; Falkov, 1996).

On the other hand, while it appears that general practitioner and psychiatrists are in a position to be able to identify those psychiatric situations where there is a risk of serious child assault, it equally appears that there is difficulty for these professionals in fulfilling this role. The Beckford inquiry (Blom-Cooper, 1985) suggested that in training, doctors should be educated

278

about the need for inter-agency work in child protection and notes that current medical training emphasises doctors being in charge, listening to other professional views, but still taking decisions based upon their own medical judgement. The Cleveland Inquiry (Butler-Sloss, 1988) makes the same observation. It is also suggested that often a doctor's assessment of a situation depends on what he/she is told by the patient (Lucy Gates inquiry: London Borough of Bexley, 1982).

Noyes (1991) points out that a theme running through the child abuse inquiries of the 1980s is the isolation of the GP and their non-involvement in the inter-agency system. It appears that psychiatrists are also often isolated from child care systems (Whipple and Webster-Stratton, 1991). It would seem sensible that adult and child psychiatrists develop a role in informing the medical professions about the association between mental health and fatal child assault. Some doctors consider that patient confidentiality prevents them alerting social services to situations of risk, but the General Medical Council in 1987 expressed the view that:

> If a doctor has reason for believing that a child is being physically or sexually abused, not only is it permissible for the doctor to disclose information to a third party, but it is a duty of the doctor to do so. (The Annual Report of the General Medical Council, 1987, cited in Home Office, DoH et al., 1991 p.120.)

It seems essential that further research be carried out to identify the persons with a psychiatric disorder who are most at risk of injuring others, and quantifying the psychosocial stresses which precipitate such violence, inlcuding the vexed question of inter-generational transmission of abuse (Langeland and Dijkstra, 1995). Sheppard (1993) points out that research on mental disorder has been carried out largely separately from child care issues: it seems the psychiatric and social work professionals must make good this omission and undertake more collaborative research. It is important that existing and future research findings are utilised in informing preventive practice.

The organisation of child care social work is an issue that requires consideration. In the last twenty years most social services departments (the lead agency for child protection) have been divided into *de facto* specialisms, and have minimised the previous psychiatric social worker role, developing instead the 'Approved Social Worker' (Mental Health Act, 1983) role.

In response to a reduction of SSD resources, the Approved Social Workers have offered the mentally ill a minimally feasible service, largely letting slip the opportunities for effective intervention which are known to be enhanced when the bio-physiological approach is teamed with the psycho-social. The result has been that child care practitioners have little relevant experience of mental health issues and may well be unable to identify and assess the relevant problems and opportunities to intervene. This situation must be remedied and a more integrated approach adopted in social work practice and education: if social work specialisms are to continue, consideration must be given to this proposal.

The significant levels of mental health difficulties experienced by physically abusive parents indicate that a more cohesive approach to intervention is required with, for example, specific psychological and medical support being readily available. To develop such an integrated approach, a substantial improvement in multi-agency working is required, with more routine liaison and co-working. There is a traditionally 'testy' relationship between doctors and social workers (Hallett et al. 1995), with general practitioners and psychiatrists rarely involved in the inter-agency system (Noyes 1991; Gibbons et al., 1995).

Conclusions: The Child Sex Abuse Offender Dimension

The key findings merit highlighting. In criminological terms, there are two distinct patterns of CSAOs i.e. the majority 'Indictable-and-Sex' group, and then the 'Sex-Only' group, with the IS group being more psycho-socially disturbed, 47 per cent having convictions for non-sexual violence. In turn, those with convictions for violence had the worst criminal and sexual profiles, especially those with Offensive Weapons and Firearms convictions. The fact that it was easier to 'defend' a sex offence charge than a non-sexual one, highlights the practice-legal-ethical dilemmas for all agencies involved. As Bagley argues in another chapter in this book, the needs of children *must* come first, and rather than subjecting the child witness to the stress of a 'failed prosecution' it seems better to proceed with the case in another way. Yet not proceeding at all can, as Sharland shows in this book, also leave the child hurt and even outraged.

While the design of the research was not set up to identify elements of 'sexual sadism' in offenders, it seems likely given the length and pattern of offending that some of the men identified could fall into this category. Fortunately however their number is small.

Ethical and Legal Dilemmas The first dilemma to address is that a substantial minority of CSAOs were themselves victims of childhood sexual abuse, and in this sense, were themselves 'failed' by child care and preventive systems. For a small minority of offenders, their sexual drives towards children are not merely cognitive and psychosocial, they may also have a biological basis (Bagley and Thurston, 1996b). Therefore it may be that some men are sexually attracted to children in very fundamental ways, and they may not ever be capable of mature, appropriate sexual relationships (Bagley 1997). For these and other sex offenders, biological treatments to reduce sex drive may be necessary.

We also have to face the dilemma that in dealing with these types of offences, there are dangers in an erosion of standards of civil liberties, if offenders are detained for long periods on the grounds of their alleged dangerousness, over and above a normal, penal sentence.

Moreover, to compound the dilemmas concerning the search for natural justice for both victim and offender in cases of CSA is the fact that cases of abuse (those who come into the ambit of the criminal justice and child protection systems) represent only a small proportion of *actual* cases. There is evidence that apprehended offenders (and those pleading guilty) are less educated and less socio-economically effective, than those who avoid detection (Bagley 1995 and 1997; Cox and Pritchard 1995; Pritchard and Bagley 1998; Bagley et. al., in this volume). Thus most data on CSAOs can only reflect those perpetrators within the system, as few men come forward entirely voluntary for treatment.

Predictions and Assessment of Dangerousness Wilkinson (1994) has demonstrated that previous convictions are a powerful predictor of subsequent behaviour; thus with respect to violence, the offender's previous track record is an important indicator of risk. We cannot predict with precision levels of re-offending, but can highlight the time span over which the men in our sample appeared to continue their sexual abuse of children. It is the Indicatable and Sexual Offences (IS) group who cause most concern, since they often appear to be 'intractable' in their sexual offending. Though the IS group were on average younger than the Sex Only (SO) group, nonetheless two-thirds of the IS group were over 30 years old and may be too old for positive reform.

When a child protection worker encounters a persistent sex offender, who began their criminal career early, has other indictable convictions (in particular for violence and especially that using an offensive weapon) then, according to our research, this man requires the most stringent in-depth risk assessment, with preventive custody (perhaps in a secure mental hospital) being a serious consideration. Based upon the Dorset data these men would represent some 0.003 per cent of the general population, or 630 men in England and Wales (a figure that must be tempered by the knowledge that some 70 per cent of all sexual assaults on children are not reported by the victim, at the time of the assault, with large numbers of assailants never coming to the notice of the authorities).

There are however, some positive findings from this study. Laying aside the issue of whether sexual assault on a child achieved by the misuse of adult authority but without physical injury, should automatically be considered a crime of violence, 60 per cent of these CSAOs were not involved in causing violent injury to their sexual and non-sexual victims; and 91 per cent were not involved with offensive weapons. Hence we should avoid blanket, indiscriminate sentences which might lead to children being more not less at risk from these men: for example, if an offender faces life without parole in sexually assaulting a child, might he not contemplate the actual murder of the only witness?

Indeterminate Sentences? With respect to the dangerous minority of CSA0s, there is need to consider how safe they may be on discharge from prison. The present Criminal Justice Act 1991 has some of the power necessary, but in some situations it may not go far enough. There is an argument for the notion (as in Canadian jurisdictions) of indeterminate sentences subject to periodic review. Such sentences would be necessary because of the nature of the offence, sexual assault combined with violent aggression, and perhaps an underlying personality disorder of sexual sadism, the person continuing to be at risk. Borrowing from the best in the forensic psychiatric field, and building upon the 1991 Criminal Justice Act after more than a third of the sentence has been served, the offender could be assessed in respect to their management and control of their sexuality, and especially their aggression. This would require individualised in-depth, multi-disciplinary assessment to determine progress.

Ethics and the Search for Social Justice The idea of renewable (or indeterminate, reviewable) sentences raises major professional/ethical problems. Indeed, the authors could make out a strong intellectual case opposed to these recommendations (e.g Cox and Pritchard 1995). But for the present group of dangerous offenders, these seem to be over-ridden by three factors.

1. The need to prevent the potentially disastrous consequence to the most vulnerable at the end of the chain-of-vulnerability, the child, especially those crimes committed by men with psychopathic or sexually sadistic personality disorders.

2. The need to help the offender avoid hiding relevant motivations and personal circumstances, which could ultimately assist in their rehabilitation and reintegration.

3. Reducing the possibility of the CSAO having to suffer the consequences of being the agent of the extremes of child sexual abuse, by providing a framework of supervision and sheltered accommodation.

For a tiny minority of citizens, their sexuality and aggression is such that until maturity arrives, they need protecting against their deviant motivations and desires through a kindly system of restraint and custody. It is prudent to maintain security to prevent the extreme consequences, rather than becoming locked into the bind of attending to conflicting 'rights' in a field where artifice and subterfuge become the child sex abuser's norm.

Equally in the humanistic model outlined by Bagley (1997), every effort must be made to ensure against inappropriate sentences imposed by a vengeful society which pays no heed to prevention or reform: in the end, the minority can also make a contribution to child protection, in the manner observed by John Milton: 'They also serve who only stand and wait'. Appealing to the spiritual nature of the offender is an idealistic plea, one that is at the heart of the humanistic model of reform.

11   Completed Suicide in Men Accused of Sexual Crimes Involving Children: Implications for a Humanistic Approach

CHRISTOPHER BAGLEY AND COLIN PRITCHARD

Introduction

Our files are full of case studies gathered from press cuttings and Medical Examiner files (Bagley and Ramsay, 1997) about men who have killed themselves after being charged with a criminal offence related to sexual assault on a child, or the possession of child pornography. The headlines related to the British reports (Canadian Medical Examiner reports are never made public) carry messages such as: "Lecturer kills self over indecent pictures" (McAdam, 1998); "Net porn charge man dies," (Johnston, 1996); and "Choir's second suicide linked to pornography," (Hornsell, 1996). In France in 1997 police raided 600 addresses and charged 208 men in a "child pornography" sweep: soon afterwards three of the men investigated killed themselves (Bell, 1997).

It is notable in these cases that the "indecent pictures" apparently displayed only nudity; there was no additional evidence that the men who killed themselves had actual contact with children. These men seemed to be cases of pathetic misfits, unable to maintain normal sexual or social relations with adult peers. In other cases known to us these "pathetic" men had sexually assaulted children, but often briefly without attempting the grosser forms of intrusion.

Prevalence Studies

The purpose of this chapter is to review studies which have produced enough data to provide prevalence rates for completed suicide to be calculated, and to report on our own data gathered in the context of a review of cases in police files of all those who were convicted of a sexual offence involving a minor, over a 10-year-period in two southern English counties.

Several published studies indicate that the completed suicide rate in men accused of sexually abusing children is much higher than in men in the general population. Certainly, men so accused often feel suicidal, or will threaten suicide if their abusive activities are exposed to the wider community (Heptinstall, 1984). Men who abuse children (physically and sexually) are according to Roberts & Hawton (1980) likely to have unstable personalities of the sociopathic type, which often involve chaotic amounts of aggression directed against others and against themselves, with attempted suicide and alcoholism in more than 20 percent.

Wild (1988) describes nine cases of perpetrator suicide in one city in England (Leeds). In the period considered there were 1,074 cases of alleged sexual assault of children reported to police, yielding a completed suicide rate in alleged perpetrators of 838 per 100,000, compared with the general population rate for suicide in males aged less than 65, of less than 40 per 100,000. These suicides usually occurred in men suffering from depressive illness and/or alcoholism following accusation of, or conviction for sexual assaults on children. Walford et al. (1990) report two similar cases in Belfast.

Two American cases are reported by Morrison (1988), suggesting a very high rate of completed suicide in alleged perpetrators (suicide in two of the 37 men investigated). Tate's (1990) British study of child pornography identified four suicides amongst 165 men arraigned on child pornography charges. Butler-Sloss (1988) in her inquiry in to the Cleveland seizures of alleged CSA victims found that two men, an uncle and a father of the alleged victim (in the series of 274 families investigated) killed themselves in prison soon after arraignment (a rate of 730 per 100,000), whilst a further man made several suicide attempts. In a study from Wales, Anthony & Watkeys (1991) identified six alleged child sexual abuse perpetrators amongst 142 investigated who committed suicide following accusation or arraignment giving a rate of 4,286 per 100,000.

In our study in two English counties, we found that police had recorded the suicide of seven out of 636 (i.e. 1,100 per 100,000) men who had been previously convicted of a sexual offence involving a minor.

Putting these various findings together (but excluding the one American study) we reach the total of 29 cases amongst 2,296 men investigated, a rate of 1,219 per hundred thousand, a rate at least thirty times that in males of a similar age in the general populations of Britain and North America (Pritchard, 1995; Bagley and Ramsay, 1997).

Discussion

It appears then that men who have been accused of sexual abuse are at greatly increased risk of completed suicide. This has unresearched consequences for victims and their families, but in the light of findings that family suicides can occur in clusters it could be that victims have elevated risk of suicidal behaviours in the months and years following perpetrator suicide. Certainly it is known that the victims of child sexual abuse have extremely high rates of suicidal gestures and attempts (Bagley, 1995; Bagley and Ramsay, 1997); but the *completed* rate of suicide is in victims is unknown. However, evidence submitted to Sir Frank Waterhouse's judicial inquiry into child sexual abuse in children's homes in Clywd found that former male residents had a suicide rate 19 times that of their age peers (Pritchard, 1998).

We are faced with the dilemma of being too concerned with the suicidal problems of offenders: clearly, our primary focus should be on victims and their mental health. Nevertheless, about a third of men who sexually abuse children were themselves victims of sexual abuse, and their lifelong suicidal personalities may have reflected this earlier abuse.

Furthermore, perpetrator suicide soon after a victim has taken the courage to reveal such abuse could leave him or her with profound feelings of remorse and guilt, especially when the abuser was a close family member. Therapists need special skills in counselling a young teenaged girl whose father has recently killed himself, apparently as the direct consequence of her revelation. According to the Giarretto model (outlined in Bagley and King, 1990) many offenders at risk of self-injury and suicide are of the "regressed" type, men whose pitifully small world of power resides in their family, over whom they exercise petty power and sexual domination. Such men have had poor mental health during the abuse, and revelation is for them (as for other family members) a psychological catastrophe.

Consider the following case, known to us in a Canadian context:

A girl of 12 revealed to her mother that she had been sexually abused by her father for the past two years. Police were informed, and prosecution of the father was set in train. When released on bail the man killed himself, leaving a note expressing guilt and shame at what he had done. Mother, daughter and other children in the family were now in great psychological distress, their victim status now confused with guilt at "causing" the suicide of the family's father.

287

Could the humanistic approach to handling cases of child sexual abuse, once revealed, advocated by Bagley (1997) have prevented this and other suicides of like type? The available clinical evidence certainly suggests that this type of suicide could be prevented, and in the process the healing of victims could be aided rather than catastrophically impaired by perpetrator suicide. Such suicide is an example of what Pritchard (1995) terms "the ultimate rejection". In the humanist model of social work elaborated in Bagley (1997), intervention in child sexual abuse, and the healing of all actors in the drama is sought. Obviously, restoring the victim to psychological health and social confidence must be the primary goal, but often this can be more readily achieved when the victim's family is also restored to health, and when a within-family abuser if not allowed to return to the family he has violated, at least faces the prospect of therapy and some forgiveness, rather than vilification and social disgrace. The offender-father who kills himself is a failure for an intervention system, and a traumatic failure for victims whose self-confidence has been undermined by prolonged sexual abuse.

An additional failure is the loss of life of men disgraced by the finding of child pornography, men whose sexual interest in children has (in our clinical experience) only atypically led them to sexually abuse a child. While they may be at risk of doing so, there is certainly a case for some therapeutic acceptance of this condition, with attempts to accommodate their impulses in the direction of non-offending (Bagley and King, 1990). Indeed, there is no evidence so far as we can discover that exposure to or use of pornography or erotica actually *causes* men to offend: indeed, the evidence reviewed in Bagley (1997) suggests that use of erotica could be an alternative to offending. The case against child pornography is of course strong, since it may depict children actually being abused. But there is a different level of non-photographic erotica which might be permitted, under the guidance of therapy. But who will accept the potential paedophile as a patient?

Putting the matter into a broader perspective, we desperately need research to help us understand the range of types of child sexual abuse, in terms of the risk to future victims; obviously a liberal or humanistic approach must act primarily on behalf of actual and potential victims, and should strive to identify dangerousness in offenders, as well as their potential for reform. Our research (and that of Pritchard and Stroud in this volume) suggests. At one end of a continuum are "pathetic" men whose conduct and demeanour cries out for help - these are men who are imposing their own, unjustified capital punishment. At the other end of the continuum are perhaps ten per cent of those who sexually offend against children in callous and sadistic ways, and who will use whatever wiles they can (including killing their victims) to avoid detection or punishment. These men have laid aside their humanity, and require maximum control.

References

Abidin, R. (1983). *Parenting Stress Index*. Richmond, VA: Institute of Clinical Psychology, University of Virginia.

Achenbach, T.M. and Edelbrock, C.S. (1983). *Manual for the Child Behaviour Checklist and Revised Child Behaviour Profile*. Burlington, VT: Department of Psychiatry, University of Vermont.

Adams-Tucker, C. (1982). Proximate Effects of Sexual Abuse in Childhood: A Report on 28 Children. *American Journal of Psychiatry*, 139, 1252-1256.

Adcock, M., (1991). Significant harm: Implications for the Exercise of Statutory Responsibilities In Adcock, M., White. R., and Hollows, A., (Eds.) *Significant Harm: Its Management and Outcome*. London: Significant Publications.

Adelson, L. (1961) Slaughter of the Innocents: A Study of Forty-six Homicides in Which the Victims were Children. *New England Journal of Medicine*, 246, 1345-1349.

Akehurst, M., Brown, I. and Wessley, S. (1995). *Dying for Help: Offenders at Risk of Suicide*. Wakefield, Association of Chief Probation Officers.

Alberman, E. and Goldstein, H. (1970). The 'At-risk' Register: A Statistical Evaluation. *British Journal of Preventive and Social Medicine*, 24, 129-135.

Aldgate, J. and Tunstill, J. (1996). *Making Sense of Section 17*. London: HMSO.

Alexander, P.C. (1985). A Systems Theory Conceptualization of Incest. *Family Process*, 24, 79-88.

Alexander, P., Neimeyer, R., Follette, V., Moore, M. and Harter, S. (1989). A Comparison of Group Treatments of Women Sexually Abused As Children. *Journal of Consulting and Clinical Psychology*, 57, 479-483.

Alexander, P.C. and Lupfer, S.L. (1987). Family Characteristics and Long-term Consequences Associated with Sexual Abuse. *Archives of Sexual Behaviour*, 16, 235-245.

Amato, P.R. (1989). Family Processes and the Competence of Adolescents and Primary School Children. *Journal of Youth and Adolescence*, 18, 39-53.

Andrews B., Brown G.W. and Creasey L. (1990). Inter-generational Links Between Psychiatric Disorder in Mothers and Daughters: The Role of Parenting Experiences. *Journal of Child Psychology and Psychiatry* 31, 1115-1129.

Anthony, G. and Watkeys, J. (1991). False Allegations of Child Sexual Abuse: the Pattern of Referral in An Area Where Reporting is Not Mandatory. *Child Abuse and Neglect*, 5, 11-122.

Appleby, L., Shaw, J. and Amos, T. (1997). Confidential Inquiry Into Suicide and Homicide by People with Mental Illness. *British Journal of Psychiatry*, 171, 391.

Arnstein, S. (1969). A Ladder of Citizen Participation. *Journal of American Institute of Planners*, 35, 4-10.

Atmore, C. (1992). *Other Halves: Lesbian-feminist Post-structuralist Readings of Some Recent Print Media Representations of 'Lesbians' in Aotearoa.* Unpublished Doctoral Dissertation, Victoria University of Wellington.

Atmore, C. (1993a). Feminism's Restless Undead: The Essential(ist) Activist. Paper Given at 'Bring a Plate': The Feminist cultural Studies Conference, University of Melbourne, December.

Atmore, C. (1993b). 'Branded': Lesbian Representation and a New Zealand Cultural Controversy. In D. Bennett (Ed.) *Cultural Studies: Pluralism and Theory* (281-292). University of Melbourne: Department of English.

Atmore, C. (1994a). Witch Hunts, Icebergs and the Light of Reason: Constructions of Child Sexual Abuse in Recent Cultural Controversies. In H. Borland (Ed.) *Communication and Identity: Local, Regional, Global. Selected Papers from the 1993 National Conference of the Australian Communication Association* (85-96). Canberra, ACT: Australian and New Zealand Communication Association.

Atmore, C. (1994b). The Mervyn Thompson Controversy: A Feminist Deconstructive Reading. *New Zealand Sociology*, 9, 2, 171-215.

Atmore, C. (1996). Cross-cultural Media-tions: Media Coverage of Two Child Sexual Abuse Controversies in New Zealand/Aotearoa. *Child Abuse Review*, 5, 334-345.

Atmore, C. (1997). Rethinking Moral Panic and Child Abuse for 2000. In J. Bessant and R. Hill (Eds.) *Reporting Law and Order: Youth, Crime and the Media.* Hobart: National Clearing House for Youth Studies.

Atmore, C. (1998). Towards 2000: Child Sexual Abuse and the Media. In A. Howe (Ed.) *Sexed Crime in the News.* Melbourne: Federation Press.

Atmore, C. (forthcoming). Sexual Abuse and Troubled Feminism: A Reply to Camille Guy. *Feminist Review*, 6.

Audit Commission, (1994). *Seen But Not Heard: Co-ordinating Community Child Health and Social Services for Children in Need*. London: HMSO.

Bach, C.M., and Anderson, S.C. (1980). Adolescent Sexual Abuse and Assault. *Journal of Current Adolescent Medicine*, 2, 11-15.

Baker, J. (1902). Female Criminal Lunatics. *Journal of Mental Science*, 48, 13-28.

Bagley, C. (1985). Child Sexual Abuse and Juvenile Prostitution: A Commentary on the Badgley Report on Sexual Offences Against Children and Youth. *Canadian Journal of Public Health*, 76, 65-66.

Bagley, C. (1988). Day Care, Maternal Health and Child Development: Evidence From A Longitudinal Study. *Early Child Development and Care*, 39, 134-161.

Bagley, C. (1989a). Development of A Short Self-esteem Measure for Use with Adults in Community Mental Health Surveys. *Psychological Reports*, 65, 13-14.

Bagley, C. (1989b). Prevalence and Correlates of Unwanted Sexual Acts in Childhood: Evidence From A National Canadian Survey. *Canadian Journal of Public Health*, 80, 295-296.

Bagley, C. (1990a). *A Long-term Study of Childhood Temperament, Disability, Mental Health and Family Structure*. London: McDonald.

Bagley, C. (1990b). Development and Validity of A Measure of Unwanted Sexual Contact in Childhood, for Use in Community Mental Health Surveys. *Psychological Reports*, 66, 401-402 and 449-450.

Bagley, C. (1990c). Is the Prevalence of Child Sexual Abuse Decreasing? Evidence From A Random Sample of 750 Young Adult Women, *Psychological Reports*, 66, 1037-1038.

Bagley, C. (1991). The Prevalence and Mental Health Sequels of Child Sexual Abuse in A Community Sample of Women Aged 18 to 27. *Canadian Journal of Community Mental Health*, 10, 103-116.

Bagley, C. (1992a). Psychological Dimensions of Poverty and Parenthood. *International Journal of Marriage and the Family*, 1, 37-49.

Bagley, C. (1992b). The Urban Setting of Juvenile Pedestrian Injuries: A Study of Behavioural Ecology and Social Disadvantage. *Accident Analysis and Prevention* 24, 673-678.

Bagley, C. (1995). *Child Sexual Abuse and Mental Health in Adolescents and Adults*. Brookfield, VT: Avebury.

293

Bagley, C. (1996). A Typology of Child Sexual Abuse: The Interaction of Emotional, Physical and Sexual Abuse As Predictors of Adult Psychiatric Sequelae in Women. *Canadian Journal of Human Sexuality*, 5, 101-112.

Bagley, C. (1997). *Children, Sex and Social Policy: Humanist Solutions for Problems of Child Sexual Abuse.* Aldershot, UK and Brookfield, VT: Avebury.

Bagley, C., Bolitho, F. and Bertrand, L. (1995). Mental Health Profiles, Suicidal Behaviour, and Community Sexual Assault in 2112 Canadian Adolescents. *Crisis: Journal of Crisis Intervention and Suicide Prevention*, 16, 126-131.

Bagley, C., Bolitho, F. and Bertrand, L. (1997). Norms and Construct Validity of the Rosenberg Self-esteem Scale in Canadian High School Populations: Implications for Counselling. *Canadian Journal of Counselling*, 31, 82-92.

Bagley, C. and Genuis, M. (1991). Sexual Abuse Recalled: Evaluation of A Computerized Questionnaire in A Population of Young Adults Males. *Perceptual and Motor Skills*, 72, 287-288.

Bagley, C., Goldberg, G. and Wellings, D. (1995). Child Sexual Abuse and Dissociative Personality Traits in Troubled Adolescents. *Child Abuse Review*, 3, 99-113.

Bagley, C. and King, K. (1990). *Child Sexual Abuse: The Search for Healing.* London: Tavistock-Routledge.

Bagley, C, and, Kufeldt K. (1989). Juvenile Delinquency and Child Pedestrian Accidents: An Ecological Analysis. *Perceptual and Motor Skills*, 69, 1281-1281.

Bagley, C. and Macdonald, M. (1984). Adult Mental Health Sequels of Child Sexual Abuse, Physical Abuse and Neglect in Maternally Separated Children. *Canadian Journal of Community Mental Health*, 3, 15-26.

Bagley, C., Madrid, S. and Bolitho, F. (1997). Filipinos Migrating: Poverty, Stress and Achievement. *International Social Work*, 40, 373-382.

Bagley, C. and Mallick, K. (1978). Development of A Short Form of the Piers Harris Self-concept Scale. *Educational Review*, 30, 265-268.

Bagley, C. and Mallick, K. (1995). Towards Achievement of Reading Skill Potential Through Peer Tutoring in Mainstream 13-year-olds. *Disability and Society*, 11, 83-89.

Bagley, C. and Mallick, K. (1997). Temperament, CNS Problems and Maternal Stressors: Interactive Predictors of Conduct Disorder in 9-year-olds. *Perceptual and Motor Skills*, 84, 617-618.

Bagley, C. and Ramsay, R. (1986). Sexual Abuse in Childhood: Psychological Outcomes and Implications for Social Work Practice. *Journal of Social Work and Human Sexuality*, 4, 33-47.

Bagley, C. and Ramsay, R. (1997). *Suicidal Behaviour in Adults and Adolescents: Research, Taxonomy and Prevention.* Brookfield, VT: Avebury.

Bagley, C. and Sewchuk-Dann, L. (1991). Characteristics of 60 Children and Adolescents Who Have A History of Sexual Assault Against Others: Evidence From A Controlled Study. *Journal of Child and Youth Care*, 9, 43-52.

Bagley, C. and Thurston, W. (1996a). *Understanding and Preventing Child Sexual Abuse. Volume I Children: Assessment, Social Work and Clinical Issues, and Prevention Education.* Aldershot, UK: Arena Social Work Series.

Bagley, C. and Thurston, W. (1996b). *Understanding and Preventing Child Sexual Abuse. Volume II Male Victims, Adolescents, Adult Outcomes and Offender Treatment.* Aldershot, UK: Arena Social Work Series.

Bagley, C. and Tremblay, P. (1998). On the Prevalence of Homosexuality: Evidence From A Random Community Sample of 750 Males Aged 18 to 27. *Journal of Homosexuality*, in Press.

Bagley, C., Wood, M. and Young, L. (1994). Victim to Abuser: Mental Health and Behavioural Sequels of the Sexual Abuse of Males in Childhood. *Child Abuse and Neglect*, 18, 683-697.

Bagley, C. and Young, L. (1987). Juvenile Prostitution and Child Sexual Abuse: A Controlled Study. *Canadian Journal of Community Mental Health*, 6, 5-26.

Bagley, C. and Young, L. (1990). Depression, Self-esteem, and Suicidal Behaviour As Sequels of Sexual Abuse in Childhood: Research and Therapy. In M. Rothery and G. Cameron (Eds.), *Child Maltreatment: Expanding Our Concepts of Helping* (183-219). Hillsdale, NJ: Lawrence Erlbaum.

Bagley, C. and Young, L. (1995). Juvenile Prostitution and Child Sexual Abuse: A Controlled Study. In C. Bagley *Child Sexual Abuse and Mental Health in Adults and Adolescent* (15-28). Brookfield, VT: Avebury.

Bagnall, J. (1990). Gang Enslaves Foster Kids. *Calgary Herald*, May 17th, 1990, p. C2.

Baker, J. (1902). Female Criminal Lunatics. *Journal of Mental Science*, 48, 13-28.

Barker M. and Morgan R. (1992). *Sex Offenders: A Framework for the Evaluation of Community Based Treatment*. London: Home Office.

Barnard, C.P. (1983). Alcoholism and Incest: Improving Diagnostic Comprehensiveness. *International Journal of Family Therapy*, 5, 136-144.

Barnes, G. and Prosen, H. (1984). Depression in Canadian General Practice Attenders. *Canadian Journal of Psychiatry*, 29, 2-10.

Barnett, J. and Hill, M. 1993. When the Devil came to Christchurch. *Australian Religion Studies Review*, 6, 2, 25-30.

Barrett, M. and McIntosh, M. (1982). *The Anti-Social Family*. London: Verso.

Barry, K. (1979). *Female Sexual Slavery*. New Jersey, Englewood Cliffs.

Bean, P. (1986). *Mental Disorder and Legal Control*. Cambridge: Cambridge University Press.

Beech, A., Fisher, D., Beckett, R. and Fordham, A. (1996). Treating Sex Offenders in the Community. In *Home Office Research Bulletin No 38*, (21-25). London: Home Office.

Bell, P. and Bell, R. (1993). *Implicated: The United States in Australia*. Melbourne: Oxford University Press.

Bell, S. (1997). France Numbed by Child Sex Scandal. *The Times*, June 21st, p. 5.

Bentovim, A., Van Elburg, A. and Boston, P. (1988). The Results of Treatment. In A. Bentovim (Ed.) *Child Sexual Abuse Within the Family: Assessment and Treatment*. London: Wright-Butterworth Scientific Books.

Berlin, F., Malin, H. and Dean, S. (1991). Effects of Statutes Requiring Psychiatrists to Report Suspected Sexual Abuse of Children. *American Journal of Psychiatry*, 148, 449-455.

Bernet, W. (1995). Running Scared: Therapists' Excessive Concerns About Following Rules. *Bulletin of the American Academy of Psychiatry and the Law*, 23, 367-374.

Bernstein, D., Fink, L., Handelsman, L. and Foote, J. (1994). Initial Reliability of A New Retrospective Measure of Child Abuse and Neglect. *American Journal of Psychiatry*, 151, 1132-1136.

Best, J. (Ed.) (1989a). *Images of Issues: Typifying Contemporary Social Problems*. New York: Aldine de Gruyter.

Best, J. (1989b). Introduction: Typification and Social Problems Construction. In J. Best (Ed.) *Images of Issues: Typifying Contemporary Social Problems*, (xv-xxii). New York: Aldine de Gruyter.

Best, J. (1989c). Claims-makers. In J. Best (Ed.) *Images of Issues: Typifying Contemporary Social Problems*, (75-77). New York: Aldine de Gruyter.

Best, J. (1989d). Afterword - Extending the Constructionist Perspective: A Conclusion - and an Introduction. In J. Best (Ed.) *Images of Issues: Typifying Contemporary Social Problems,* (243-253). New York: Aldine de Gruyter.

Best, J. (1990). *Threatened Children: Rhetoric and Concern about Child-Victims.* Chicago and London: University of Chicago Press.

Best, J. (1994). Troubling Children: Children and Social Problems. In J. Best (Ed.) *Troubling Children: Studies of Children and Social Problems* (3-19). New York: Aldine de Gruyter.

Bifulco, A., Brown, G., Lillie, A. and Jarvis, J. (1997). Memories of Childhood Neglect and Abuse: Corroboration in A Series of Sisters. *Journal of Child Psychology and Psychiatry,* 38, 365-374.

Bigras, J., Bouchard, C., Coleman-Porter, N. and Tasse, Y. (1966). En Deca et au Dela de l'incest chez l'Adolescente. *Canadian Psychiatric Association Journal,* 11, 189-209.

Bishop, S.M. and Ingersoll, G.M. (1989). Effects of Marital Conflict and Family Structure on the Self-concepts of Pre- and Early Adolescents. *Journal of Youth and Adolescence,* 18, 25-37.

Blick, L.C. and Porter, F.S. (1982). Group Therapy with Female Adolescent Incest Victims. In S.M. Sgroi (Ed.). *Handbook of Clinical Intervention in Child Sexual Abuse* (147-175). Toronto: Lexington.

Blishen, B.R., Carroll, W.K. and Moore, C. (1987). The 1981 Socioeconomic Index for Occupations in Canada. *Canadian Review of Sociology and Anthropology,* 24, 465-488.

Blom-Cooper, L. (1985). *A Child in Trust. The Report of the Inquiry into the Circumstances Surrounding the Death of Jasmine Beckford.* Wembley: London Borough of Brent.

Bluglass, K. (1988). Infant Deaths: Categories, Causes and Consequences in Kumar, R. and Brockington, I (Eds.) *Motherhood and Mental Illness 2: Causes and Consequences,* (212-235). Cambridge: Cambridge University Press.

Bogopolski, N. and Cormier, B.M. (1979). Economie Relationelle De Chacun Des Membres Dans Une Famille Incestueuse. *Canadian Journal of Psychiatry,* 24, 65-70.

Boney-McCoy, S. and Finkelhor, D. (1996). Is Youth Victimization Related To Trauma Symptoms and Depression After Controlling for Prior Symptoms and Family Relationships? *Journal of Consulting and Clinical Psychology,* 64, 1406-1416.

Boney-McCoy, S., and Finkelhor, D. (1998). Psychopathology Associated With Sexual Abuse: A Reply to Nash, Neirmeyer, Hulsey, and Lambert (1998). *Journal of Consulting and Clinical Psychology*, 66, 572-573.

Bourget, D and Bradford, J. (1986). Affective Disorder and Homicide: A Case of Familial Filicide Theoretical and Clinical Considerations. *Canadian Journal of Psychiatry*, 32, 222-225.

Bourget D. and Bradford J. (1990). Homicidal Parents. *Canadian Journal of Psychiatry*, 35, 233-238.

Bourget, D. and Labelle, A. (1992). Homicide, Infanticide and Filicide. *Psychiatric Clinics of North America*, 15, 661-673.

Bowden, P. (1990). Homicide. In Bluglass, R. And Bowden, P. (Eds.) *Principles and Practice of Forensic Psychiatry*, (507-521). London and Edinburgh: Churchill Livingstone.

Brand, A.H. and Johnson, J.H. (1982). Note on the Reliability of the Life Events Checklist. *Psychological Reports*, 50, 1274.

Brandon, S., Boakes, J., Glaser, D. and Green, R. (1998). Recovered Memories of Childhood Sexual Abuse. *British Journal of Psychiatry*, 172, 296-307.

Briere, J. (1988). Controlling for Family Variables in Abuse Effects Research. A Critique of the 'Partialling' Approach. *Journal of Interpersonal Violence*, 3, 80-89.

Briere, J. and Runtz, M. (1988). Symptomatology Associated with Childhood Sexual Victimization in A Nonclinical Adult Sample. *Child Abuse and Neglect*, 12, 51-59.

Briere, J. and Elliott, D.M. (1993). Sexual Abuse, Family Environment and Psychological Symptoms: On The Validity of Statistical Control. *Journal of Consulting and Clinical Psychology*, 61, 284-288.

Brindle, D. (1993). Supervised Hospital Discharge for the Mentally Ill, *Guardian*, August 13th, p.4.

Brindle D. (1995). Support Versus An Inquisition. *The Guardian*, June 21st, p.5

Brogi, L. and Bagley, C. (1998). Abusing Victims: Detention of Victims of Child Sexual Abuse in Secure Residential Centres. *Child Abuse Review*, 7, 315-239.

Brockington, I. and Cox-Roper, A. (1988). The Nosology of Puerperal Mental Illness. In Kumar, R and Brockington I. (Eds.) *Motherhood and Mental Illness 2: Causes and Consequences* (1-16). Cambridge: Cambridge University Press.

Bromley, D. (1991). Satanism: The New Cult Scare. In J. Richardson, J. Best and D. Bromley (Eds.) *The Satanism Scare* (49-72). New York: Aldine de Gruyter.

Brown, G.W. (1987). Social Factors and the Development and Cause of Depression in Women. *British Journal of Social Work* Special Supplement, 615-634.

Brown, G.W., Andrews, B., Bifulco, A., Veiel, H. (1990). Self Esteem and Depression. *Social Psychiatry and Psychiatric Epidemiology,* 25, 200-249.

Brown, G., Andrews, B., Harris, T., Adler, Z. and Bridge, L. (1986). Social Support, Self-esteem and Depression. *Psychological Medicine,* 16, 813-831.

Brown, G.W., Bifulco, A and Harris, T. (1987). Life Events, Vulnerability and Onset of Depression: Some Refinements. *British Journal of Psychiatry,* 150, 30-42.

Brown, G.W. and Harris, T. (1978). *Social Origins of Depression. A Study of Psychiatric Disorders in Women.* London: Tavistock.

Browne, A. and Finkelhor, D. (1986). Impact of Child Sexual Abuse: A Review of the Research. *Psychological Bulletin,* 99, 66-77.

Browne, K. and Felshaw, L. (1996). Factors Related to Bullying in Secure Accommodation. *Child Abuse Review,* 5, 123-127.

Brownmiller, S. (1975). *Against Our Will: Men, Women and Rape.* New York: Simon and Shuster.

Buchanan, A. (1998). Criminal Conviction After Discharge From Special (High Security) Hospital: Incidence in the First 10 Years. *British Journal of Psychiatry,* 172, 472-476.

Butler-Sloss, Justice (1988). *Report of the Inquiry into Child Abuse in Cleveland.* London: HMSO.

Bybee, J., Kramer, A. and Zigler, E. (1997). Is Repression Adaptive? Relationships to Socioemotional Adjustment, Academic Performance, and Self-image. *American Journal of Orthopsychiatry,* 67, 59-69.

Byles, J.A., Byrne, C., Offord, D.R. and Boyle, M.H. (1988). Ontario Child Health Study: Family Functioning and Emotional/Behaviour Disorders in Children. *Family Process,* 27, 97-104.

Callero, L.P. and Howard, A.J. (1989). Biases of the Scientific Discourses of Human Sexuality: Toward A Sociology of Sexuality. In Kathleen Mckinney and Susan Sprecher (Eds.) *The Societal Context* (370-425). Norwood New Jersey: Ablex Publishing Corporation.

Canadian Child Welfare Association (1987). *Proceedings of the National Consultation on Adolescent Prostitution.* Mont Tremblant, Quebec, CCWA.

Cammaert, L.P. (1988). Non-offending Mothers: A New Conceptualization, in L.E.A. Walker (Ed.). *Handbook on Sexual Abuse of Children* (309-325), New York: Springer.

Carlton (1995). *Defender of the Children.* London: Carlton TV Documentary. October 31st, 1995.

Cavaiola, A.A. and Schiff, N. (1988). Behavioural Sequelae of Physical And/or Sexual Abuse in Adolescents. *Child Abuse and Neglect,* 12, 181-188.

Cavaiola, A.A. and Schiff, M. (1989). Self-esteem in Abused Chemically Dependent Adolescents. *Child Abuse and Neglect,* 13, 327-334.

Chambers, J. (1955). *Statistical Calculations.* Cambridge: Cambridge University Press.

Chess, S. And Thomas, A. (1984). *Origins and Evolution of Behaviour Disorders.* New York: Brunner-Mazel.

Children Act 1989. London: HMSO.

Cleaver, H. and Freeman, P. (1995). *Parental Perspectives in Cases of Suspected Child Abuse,* London: HMSO 1995.

Cohen, J.A. and Mannarino, A.P. (1988). Psychological Symptoms in Sexually Abused Girls. *Child Abuse and Neglect,* 12, 571-577.

Cohen, P. and Brook, J. (1987). Family Factors Related to the Persistence of Psychopathology in Childhood and Adolescence. *Psychiatry,* 50, 332-345.

Cole, P.M. and Woogler, C. (1989). Incest Survivors: the Relation of Their Perceptions of Their Parents and Their Own Parenting Attitude. *Child Abuse and Neglect,* 13, 409-416.

Conte, J.R. (1986). Sexual Abuse and the Family: A Critical Analysis. In T.S. Trepper and M.J. Barrett (Eds.) *Treating Incest: A Multiple System Perspective,* (113-126). New York: Haworth Press.

Conte, J.R. and Schuerman, J.R. (1987). Factors Associated With an Increased Impact of Child Sexual Abuse. *Child Abuse and Neglect,* 11, 201-211.

Conte, J., Wolfe, S., and Smith, T. (1989). What Sexual Offenders Tell Us About Prevention Strategies. *Child Abuse and neglect,* 13, 293-301.

Courtois, C.A. (1979). The Incest Experience and Its Aftermath. *Victimology,* 4, 337-347.

Cox, M. and Pritchard, C. (1995). The Pursuit of Social Justice and the Probation Service. In Ward, D. and Lacy, M. (Eds) *Probation: Working for Justice,* (88-122). London: Whiting and Birch.

CPS. (1998). *Report on the Prosecution of Child Abuse Cases*. London: The Crown Prosecution Service.

Creighton, J. (1993). Childrens' Homicide: An Exchange. *British Journal of Social Work*, 23, 643-644.

Croft, S. and Beresford, P. (1990). *From Paternalism to Participation*. London: Open Services Project.

Cupoli, J.M. and Sewell, P.M. (1988). One Thousand Fifty-nine Children with a Chief Complaint of Sexual Abuse. *Child Abuse and Neglect*, 12, 151-162.

Dadds, M.R. (1987). Families and the Origins of Child Behaviour Problems. *Family Process*, 26, 341-357.

Davies C. and Little M. (1995). Family Circle. *Community Care*, 22 June, 18-19.

Davies, G.M., Wilson, C., Mitchell, R. and Milsom, J. (1995). *Videotaping Children's Evidence: An Evaluation*. London; Home Office.

Deblinger, E., McLeer, S.V., Atkins, M.S., Ralphe, D., and Foa, E. (1989). Post-traumatic Stress in Sexually Abused, Physically Abused, and Non-Abused Children. *Child Abuse and Neglect*, 13, 403-408.

de Jong, T. and Gorey, K.(1996). Short-term Versus Long-term Work with Female Survivors of Childhood Sexual Abuse: A Brief Meta-analytic Review. *Social Work with Groups*, 19, 19-27.

de Lauretis, T. (1987). *Technologies of Gender: Essays on Theory, Film and Fiction*. Bloomington and Indianapolis: Indiana University.

de Lauretis, T. (1993). Upping the Anti [sic] in Feminist Theory. In S. During (Ed.) *The Cultural Studies Reader*, (74-99). New York: Routledge.

de Mause (1991). The Universality of Incest. *Journal of Psychohistory*, 19, 123-164 .

Department of Health (1991a). *Working Together Under the Children Act 1989*, London: HMSO.

Department of Health (1991b). *Patterns and Outcomes in Child Placement*. London: HMSO.

Department of Health (1991c). *Working Together Under the Children Act 1989: A Guide to Arrangements for Inter-Agency Cooperation for the Protection of Children from Abuse*. London: HMSO.

Department of Health (1994). *Children Act Report 1993*, London: HMSO.

Department of Health (1995). *Child Protection: Messages From Research*. London: HMSO.

DeYoung, M. (1982). *The Sexual Victimisation of Children*. Jefferson, N.C.: McFarland.

Dingwall, R., Eekelaar, J., and Murray, T., (1983). *The Protection of Children: State Intervention in Family Life*. London; Blackwell.

Dobson, R. (1996). Gagged: Insurers Silence Social Service Results of Enquiries. *Community Care,* May 11th, 18-19.

Dolik, H. (1993). Pimp Gets Prison Term. *Calgary Herald*, December 6th, B4.

Dominelli, L. (1991). *Gender, Sex Offenders and Probation Practice*. Norwich, Novata Press.

Donzelot, J. (1979). *The Policing of Families: Welfare Versus the State*. New York: Pantheon.

d'Orban P. (1979). Women Who Kill Their Children. *British Journal of Social Psychiatry*, 134, 560-571.

d'Orban, P. (1990). Female Homicide. *Irish Journal of Psychological Medicine*, 7, 64-70.

Draucker, C. (1995). A Coping Model for Adult Survivors of Childhood Sexual Abuse. *Journal of Interpersonal Violence*, 10, 159-175.

Dworkin, A. (1981). *Pornography: Men Possessing Women*. London Women Press.

Dwyer, S. (1997). Treatment Outcome Study: Seventeen Years After Sexual Offender Treatment. *Sexual Abuse: A Journal of Research and Treatment*, 9, 149-160.

Eckenrode, J., Munsch, J., Powers, J. and Doris, J. (1988). The Nature and Substantiation of Official Sexual Abuse Reports. *Child Abuse and Neglect*, 12, 311-319.

Edwards, J. and Alexander, P. (1992). The Contribution of Family Background to the Long-term Adjustment of Women Sexually Abused As Children. *Journal of Interpersonal Violence*, 7, 306-320.

Egeland, B., Breitenbucher, M. and Rosenbury, D. (1980). Prospective Study of the Significance of Life Stress in the Etiology of Child Abuse. *Journal of Consulting and Clinical Psychology,* 48, 195-205.

Einbender, A.J. and Friedrich, W.N. (1989). Psychological Functioning and Behaviour of Sexually Abused Girls. *Journal of Consulting and Clinical Psychology*, 57, 155-157.

Eist, H.I. and Mandel, A.V. (1968). Family Treatment of Ongoing Incest Behaviour. *Family Process*, 7, 216-232.

Emery, R.E. (1982). Interparental Conflict and the Children of Discord and Divorce. *Psychological Bulletin*, 92, 310-330.

Emery, R.E. and O'Leary, K.D. (1982). Children's Perception of Marital Discord and Behaviour Problems of Boys and Girls. *Journal of Abnormal Psychology*, 10, 11-24.

Emslie, G.J. and Rosenfeld, A. (1983). Incest Reported by Children and Adolescents Hospitalised for Severe Psychiatric Problems. *American Journal of Psychiatry*, 40, 708-711.

Epstein, N., Baldwin, L. and Bishop, W. (1983). The McMaster Family Assessment Device. *Journal of Marital and Family Therapy*, 9, 171-180.

Erikson, E. (1968). *Identity, Youth and Crisis*. London: Faber.

Ethier, L.S., Lacharite, C. and Couture, G. (1995). Childhood Adversity, Parental Stress and Depression of Negligent Mothers. *Child Abuse and Neglect*, 19, 619-632.

Everson, M., Hunter, W., Runyon, D., Edelsohn, G. and Coulter, M. (1989). Maternal Support Following Disclosure of Incest. *American Journal of Orthopsychiatry*, 59, 197-207.

Everson, M.D., Hunter, W.M., Runyon, D.R. Edelsohn, G.A. and Coulter, M.L. (1989). Maternal Support Following Disclosure of Incest. *American Journal of Orthopsychiatry*, 59, 197-207.

Everstine, D.S. and Everstine, L. (1989). *Sexual Trauma in Children and Adolescents*. New York: Brunner/Mazel.

Falkov, A. (1996). *Study of Working Together. Part 8 Reports of Fatal Abuse and Parental Psychiatric Disorder: An analysis of 100 Area Child Protection Committee Reviews*. London: Dept of Health.

Falkov, A. (1997). Adult Psychiatry: A Missing Link in the Child Protection Network: A Response to Reder and Duncan. *Child Abuse Review*, 6 41-45.

Famularo, R., Kinscherff, R. and Fenton, T. (1992). Psychiatric Diagnoses of Abusive Mothers: A Preliminary Report. *Journal of Nervous and Mental Disease*, 180, 658-661.

Farmer, E. and Owen, M. (1995). *Child Protection Practice: Private Risks and Public Remedies - Decision Making, Intervention and Outcome in Child Protection Work*. London: HMSO.

Fernando, S. (1988). *Mental Health, Race and Culture*. London: MacMillan.

Finkelhor, D. (1979). *Sexually Victimized Children*. New York: Free Press.

Finkelhor, D. (1984). *Child Sexual Abuse: New Theory and Research*. New York: Free Press.

Finkelhor, D and Browne, A. (1985). The Traumatic Impact of Child Sexual Abuse: A Conceptualisation. *American Journal of Orthopsychiatry*, 530, 541.

Finkelhor, D. and Zellman, G. (1991). Flexible Reporting Options for Skilled Child Abuse Professionals. *Child Abuse and Neglect*, 15, 344-351.

Firestone, R. (1987). *Voice Therapy: A Psychotherapeutic Approach to Self-destructive Behaviour*. New York: Human Sciences Press.

Fitts, W. (1965). *Manual for the Tennessee Self-concept Scale*. Los Angeles: Western Psychological Services.

Flaherty, E. (1992). Task Force to Tackle Youth Prostitution: Young Women Grabbed Off the Streets, Coerced Into Prostitution and Kept in Line by Beatings and Torture. *Calgary Herald*, October 1st, C4.

Flin, R. and Boon, J. (1989). The child witness in court. In Blagg, H., Hughes, J. and Wattam, C. (eds.) *Child Sexual Abuse: Listening, Hearing and Validating the Experiences of Children*. Harlow: Longman.

Flin, R., Davies, G. and Tarrant, A. (1988). *Children as Witnesses*. Edinburgh: Scottish Home and Health Department.

Follette, V., Alexander, P. and Follette, W. (1991). Individual Predictors of Outcome in Group Treatment for Incest Survivors. *Journal of Consulting and Clinical Psychology*, 59, 150-155.

Ford, P., Cox, M. and Pritchard, C. (1997). Consumer Opinions of the Probation Service: Advice, Assistance, Befriending and the Reduction of Crime. *Howard Journal Criminal Justice*, 36, 42-60.

Foucault, M. (1980). *Power/Knowledge: Selected Interviews and Other Writings 1972-1977*. Brighton: Harvester.

Fox-Harding, L. (1997). *Perspectives in Childcare Policy*. London: Longman.

Fraser, K. (1988). Bereavement in Those Who Have Killed. *Medicine, Science and the Law*, 28, 127-130.

Friedman, S. (1988). A Family Systems Approach to Treatment. In L.E.A. Walker (Ed.) *Handbook on Sexual Abuse of Children*, (326-349). New York: Springer.

Friedrich, W.N. (1988). Behaviour Problems in Sexually Abused Children: An Adaptational Perspective. In G.E. Wyatt and G.J. Powell (Eds.), *Lasting Effects of Child Sexual Abuse*, (171-191). Newbury Park, CA: Sage.

Friedrich, W. (1998). Behavioral Manifestations of Child Sexual Abuse. *Child Abuse and Neglect*, 6, 523-531.

Friedrich, W.N., Beilke, R.L. and Urquiza, A.J. (1987). Children From Sexually Abusive Families: A Behavioural Comparison. *Journal of Interpersonal Violence*, 2, 391-402.

Friedrich, W.N. and Luecke, W.J. (1988). Young School-Age Sexually Aggressive Children. I: Assessment and Comparison. *Professional Psychology*, 19, 155-164.

Friedrich, W.N., Urquiza, A.J. and Beilke, R.L. (1986). Behaviour Problems in Sexually Abused Young Children. *Journal of Paediatric Psychology*, 11, 47-57.

Fritz, G.S., Stoll, K. and Wagner, N.N. (1981). A Comparison of Males and Females Who Were Sexually Molested as Children. *Journal of Sex and Marital Therapy*, 7 54-59.

Frodi, A. and Smetena, J. (1984). Abused, Neglected and Nonmaltreated Preschoolers' Ability to Discriminate Emotions in Others: The Effects of IQ. *Child Abuse and Neglect*, 8, 459-465.

Fromuth, M.E. (1986). The Relationship of Childhood Sexual Abuse with Later Psychological and Sexual Adjustment in a Sample of College Women. *Child Abuse and Neglect*, 10, 5-15.

Furniss, T. (1983). Family Process and the Treatment of Intrafamilial Child Sexual Abuse. *Journal of Family Therapy*, 5, 263-278.

Furniss, T. (1985). Incest and Child Sexual Abuse. Conflict-avoiding and Conflict-regulating Patterns. *Acta Paedopsychiatrica*, 50, 299-313.

Furniss, T. (1991). *The Multi-professional Handbook of Child Sexual Abuse*. London: Routledge.

Furniss, T., Bingley-Miller, L. and Van Elburg, A. (1988). Goal-oriented Treatment for Sexually Abused Girls. *British Journal of Psychiatry*, 152, 97-106.

Gad, M.T. and Johnson, J.H. (1980). Correlates of Adolescent Life Stress as Related to Race, SES, and Perceived Social Support. *Journal of Clinical Child Psychology*, 9, 13-16.

Gale, J., Thompson, R.J., Moran, T. and Sack, W.H. (1988). Sexual Abuse in Young Children: Its Clinical Presentation and Characteristic Patterns. *Child Abuse and Neglect*, 12 163-170.

Garmezy, N (1983). Stressors of Childhood. In N. Garmezy and M. Rutter (Eds.), *Stress, Coping and Development in Children*, (43-84). New York: McGraw-Hill.

Garmezy, N., Masten, A.S. and Tellegen, A. (1984). The Study of Stress and Competence in Children: A Building Block for Developmental Psychopathology. *Child Development*, 55, 97-111.

Gelinas, D.J. (1983). The Persisting Negative Effects of Incest. *Psychiatry*, 46, 312-332.

Gelsthorpe, L. (1990). *Feminist Perspectives in Criminology*. Milton Keynes: Open University Press.

Giarretto, H. (1982). *Treatment of Child Sexual Abuse: A Treatment and Training Manual*. Pal Alto, CA: Science and Behaviour Books.

Gibbons, J., Thorpe, S. and Wilkinson, P. (1990). *Family Support and Prevention: Studies in Local Areas*. London: National Institute of Social Work.

Gibbons, J. Gallagher, B., Bell, C. and Gordon, D. (1995a). *Development After Physical Abuse in Early Childhood*. London: HMSO.

Gibbons, J., Conroy, S. and Bell, C. (1995b). *Operating the Child Protection System: A Study of Child Protection Practices in English Local Authorities*. London; HMSO.

Gibson, R. and Hartshorne, T. (1996). Childhood Sexual Abuse and Adult Loneliness and Network Orientation. *Child Abuse and Neglect*, 20, 1087-1093.

Glaser, D. (1995). Children's Evidence - State of the Art? A Commentary on Videotaping Children's Evidence: An Evaluation. *Child Abuse Review*, 4, 4-14.

Glaser, G.B. and Strauss, L.A. (1967). *The Discovery of Grounded Theory: Strategies for Qualitative Research*. Chicago: Aldine Publishing Company.

Glover, E. (1969). *The Psychopathology of Prostitution*. London: Institute for Study and Treatment of Delinquency.

Gold, E.R. (1986). Long-term Effects of Sexual Victimisation in Childhood: An Attributional Approach. *Journal of Consulting and Clinical Psychology*, 54, 471-475.

Goldberg, D. (1978). *Manual of the General Health Questionnaire*. Windsor: NFER.

Goldston, D.B., Tunrquist, D.C. and Knutson, J.F. (1989). Presenting Problems of Sexually Abused Girls Receiving Psychiatric Services. *Journal of Abnormal Psychology*, 98, 314-317.

Goodman, G., Quin, G., Bottoms, B. and Shaver, R. (1995). *Characteristics and Sources of Ritualistic Abuse*. Chicago: National Center on Child Abuse and Neglect.

Goodwin, J. (1985). Post-traumatic Symptoms in Incest Victims. In S. Eth and R.S. Pynoos (Eds.), *Post-traumatic Stress Disorder in Children*, (157-165). Washington, DC: American Psychiatric Press.

Goodwin, J., Cormier, L., and Owen, J. (1983). Grandfather-granddaughter Incest: A Trigenerational View. *Child Abuse and Neglect*, 7, 163-170.

Goodyer, I.M. (1990). Family Relationships, Life Events, and Childhood Psychopathology. *Journal of Child Psychology and Psychiatry*, 31, 161-192.

Gordon, L. (1988a). The Politics of Child Sexual Abuse: Notes from American History. *Feminist Review*, 28, Spring, 56-64.

Gordon, L. (1988b). *Heroes of Their Own Lives: The Politics and History of Family Violence: Boston 1900-1960*. New York: Viking.

Gough, D., *Child Abuse Interventions: A Review of the Research Literature.* London: HMSO 1993.

Gratzer, T. and Bradford, J. (1995). Offender and Offence Characteristics of Sexual Sadists. *Journal of Forensic Science*, 40, 430-455.

Greenland, C. (1987). *Preventing Child Abuse and Neglect Deaths.* London: Tavistock.

Greer, G. (1975), Seduction is A Four Letter Word. In L.G. Schultz (Ed.), *Rape Victimology*. (372-289). Illinois: C.C. Thomas.

Groth, A.N. (1982). The Incest Offerender. In S.M. Sgroi (Ed.), *Handbook of Clinical Intervention in Child Sexual Abuse*, (215-239). Toronto: Lexington.

Gruber, K.J. and Jones R.J. (1983). Identifying Determinants of Risk of Sexual Victimisation of Youth: A Multivariate Approach. *Child Abuse and Neglect*, 7, 17-24.

Grubin, D. (1994). Sexual Sadism. *Criminal Behaviour and Mental Health*, 4, 3-9.

Grunfeld, B. and Steen, J. (1984). Faal Barnemishandling: Barnedrap I Norgei. *Tidskrift for Norsk Laegeforening*, 104, 289-292

Guy, C. (1996). Feminism and Sexual Abuse: Troubled Thoughts on Some New Zealand Issues. *Feminist Review*, 52, Spring, 154-168.

Hallett C. and Birchall E. (1995). Inter-agency Co-ordination in Child Protection. In *Child Protection. Messages From Research*, (70-73) London: HMSO.

Handy, L.C. (1988). A Developing Behavioural Treatment Model: One Therapist's Perspective Within a Community's Evolving Response. In L.E.A. Walker (Ed.), *Handbook on Sexual Abuse of Children*, (350-364). New York: Springer.

Handy, L.C. and Cammaert, L.P. (1985, June). *Power: A Major Construct of Child Sexual Abuse.* Paper presented at the Meeting of the Canadian Psychological Association, Halifax, Nova Scotia.

Handy, L.C. and Pelletier, G. (1988). Child Sexual Abuse: A Selective Review and Behavioural Treatment Perspective. In R. Dev. Peters and R.J. McMahon, (Eds.), *Social Learning and Systems Approaches to Marriage and the Family.* (168-192). New York: Brunner/Mazel.

Haraway, D. (1985). A Manifesto for Cyborgs: Science, Technology, and Socialist Feminism in the 1980s. *Socialist Review*, 15, March/April, 65-107.

Haraway, D. (1988). Situated Knowledges: The Science Question in Feminism and the Privilege of Partial Perspective. *Feminist Studies*, 14, 575-99.

Harder, T. (1967). The Psychopathology of Infanticide. *Act Psychiatria Scandinavia*, 43, 196-245.

Harter, S. (1985). *Manual for the Self-Perception Profile for Children*. Denver, CO: University of Denver.

Harter, S. (1988). *Manual for the Self-Perception Profile for Adolescents*. Denver, CO: University of Denver.

Harter, S., Alexander, P.C. and Niemeyer, R.A. (1988). Long-term Effects of Incestuous Child Abuse in College Women: Social Adjustment, Social Cognition, and Family Characteristics. *Journal of Consulting and Clinical Psychology*, 56, 5-8.

Hart-Hansen, J.P. (1977). *Drabi I Danmark* 1946-1970. Kopenhagen: Munksgaard.

Hartman, M, Finn, S.E. and Leon, G.R. (1987). Sexual-abuse Experiences in a Clinical Population: Comparison of Familial and Non-familial Abuse. *Psychotherapy*, 24, 154-159.

Haugaard, J.J. and Repucci, N.D. (1988). *The Sexual Abuse of Children*. San Francisco: Jossey-Bass.

Hawton, K. And Roberts, J. (1981). The Association Between Child Abuse and Attempted Suicide. *British Journal of Social work*, 11, 415-420.

Hawton, K., Roberts, J. and Goodwin, G. (1985). The Risk of Child Abuse Among Mothers Who Attempt Suicide. *British Journal of Psychiatry*, 146, 486-489.

Henderson, J. (1983). Is Incest Harmful? *Canadian Journal of Psychiatry*, 28, 34-40.

Henggeler, S.W., Edwards, J. and Borduin, C.M. (1987). The Family Relations of Juvenile Delinquents. *Journal of Abnormal Child Psychology*, 15, 199-209.

Heptinstall, W. (1984). Sexual Abuse of Children. *Community Care*, 541, 32-34.

Heriot, J. (1996). Maternal Protectiveness Following the Disclosure of Intrafamilial Sexual Abuse. *Journal of Interpersonal Violence*, 11. 181-194.

Herman, J.L. (1981). *Father-daughter Incest*. Cambridge: Harvard University Press.

Higgins, G. (1994). *Resilient Adults: Overcoming a Cruel Past*. San Francisco: Jossey-Bass.

Himmelein, M. and McElrath, J. (1996). Resilient Child Sexual Abuse Survivors: Cognitive Coping and Illusion. *Child Sexual Abuse and Neglect*, 8, 747-758.

Hoagwood, K., and Stewart, J.M. (1989). Sexually Abused Children's Perceptions of Family Functioning. *Child and Adolescent Social Work*, 6, 139-149.

Hoddinott, J.C. and Neyroud, P.W. (1995). *In Search of Criminal Justice*. London: Association of Chief Police Officers.

Hollows, A. and Wonnacott, J. (1994). Protect by Prevention. *Community Care*, 30 April, 22-23.

Home Office, Department of Health, Department of Education and Science, and Welsh Office (1991). *Working Together*. London: HMSO.

Home Office (1992). *Memorandum of Good Practice on Video Recorded Interviews with Child Witnesses for Criminal Proceedings*. London: HMSO.

Home Office (1993). *Criminal Statistics England and Wales 1991*. London: HMSO.

Hooper, C.A. (1992). *Mothers Surviving Child Sexual Abuse*. London: Routledge.

Hopwood, J. (1927). Child Murder and Insanity. *Journal of Mental Science*, 73, 95-108.

Hornsell, M. (1996). Choir's Second Suicide Linked to Pornography. *The Times*, December 9th, p.3.

Hughes, R. (1996). The Department of Health Research Studies in Child Protection: A Response to Parton. *Child and Family Social Work*, 1, 2.

Husain, A. and Chapel, J.L. (1983). History of Incest in Girls Admitted to a Psychiatric Hospital. *American Journal of Psychiatry*, 140, 591-593.

Hutchison, E. (1993). Mandatory Reporting Laws: Child Protective Case Work Awry? *Social Work*, 38, 56-63.

Huxley, P., Korer, J and Toley, S. (1987). The Psychiatric 'Cases' of Clients Referred to An Urban Social Services Department. *British Journal of Social Work*, 17, 507-520.

Jackson, S. (1994) Partnership With Families. In A. Buchanan (Ed.). *Partnership in Practice*, Aldershot: Avebury.

Jackson, S. and Morris, K. (1994). *Looking At Partnership Teaching in Social Work Qualifying Programmes*. London: Central Council for Education and Training in Social Work.

James, J. (1978). The Prostitute As Victim. In R. Fane and M. Gates (Eds.), *The Victimisation of Women*, (175-201). Beverley Hills, CA.: Sage Publications.

Jason, J. (1983). Child Homicide Spectrum. *American Journal of Diseases of Childhood*, 137, 578-581.

Jenkins, P. (1992). *Intimate Enemies: Moral Panics in Contemporary Great Britain*. New York: Aldine de Gruyter.

Johnson, J. (1989). Horror Stories and the Construction of Child Abuse. In J. Best (Ed.) *Images of Issues: Typifying Contemporary Social Problems*, (5-19). New York: Aldine de Gruyter.

Johnson, J.H. (1986). *Life Events as Stressors in Childhood and Adolescence*. Newbury Park, CA: Sage.

Johnson, J.H. and McCutcheon, S.M. (1980). Assessing Life Stress in Older Children and Adolescents: Preliminary Findings with the Life Events Checklist. In I.G. Sarason and C.D. Spielberger (Eds.) *Stress and Anxiety*, (111-125). Washington, DC: Hemisphere.

Johnston, C. (1996). Net Porn Charge Man Dies. *Times Higher Educational Supplement*, August 30th, p.3.

Johnston, W.C (1967). Releasing the Dangerous Offender. In Rappoport, J.R. (Ed.) *The Clinical Evaluation of the Dangerousness of the Mentally Ill*. Illinois: Charles C. Thomas.

Jones, A. (1990). Am 'I' in the Text? The Positioned/Partial Subject and Writing in the Feminist Classroom. Paper Given at National Women's Studies Association Conference, Akron, Ohio, June.

Joseph, C. (1995). Scarlet Wounding: Issues of Child Prostitution. *The Journal of Psychohistory*, 23, 2-18.

Justice, B., Calvert, A. and Justice, R. (1985). Factors Mediating Child Abuse As A Response to Stress. *Child Abuse and Neglect* 9, 359-363.

Kelly, L. (1988). *Understanding Sexual Violence*. Cambridge: Polity Press.

Kelly, L., Regan, L. and Burton, S. (1991). *An Exploratory Study of the Prevalence of Sexual Abuse in A Sample of 16-21 Year Olds*. London: Child and Woman Abuse Studies Unit, University of North London.

Kempe, C.H. (1980). Incest and Other Forms of Sexual Abuse. In C.H. Kempe and R.E. Helfer (Eds.) *The Battered Child* (3rd ed., 198-214). Chicago, IL: The University of Chicago Press.

Kempe, C.H., Silverman, F.N., Steele, B.F., Droegemueller, W. and Silver, H.K. (1962). The Battered Child Syndrome. *Journal of the American Medical Association*, 181, 17-24.

Kendall-Tackett, K.A., and Simon, A.F. (1988). Molestation and the Onset of Puberty: Data From 365 Adults Molested as Children. *Child Abuse and Neglect*, 12, 73-81.

Kirk, R.E. (1982). *Experimental Design: Procedure For the Behavioural Sciences*, (2nd ed.). Belmont, CA: Brooks/Cole.

Kiser, L.J., Ackerman, B.J., Brown, E., Edwards, N.B., McColgan, E., Pugh, R., and Pruitt, D.B. (1988). Post-traumatic Stress Disorder in Young Children: A Reaction to Purported Sexual Abuse. *Journal of the American Academy of Child and Adolescent Psychiatry*, 27, 645-649.

Kitsuse, J. And Schneider, J. (1989). Preface. In J. Best (Ed.) *Images of Issues: Typifying Contemporary Social Problems* (xi-xiv). New York: Aldine de Gruyter.

Kitzinger, C. (1987). *The Social Construction of Lesbianism*. London: Sage.

Kitzinger, J. and Skidmore, P. (1995). Playing Safe: Media Coverage of Child Sexual Abuse Prevention Strategies. *Child Abuse Review*, 4, 47-56.

Korbin J.E. (1986). Childhood Histories of Women Imprisoned for Fatal Child Maltreatment. *Child Abuse and Neglect* 8, 387-392.

Kovacs, M. (1980/1981). Rating Scales to Assess Depression in School Aged Children. *Acta Paedopsychiatrica*, 46, 305-315.

Kovacs, M. and Beck, A.T. (1977). An Empirical Clinical Approach Towards a Definition of Childhood Depression. In Schulterbrandt, J.G. and Raskin, A. (Eds.). *Depression in Children: Diagnosis, Treatment and Conceptual Models*. New York: Raven.

Krieger, M. and Robbins, J. (1985). The Adolescent Incest Victim and the Judicial System. *American Journal of Orthopsychiatry*, 55, 419-425.

LaBarbera, J.D., Martin, J.E. and Dozier, J.E. (1980). Child Psychiatrists' View of Father-Daughter Incest. *Child Abuse and Neglect*, 4, 147-151.

La Fontaine, G. (1998). *Speak of the Devil: Tales of Satanic Abuse in Contemporary Society*. Cambridge: University of Cambridge Press.

Langeland W. and Dijkstra S. (1995). Breaking the Inter-generational Transmission of Child Abuse: Beyond the Mother-Child Relationship. *Child Abuse Review*, 4, 4-13.

Larson, N.R. and Maddock, J.W. (1986). Structural and Functional Variables in Incest Family Systems: Implications for Assessment and Treatment. In T.S. Trepper and N.J. Barrett (Eds.) *Treating Incest: A Multiple Systems Perspective*, (27-44). New York: Haworth Press.

Lealand, G. (1988). *A Foreign Egg in Our Nest? American Popular Culture in New Zealand*. Wellington: Victoria University Press.

Lee, A. (1998). 'Rape' Schoolgirl Tells Court She Was Assaulted Aged Six. *The Times*, January 17th, p. 3.

Lerman, H. (1988). The Psychoanalytic Legacy: From Whence We Come. In L.E.A. Walker (Ed.), *Handbook on Sexual Abuse of Children*, (37-52). New York: Springer.

Levang, C.A. (1989). Interactional Communication Patterns in Father/ Daughter Incest Families. *Journal of Psychology and Human Sexuality*, 1, 53-68.

Lewis, L. (Ed.) (1992). *The Adoring Audience: Fan Culture and Popular Media*. London and New York: Routledge.

Liem, J., James, J., O'Toole, J. and Boudewyn, A. (1997). Assessing Resilience in Adults with Histories of Childhood Sexual Abuse. *American Journal of Orthopsychiatry*, 67, 594-606.

Lindsey, D. and Trocme, N. (1994). Have Child Protection Efforts Reduced Child Homicides? An Examination of Data from Britain and North America. *British Journal of Social Work*, 24, 715-732.

Linedecker, C. (1981). *Children in Chains*. New York: Everest House.

Lister, E.D. (1982). Forced Silence: A Neglected Dimension of Trauma. *American Journal of Psychiatry*, 139, 872-876.

Little, M. (1998). Whispers in the Library: A Response to Liz Trinder's Article on the State of Social Work Research. *Child and Family Social Work*, 3, 49-56.

London Boroughs of Bexley and Greenwich and Bexley Heath (1982). *Lucy Gates Inquiry: Chairman's Report*. London: L.B. of Bexley.

Long, N., Forehand, R., Fauber, R. and Brody, G.H. (1987). Self-perceived and Independently Observed Competence of Young Adolescents as a Function of Parental Marital Conflict and Recent Divorce. *Journal of Abnormal Child Psychology*, 15, 15-27.

Lowman, J. (1987). Taking Young Prostitutes Seriously. *Canadian Review of Sociology and Anthropology*, 24, 98-116.

Lynskey, M. and Fergusson, D. (1997). Factors Protecting Against the Development of Adjustment Difficulties in Young Adults Exposed to Childhood Sexual Abuse. *Child Abuse and Neglect*, 12, 1177-1190.

MacKinnon, C. (1990). Sexuality, Pornography and Method: Pleasure Under Patriarchy. In Cass, R. Sunstein (Ed.), *Feminism and Political Theory*, (207-239). Chicago, University of Chicago Press.

Maddock, J. (1988). Child Reporting and Testimony in Incest Cases: Comments on the Construction and Reconstruction of Reality. *Behavioural Sciences and the Law*, 6, 201-220.

Maddock, J. and Larson, N. (1995). *Incestuous Families: An Ecological Approach to Understanding and Treatment*. New York: Norton.

312

Manly, J., Cichetti, D., and Barnett, D. (1994). The Impact of Subtype, Frequency, Chronicity, and Severity of Child Maltreatment on Social Competency and Behaviour Problems. *Development and Psychopathology*, 6, 121-124.

Mannarino, A.P. and Cohen, J.A. (1986). A Clinical-demographic Study of Sexually Abused Children. *Child Abuse and Neglect*, 10, 17-23.

Margolin, L. (1992). Deviance on Record: Techniques for Labelling Child Abusers in Official Documents. *Social Problems*, 39, 58-70.

Marsh, P. and Fisher, M. (1992). *Good Intentions: Developing Partnership in Social Services*. Joseph York: Rowntree Foundation.

Marshall, W. and Anderson, D. (1996). An Evaluation of Relapse Prevention Programs with Sexual Offenders. *Sexual Abuse: A Journal of Research and Treatment*, 8, 209-221.

Martin, M.J. and Walters, J. (1982). Family Correlates of Selected Types of Child Abuse and Neglect. *Journal of Marriage and the Family*, 44, 267-276.

Martone, M., Jaudes, P., and Cavins, M. (1996). Criminal Prosecutions of Child Sexual Abuse Cases. *Child Abuse and Neglect*, 20, 5, 457-464.

McAdam, N. (1998). University of Ulster Lecturer Kills Self. *Times Higher Educational Supplement*, January 23rd, p.4.

McCauley, J., Kern, D., Kolodner, K. and Dill, L. (1997). Clinical Characteristics of Women with A History of Childhood Abuse: Unhealed Wounds. *Journal of the American Medical Association*, 277, 1362-1368.

McGee, R., Wolfe, D. and Wilson, S. (1997). Multiple Maltreatment Experiences and Adolescent Behaviour Problems: Adolescent's Perspectives. *Development and Psychopathology*, 9, 131-149.

McGee, D., Wolfe, D., Yuen, S., Wilson, K., and Carnochan, J. (1995). The Measurement of Maltreatment: A Comparison of Approaches. *Child Abuse and Neglect*, 19, 233-249.

McGovern, K. (1991). Understanding False and Mistaken Reports of Child Sexual Abuse. In R. Ten Bensel (Ed.) *Whole Issue of Child and Youth Services*, 15, 1-157.

McInnes, R. (1995). *Children on the Game*. Calgary, AB: The Exit Foundation.

McIntosh, M. (1976). Who Needs Prostitutes? The Ideology of Male Sexual Needs in Women. In C. Smart and B. Smart (Eds.), *Sexuality and Social Control*, (71-92). London: Routledge and Keegan Paul.

McIntyre, S. (1983). *Theoretical and Policy Issues of Child Sexual Abuse of England and Canada*. Sheffield: University of Sheffield, M.A. Thesis.

313

McIntyre, S. (1994). *The Youngest Profession: the Oldest Oppression.* Sheffield: University of Sheffield Doctoral Thesis.

McIntyre, S. (1995). *Juvenile Prostitution.* Presentation to A Professional Forum on Prostitution. Calgary, June.

McKinnon, M. (Ed.) (1988). *American Connection: Essays from the Stout Centre Conference.* Wellington: Allen and Unwin/Port Nicholson Press.

McLeer, S.V., Deblinger, E., Atkins, M.S., Foa, E.B. and Ralphe, D.L. (1988). Post-traumatic Stress Disorder in Sexually Abused Children. *Journal of the American Academy of Child and Adolescent Psychiatry,* 27, 650-654.

McLeod, E. (1982). *Women Working Prostitution.* London: Croom Helm Limited.

McRobbie, A. (1984). *Postmodernism and Popular Culture.* London and New York: Routledge.

McRobbie, A. and Thornton, S. (1995). Rethinking 'Moral Panic' For Multi-mediated Social Worlds. *British Journal of Sociology,* 46, 559-574.

Meiselman, K.C. (1978). *Incest: A Psychological Study of Causes and Effects With Treatment Recommendations.* San Francisco: Jossey Bass.

Mental Health Act (1983): London: HMSO.

Mental Health (Patients in the Community) Act (1995): London HMSO.

Miles, A. (1987). *The Mentally Ill in Contemporary Society.* Oxford: Basil Blackwell.

Millett, K. (1971). *The Prostitution Papers: A Quartet for Female Voice.* New York: Ballantine Books.

Minuchin, S. (1974). *Families and Family Therapy.* Cambridge, MA: Harvard University Press.

Modleski, T. (1982). *Loving With a Vengeance: Mass-Produced Fantasies for Women.* Hamden, CN: Archon Books.

Modleski, T. (Ed.) (1986). *Studies in Entertainment: Critical Approaches to Mass Culture.* Bloomington and Indianapolis: Indiana University Press.

Modleski, T. (1991). *Feminism Without Women: Culture and Criticism in a 'Postfeminist' Age.* New York and London: Routledge.

Mofina, R. (1993). Hooker Tells Seminar of Initiation At Age 14: She Worked in Cellar At Back of Restaurant While Diners Ate in Front. *Calgary Herald,* September 30th, p. B1.

Monck, E. and New, M. (1995). *Sexually Abused Children and Adolescents and Young Perpetrators of Sexual Abuse Who Were Treated in Voluntary Community Facilities.* London: HMSO.

Morgan, S. and Righton, P. (1989). *Child Care: Concerns and Conflicts.* London: Hodder and Stoughton.

Morris, T. and Blom-Cooper, L. (1964). *A Calendar of Murder*. London: Michael Joseph.

Morrison, J. (1988). Perpetrator Suicide Following Incest Reporting: Two Case Studies. *Child Abuse and Neglect*, 12, 115-117.

Morton, J.H. (1934). Female Homicides. *Journal of Mental Science*, 80, 64-74.

Morrow, K.B. and Sorrell, G.T. (1989). Factors Affecting Self-Esteem, Depression, and Negative Behaviours in Sexually Abused Female Adolescents. *Journal of Marriage and the Family*, 51, 677-686.

Mrazek, P.B. and Bentovim, A. (1981). Incest and the Dysfunctional Family System. In P.B. Mrazek and C.H. Kempe (Eds.), *Sexually Abused Children and Their Families*, (167-177). New York: Pergamon.

Mrazek, P.B. and Mrzaek, D.A. (1981). The Effects of Child Sexual Abuse: Methodological Considerations. In P.B. Mrazek and C.H. Kempe (Eds.), *Sexually Abused Children and Their Families*, (235-245). New York: Pergamon Press.

Mrazek, P.J. and Mrazek, D.A. (1987). Resilience in Child Maltreatment Victims: A Conceptual Exploration. *Child Abuse and Neglect*, 11, 357-366.

Mullen, P., Martin, J.L., Anderson, J.C., Romans, S.E. and Herbison, P. (1993). Childhood Sexual Abuse and Mental Health in Adult Life. *British Journal of Psychiatry*, 163, 721-732.

Munro, E. (1998). Improving Social Worker's Knowledge Base in Child Protection Work. *British Journal of Social Work*, 28, 89-105.

Murphy, E., Brewin, C. and Silka, I. (1997). The Assessment of Parenting Using the Parental Bonding Instrument: Two Or Three Factors? *Psychological Medicine*, 27, 333-342.

Myers, S. (1970). Maternal Filicide. *American Journal Diseases of Childhood*, 120, 534-536.

Myers, J. (1994). *The Backlash: Child Protection Under Fire*. London: Sage.

Nash, M.R., Hulsey, T.L., Sexton, M.C., Harralson, T.L. and Lambert, W. (1993). Long-term Sequelae of Childhood Sexual Abuse: Perceived Family Environment, Psycho-pathology and Dissociation. *Journal of Consulting and Clinical Psychology, 61, 276-283.*

Nash, M.R., Hulsey, T.L., Sexton, M.C., Harralson, T.L. and Lambert, W. (1993). Reply to Comment by Briere and Elliott. *Journal of Consulting and Clinical Psychology*, 61, 289-290.

National Health Service Act (1977). London: HMSO.

Nathan, D. (1991). Satanism and Child Molestation: Constructing the Ritual Abuse Scare. In J. Richardson, J. Best and D. Bromley (Eds.) *The Satanism Scare*, (75-94). New York: Aldine de Gruyter.

Nava, M. (1988). Cleveland and the Press: Outrage and Anxiety in the Reporting of Child Sexual Abuse. *Feminist Review*, 28 Spring, 103-32.

Nelander, J. (1994). Kidnapped Children Are Sold As Slaves: Innocent Little Girls Are Being Tortured, Starved and Locked in Filthy Dungeons of Despair. *National Examiner*, February 15th, 1, 7 and 8.

Nelson, S. (1982). *Incest: Fact and Myth*. Edinburgh: Stramullion.

Nelson, B. (1984). *Making an Issue of Child Abuse: Political Agenda Setting for Social Problems*. Chicago: University of Chicago Press.

Newberger, C.M. and DeVos, E. (1988). Abuse and Victimisation: A Life-span Development Perspective. *American Journal of Orthopsychiatry*, 58, 505-511.

Noam, G. and Valiant, G. (1994). Clinical-developmental Psychology in Developmental Psychopathology: Theory and Research of An Emerging Perspective. In D. Cichetti and S. Toth (Eds.) *Disorders and Dysfunctions of the Self*, (299-332). Rochester, NY: University of Rochester Press.

Noyes P. (1991). *Child Abuse - A Study of Inquiry Reports*. London: HMSO.

Okami, P. (1990). Sociopolitical Biases in the Contemporary Scientific Literature on Adult Human Sexual Behavior with Children and Adolescents. In J. Feierman (Ed.) *Pedophilia: Biosocial Dimensions,* (91-119). New York: Springer Verlag.

O'Leary, K.D. (1984). Marital Discord and Children: Problem Strategies, Methodologies, and Results. *New Directions for Child Development*, 24, 35-46.

Orr, D.P. and Downes, M.C. (1985). Self-concept of Adolescent Sexual Abuse Victims. *Journal of Youth and Adolescence*, 14, 401-410.

Owen, M. (1996). Child Protection and Research: Understanding the Messages. *Child and Family Social Work*, 1, 4.

Painter, S.L. (1986). Research on the Prevalence of Child Sexual Abuse: New Directions. *Canadian Journal of Behavioural Sciences*, 18, 323-339.

Paradise, J.E., Rose, L., Sleeper, L.A., and Nathanson, M. (1994). Behavior, Family Function, School Performance and Predictions of Persistent Disturbance in Sexually Abused Children. *Pediatrics*, 93, 452-459.

Parker, G., Tupling, H. and Brown, L. (1979). A Parental Bonding Instrument. *British Journal of Medical Psychology*, 52, 1-10.

Parker, R., Ward, H., Jackson, S., Aldgate, J. and Wedge, P. (1991). *Assessing Outcomes in Child Care*. London: HMSO.

Parton, N. (1991). *Governing the Family: Child Care, Child Protection and the State*. London: Macmillan.

Parton, N. (1996). Child Protection, Family Support and Social Work: A Critical Appraisal of the Department of Health Studies in Child Protection. *Child and Family Social Work*, 1, 3-11.

Parton, N. (ed.) (1997). *Child Protection and Family Support: Tensions, Contradictions and Possibilities*. London: Routledge.

Pateman, C. (1990). Defending Prostitution: Charges Against Ericsson. In Cass, R. Sunstein (Ed.), *Feminism and Political Theory*, (201-206). Chicago: University of Chicago Press.

Pedhazur, E.J. (1982). *Multiple Regression in Behavioural Research* (2nd ed.). New York: Holt, Reinhart E. Winston.

Pelletier, G. and Handy, L.C. (1986). Family Dysfunction and the Psychological Impact of Child Sexual Abuse. *Canadian Journal of Psychiatry*, 31, 407-412.

Pelletier, R. (1980). Advantages for Children of A Non-judiciary and Family Approach to Cases of Sexual Abuse. In J.M. Samson (Ed.) *Enfance Et Sexualite*. Montreal: Editions Etudes.

Pelton, L. (1981). Child Abuse and Neglect: The Myth of Classlessness. In L. Pelton (Ed.) *The Social Context of Child Abuse*, (23-38). New York: Human Sciences Press.

Plant, M. (1990). *AIDS, Drugs and Prostitution*. London: Tavistock/ Routledge.

Platt, D. and Shemmings, D. (Eds.) (1996). *Making Enquiries into Alleged Child Abuse and Neglect: Partnership with Families*. Brighton: Pennant/ NSPCC.

Pomeroy, J.C., Behar, D. and Stewart, M.A. (1981). Abnormal Sexual Behaviour in Pre-pubescent Children. *British Journal of Psychiatry*, 138, 199-125.

Powell, G.E. and Chalkley, A.J. (1981). The Effects of Paedophile Attention on the Child. In B. Taylor (Ed.), *Perspectives on Paedophilia*, (59-76). London: Batford.

Prins, H. (1981). Dangerous People or Dangerous Situation/Some Implications For Assessment and Management. *Medicine, Science and the Law*, 21, 125-135.

Prins, H. (1991). Dangerous People of Dangerous Situation? Some Further Thoughts. *Medicine, Science and the Law*, 31, 25-37.

Pritchard, C. (1991). Levels of Risk and Psychosocial Problems of Families on the At Risk of Abuse Register: Some Indications of Outcome Two Years After Case Closure. *Research, Policy and Planning*, 9, 19-26.

Pritchard, C. (1992). Children's Homicide As An Indicator of Effective Child Protection: A Comparative Study of Western European statistics. *British Journal of Social Work*, 22, 663-684.

Pritchard, C. (1993). Re-Analyzing Children's Homicide and Undetermined Death Rates As An Indication of Improved Child Protection: A Reply to Creighton. *British Journal of Social Work*, 23, 645-652.

Pritchard, C. (1995). *Suicide: The Ultimate Betrayal*. Buckingham: Open University Press.

Pritchard, C. (1998). Suicide in Ex-Clywd Children's Home Residents. *Community Care*, May.

Pritchard, C. and Bagley, C. (1998). Profiles of Men Who Sexually Offend Against Children: A Two County Study. Unpublished paper.

Pritchard, C., Cotton, A., Godson, D., Cox, M. and Weeks, S. (1993). Mental Illness, Drug and Alcohol Misuse and HIV Risk Behaviour in 214 Young Adult Probation Clients. *Social Work and Social Science Review*, 3, 150-162.

Quinton, D. and Rutter, M. (1984). Parental Psychiatric Disorder: Effects on Children. *Psychological Medicine*, 14, 853-880.

Radloff, L. (1977). The CESD Scale: A Self-report Depression Scale for Research in the General Population. *Applied Psychological Research*, 1, 385-401.

Rae-Grant, N., Thomas, B.H., Offord, D.R. and Boyle, M.H. (1989). Risk, Protective Factors, and the Prevalence of Behavioural and Emotional Disorders in Children and Adolescents. *Journal of the American Academy of Child and Adolescent Psychiatry*, 28, 262-268.

Reder, P. and Duncan, S. (1997). Adult Psychiatry: A Missing Link in the Child Protection Network: Comments on Falkov's Fatal Child Abuse and Parental Psychiatric Disorder. *Child Abuse Review*, 6, 35-40.

Renshaw, D.C. (1982). *Incest*. Boston: Little Brown.

Resnick, P. (1969). Child Murder by Parents: A Psychiatric Review of Filicide. *American Journal of Psychiatry*, 126, 325-334.

Resnick, P. (1970). Murder of the Newborn: A Psychiatric Review of Neonaticide. *American Journal of Psychiatry*, 126, 1414-1420.

Reynolds, H. (1986). *The Economics of Prostitution*. Springfield, Ill: Charles C. Thomas.

Rich, A. (1987). Notes Toward a Politics of Location. In A. Rich *Blood, Bread and Poetry*, (210-31). London: Virago.

Richardson, J. (1994). The Satanism Scare: Social Construction of an International Social Problem. Paper Given in Department of Anthroplogy and Sociology Departmental Seminar Programme. Monash University, Melbourne, 10 May.

Richardson, J., Best, J. and Bromley, D. (Eds.) (1991). *The Satanism Scare*. New York: Aldine de Gruyter.

Richter, N., Snider, E. and Gorey, K. (1997). Group Work Intervention with Female Survivors of Childhood Sexual Abuse. *Research on Social Work Practice*, 7, 53-69.

Roberts, J. And Hawton, K. (1989). Child Abuse and Attempted Suicide. *Lancet*, April 19th, 882.

Rodenburg, M. (1971). Child Murder By Depressed Parents. *Canadian Psychiatric Association Journal,* 16, 41-53.

Rubin, G. (1984). Thinking Sex: Notes for a Radical Theory of the Politics of Sexuality. In C. Vance (Ed.) *Pleasure and Danger: Exploring Female Sexuality,* (267-319). Boston: Routledge and Kegan Paul.

Runtz, M. and Briere, J. (1986). Adolescent "Acting-out" and Childhood History of Sexual Abuse. *Journal of Interpersonal Violence*, 1, 326-334.

Runyon, D., Everson, M., Edelsohn, G., Hunter, W. and Coutler, M.L. (1988). Impact of Legal Intervention on Sexually Abused Children. *Journal of Paediatrics*, 133, 647-653.

Russell, D.E.H. (1986). *The Secret Trauma: Incest in the Lives of Girls and Women*. New York: Basic Books.

Rust, J. and Troupe, P. (1991). Relationships of Treatment of Child Sexual Abuse with School Achievement and Self-concept. *Journal of Early Adolescence*, 11, 420-439.

Rutter, M. (1979a). Maternal Deprivation, 1972-78: New Findings, New Concepts, New Approaches. *Child Development*, 50, 283-305.

Rutter, M. (1979b). Protective Factors in Children's Responses to Stress and Disadvantage. In M.W. Kent and J.E. Rolf (Eds.), *Primary Prevention of Psychopathology,* (Vol. 3, 49-74). Hanover, N.H.: University Press of New England.

Rutter, M. (1985). Resilience in the Face of Adversity. *British Journal of Psychiatry*, 147, 598-611.

Rutter, M. (1987). Psychosocial Resilience and Protective Mechanisms. *American Journal of Orthopsychiatry*, 57, 316-331.

Sanford, M., Offord, D., Boyle, M. and Pearce, A. (1992). Ontario Child Health Study: Social and School Impairment in Children Aged 6 to 16. *Journal of the American Academy of Child and Adolescent Psychiatry*, 199, 60-67.

Sansfacon, D. and Presentey, F. (1993). *Processing of Child Sexual Abuse Cases in Selected Sites in Quebec*. Ottawa: Federal Department of Justice.

Sansonnet-Hayden, H., Haley, G., Marriage, K. and Fine, S. (1987). Sexual Abuse and Psychopathology in Hospitalised Adolescents. *Journal of the American Academy of Child and Adolescent Psychiatry*, 26, 753-757.

Sas, L. (1991). *Reducing the System-induced Trauma for Child Sexual Abuse Victims: Preparation, Assessment and Follow-up*. London, ONT: The Family Court Clinic.

Sauzier, M. (1989). Disclosure of Child Sexual Abuse: for Better Or Worse. *Psychiatric Clinics of North America*, 12, 455-469.

Saywitz, K. and Nathanson, R. (1993). Children's Testimony and Their Perceptions of Stress In and Out of the Courtroom. *Child Abuse and Neglect*, 17, 613-622.

Scott, P.D. (1973a). Parents Who Kill Their Children. *Medicine, Science and The Law*, 13, 120-126.

Scott, P.D. (1973b). Fatal Battered Baby Cases. *Medicine, Science and the Law*, 13, 197-206.

Seagull, E.A.W. (1987). Social Support and Child Maltreatment: A Review of the Evidence. *Child Abuse and Neglect*, 11, 41-52.

Sedney, M.A. and Brooks, B. (1984). Factors Associated with a History of Childhood Sexual Experiences in a Non-clinical Female Population. *Journal of the American Academy of Child Psychiatry*, 23, 215-218.

Seng, M.J. (1989). Child Sexual Abuse and Adolescent Prostitution: A Comparative Analysis. *Adolescence*, 24, 665-675.

Server, J.C. and Janzen, C. (1982). Contraindications to Reconstruction of Sexually Abusive Families. *Child Welfare*, 61, 279-288.

Sgroi, S.M. (1982). The State of the Art in Child Sexual Abuse Intervention. In S.M. Sgroi (Ed.), *Handbook of Clinical Intervention in Child Sexual Abuse*, (1-8). Toronto: Lexington.

Sharland, E., Jones, D., Aldgate, J. Seal, H. and Coucher, M. (1995). *Professional Intervention in Child Sexual Abuse*. London: HMSO.

Sharland, E., Seal, H., Croucher, M., Aldgate, J. and Jones, D. (1996). *Professional Interventions in Child Sexual Abuse*. London; HMSO.

Shaw, D.S. and Emery, R.E. (1987). Parental Conflict and Other Correlates of the Adjustment of School Age Children Whose Parents Have Separated. *Journal of Abnormal Child Psychology*, 15, 269-281.

Sheppard, M. (1993) Maternal Depression and Child Care: the Significance for Social Work and Social Work Research. *Adoption and Fostering*, 17, 10-16.

Shrage, L. (1990). Should Feminists Oppose Prostitution? In R. Cass, (Ed.). *Feminism and Political Theory*, (185-200). Chicago: University of Chicago Press.

Silbert, M. and Pines, A. (1981). Sexual Abuse As An Antecedent to Prostitution. *Child Abuse and Neglect*, 5, 407-411.

Sillars, L. (1995). A New Player in the Game: Street Teams Bring A Sense of Family to Calgary's Child Prostitutes. *Alberta Report* (Edmonton), November 20th, 28-31.

Simon, L.M.J., Sales, B., Kaszniak, A. and Kahn, M. (1992). Characteristics of Child Sex Molesters: Implications for the Fixated-regressed Dichotomy. *Journal of Interpersonal Violence*, 7, 211-225.

Simrel, K., Berg, R. and Thomas, J. (1979). Crisis Management of Sexually Abused Children. *Pediatric Annals*, 8, 59-72.

Sines, J.O. (1987). Influences of the Home and Family Environment on Childhood Dysfunction. In B.B. Lahey and A.E. Kazdin (Eds.), *Advances in Child Clinical Psychology*, (Vol. 10, 1-54). New York: Plenum.

Singer, M.I., Petchers, M.K. and Hussey, D. (1989). The Relationship Between Sexual Abuse and Substance Abuse Among Psychiatrically Hospitalised Adolescents. *Child Abuse and Neglect*, 13, 319-235.

Sirles, E. and Franke, P. (1989). Factors Influencing Mothers Reactions to Intrafamily Sexual Abuse. *Child Abuse and Neglect*, 13, 131-139.

Skidmore, P. (1995). Telling Tales: Media Power, Ideology and the Reporting of Child Sexual Abuse in Britain. In D. Kidd-Hewitt and R. Osborne (Eds.). *Crime and the Media: The Post-Modern Spectacle*, (78-106). London: Pluto Press.

Skinner, H.A., Steinhauer, P.D. and Stana-Barbara, J. (1983). The Family Assessment Measure. *Canadian Journal of Community Mental Health*, 2, 91-105.

Skinner, H.A., Steinhauer, P.D. and Santa-Barbara, J. (1984). *The Family Assessment Measure: Administration and Interpretation Guide*. Toronto, Ontario: Addiction Research Foundation.

321

Smale, G.,Tuson, G., Ahmad, B., Darvill, G., Domoney, L. and Sainsbury, E. (1994). *Negotiating Care in the Community: Implications of Research Findings on Community Based Practice for the Implementation of the Community Care and Children Acts*. London: HMSO.

Smale, G. and Tuson, G. (1993). *Empowerment Assessment, Care Management and the Skilled Worker*. London: HMSO.

Smets, A.C. and Hartup, W.W. (1988). Systems and Symptoms: Family Cohesion/Adaptability and Childhood Behaviour Problems. *Journal of Abnormal Child Psychology*, 16, 233-246.

Smith, C. and Carlson, B. (1997). Stress, Coping and Resilience in Children and Youth. *Social Service Review*, June, 231-257.

Smucker, M.R., Craighead, W.E., Craighead, L.W. and Green B.J. (1986). Normative and Reliability Data for the Children's Depression Inventory. *Journal of Abnormal Child Psychology*, 14, 25-39.

Social Services Inspectorate, (1995). *Draft Circular on Children's Services Plans*. London: HMSO.

Solin, C.A. (1986). Displacement of Affect in Families Following Incest Disclosure. *American Journal of Orthopsychiatry*, 56, 570-580.

Somander, L. and Rammer, L. (1991). Intra-and Extra-familial Child Homicide in Sweden 1971-1989. *Child Abuse and Neglect*, 15, 44-55.

Soothill, K. and Walby, S. (1991). *Sex Crime in the News*. London and New York: Routledge.

Sorrenti-Little, L., Bagley, C. and Robertson, S. (1986). An Operational Definition of the Long-term Harmfulness of Sexual Relations with Peers and Adults by Young Children. *Canadian Children*, 9, 46-47.

Spanier, G.B. (1976). Measuring Dyadic Adjustment: New Scales for Assessing Quality of Marriage and Similar Dyads. *Journal of Marriage and the Family*, 38, 15-28.

Spanier, G.B. and Filsinger, E.E. (1983). The Dyadic Adjustment Scale. In E.E. Filsinger (Ed.), *Marriage and Family Assessment: A Source Book for Family Therapy*, (155-168). Beverly Hills, CA: Sage.

Steinhauer, P.D., Santa-Barbara, J. and Skinner, H. (1984). The Process Model of Family Functioning. *Canadian Journal of Psychiatry*, 29, 77-88.

Stern, M.J. and Meyer, L.C. (1980). Family and Couple Interactional Patterns in Cases of Father/Daughter Incest. In B.M. Jones, L.L. Jenstrom and K. McFarlane (Eds.), *Sexual Abuse of Children: Selected Readings*. (U.S. Department of Health and Human Services Publication No. OHDS 78-30261, 83-86). Washington, D.C.: U.S. Government Printing Office.

322

Stewart, A. and Stewart, D. (1993). *Social Backgrounds of Young Offenders*. London: Association of Chief Probation Officers.

Stoneman, Z., Brody, G.H. and Burke, M. (1989). Marital Quality, Depression and Inconsistent Parenting: Relationship With Observed Mother-Child Conflict. *American Journal of Orthopsychiatry*, 59, 105-117.

Stroud J. (1998). Child Homicide and Mental Disorder: A Review (Forthcoming).

Summit, R.C. (1983). The Child Sexual Abuse Accommodation Syndrome. *Child Abuse and Neglect*, 7, 177-193.

Tabachnick, B.G. and Fidell, L.S. (1983). *Using Multivariate Statistics*. New York: Harper and Row.

Tate, T. (1990). *Child Pornography*. London: Methuen.

Tedesco, J. and Schnell, S. (1987). Children's Reactions to Sex Abuse Investigation and Litigation. *Child Abuse and Neglect*, 11, 267-272.

Tennent, G. and Way, C. (1984). The English Special Hospital - A 12-17 Year Follow-up Study: A Comparison of Violent and Non-violent Re-offenders and Non-offenders. *Medicine, Science and the Law*, 24, 81-91.

Terman, H. (1988). The Psychoanalytic Legacy: From Whence We Come. In L.E.A. Walker (Ed.), *Handbook on Sexual Abuse of Children*, (37-52). New York: Springer.

Thoburn, J. Lewis, A. and Shemmings, D. (1995). *Paternalism Or Partnership: Family Involvement in the Child Protection Process*. London: HMSO.

Thoburn, J. and Lewis, A. (1992). Parentership with Parents of Children in Need of Protection. In Gibbons, J. (Ed.) *The Children Act 1989 and Family Support: Principles into Practice*. London: HMSO.

Thompson-Cooper, I., Fugere, R. and Cormier, B. (1993). The Child Abuse Reporting Laws: An Ethical Dilemma for Professionals. *Canadian Journal of Psychiatry*, 38, 557-562.

Thorman, G. (1983). *Incestuous Families*. Springfield, MA: Charles C. Thomas.

Toneguzzi, M. (1993). Trick Pad Busted: Teen Girls Held Captive in Basement. *Calgary Herald*, December 29th, p. 1.

Tong, L., Oates, K., McDowell, M. (1987). Personality Development Following Sexual Abuse. *Child Abuse and Neglect*, 11, 371-383.

Trepper, T.S. (1986). The Apology Session. In T.S. Trepper and M.J. Barrett (Eds.), *Treating Incest: A Multiple System Perspective*, (93-101). New York: Haworth Press.

Trepper, T.S. and Barrett, M.J. (1986). Vulnerability to Incest: A Framework For Assessment. In T.S. Trepper and M.J. Barrett (Eds.), *Treating Incest: A Multiple System Perspective,* (13-25). New York: Haworth Press.

Trinder, L. (1996). Social Work Research: The State of the Art (or Science). *Child and Family Social Work,* 1, 233-242.

Tsai, M., Feldman-Summers, S. and Edgar, M. (1979). Childhood Molestation: Variables Related to Differntial Impacts on Psychosexual Functioning in Adult Women. *Journal of Abnormal Psychology,* 88, 407-417.

Tunstill, J. (1992). Local Authority Policies on Children in Need. In J. Gibbons, (Ed.) *The Children Act 1989 and Family Support: Principles into Practice.* London: HMSO.

Tufts' New England and Medical Center, Division of Child Psychiatry (1984). *Sexually Exploited Children: Service and Research Project.* Final Report for the Office of Juvenile Justice and Delinquency Prevention. Washington, D.C.: U.S. Department of Justice.

van der Kolk, B. (1994). The Body Keeps the Score: Memory and the Emerging Psychobiology of Post Traumatic Stress. *Harvard Review of Psychiatry,* 1, 253-265.

van Egmond, M., Garnefski, N., Jonker, D. and Kerkof, A. (1993). The Relationship Between Sexual Abuse and Female Suicidal Behaviour. *Crisis,* 14, 129-139.

Verleur, D., Hughes, R. and De Rios, M. (1986). Enhancement of Self-esteem Among Female Adolescent Incest Victims: A Controlled Comparison. *Adolescence,* 21, 843-854.

Villeneuve, C. and Roy, L. (1984). Psychological Distance in 'Clinic' and Control Families. *Canadian Journal of Behavioural Sciences,* 16, 216-223.

Violence Against Children Study Group (1990). *Taking Child Abuse Seriously: Contemporary Issues in Child Protection Theory and Practice.* London: Unwin Hyman.

Walford, G., Kennedy, M., Manwell, M. and McCune, N. (1990). Father-perpetrators of Child Sexual Abuse Who Commit Suicide. *Irish Journal of Psychological Medicine,* 7, 144-145.

Wallace, A. (1986). *Homicide, The Social Reality.* Sydney: NSW Bureau of Crime Statistics and Research, Attorney General's Department, Research Study No. 5.

Wallerstein, J.S. (1983). Children of Divorce: Stress and Developmental Tasks. In N. Garmezy and M. Rutter (Eds.), *Stress, Coping and Development in Children*, (265-302). New York: McGraw-Hill.

Waterhouse, L., Dobash, R. and Carnie, J. (1994). *Child Sexual Abusers*. Edinburgh: The Scottish Office Central Research Unit.

Waterhouse L., Pitcairn T., McGhee J., Secker J. and Sullivan C. (1995). Evaluating Parenting in Child Physical Abuse. In *Child Protection. Messages From Research*, (91-92). London: HMSO.

Watney, S. (1987). *Policing Desire: Pornography, AIDS and the Media*. London: Methuen.

Wattam, C. (1997). Is the Criminalisation of Child Harm and Injury in the Interests of the Child? *Children and Society*, 11, 97-107.

Wattam, C. (1992). *Making a Case in Child Protection*. Harlow; Longman.

Wattam, C. (1991). *Truth and Belief in the Disclosure Process*. London: NSPCC.

Webster, R. (1998). *The Great Children's Home Panic*. Oxford: The Orwell Press.

Weeks, J. (1985). *Sexuality and its Discontents: Meanings, Myths and Modern Sexualities*. London: Routledge and Kegan Paul.

Weisberg, D.K. (1985). *Children of the Night: A Study of Adolescent Prostitution*. Lexington, D.C. Heath.

West, D.J. (1965). *Murder Followed by Suicide*. London: Heinemann.

Westen, D. (1994). The Impact of Sexual Abuse on Self-structure. In D. Cicchetti and S. Toth (Eds.) *Disorders and Dysfunctions of the Self*, (223-250). Rochester, NY: University of Rochester Press.

Whipple, E.E. and Webster-Stratton, C. (1991). The Role of Parental Stress in Physically Abusive Families. *Child Abuse and Neglect*, 15, 279-291.

White, S. (1997). Beyond Retroduction? Hermeneutics, Reflexivity and Social Work Practice. *British Journal of Social Work*, 27, 739-753.

White, S. (1998). Social Work Practice as a Practical Moral Activity. Unpublished paper, presented at University of Southampton, 26 February 1998.

White, S., Halpin, B.M., Strom, G.A. and Santilli, G. (1988). Behavioural Comparisons of Young Sexually Abused, Neglected, and Non-referred Children. *Journal of Clinical Child Psychology*, 17, 53-61.

Widom, C.S. (1988). Sampling Biases and Implications for Child Abuse Research. *American Journal of Orthopsychiatry*, 58, 160-270.

Widom, C. and Morris, S. (1997). Accuracy of Adult Recollections of Childhood Victimization: Part 2 Childhood Sexual Abuse. *Psychological Assessment*, 9, 1, 34-46.

Widra, J. and Amidon, E. (1987). Improving Self-concept Through Intimacy Group Training. *Small Group Behaviour*, 4, 269-279.

Wierson M., Forehand, R. and McCombs, A. (1988). The Relationship of Early Adolescent Functioning to Parent-reported and Adolescent-perceived Interparental Conflict. *Journal of Abnormal Child Psychology*, 16, 707-718.

Wilczynski, A. and Morris, A. (1993). Parents Who Kill Their Children, *Criminal Law Review*, January, 31-36.

Wild, N. (1988). Suicide of Perpetrators After Disclosure of Child Sexual Abuse. *Child Abuse and Neglect*, 12, 119-121.

Wilkinson, J. (1994). Using A Reconviction Predictor to Make Sense of Reconviction Rates in the Probation Service. *British Journal of Social Work*, 24, 461-475.

Will, D. (1983). Approaching the Incestuous and Sexually Abusive Family. *Journal of Adolescence*, 6, 229-246.

Wolfe, D.A. and Mosk, M.D. (1983). Behavioural Comparisons of Children from Abusive and Distressed Families. *Journal of Consulting and Clinical Psychology*, 51, 702-708.

Wolfe, V.V., Gentile, C. and Wolfe, D.A. (1989). The Impact of Sexual Abuse on Children: A PTSD Formulation. *Behaviour Therapy*, 20, 215-228.

Woods, P. (1993). Overview of an Adolescent Sadistic Sex Offender. *Issues in Criminological and Legal Psychology*, 19, 33-36.

World Health Organisation (1992). *The ICID-10 Classification of Mental and Behaviour Disorders*. Geneva: World Health Organization.

Wyatt, G., Newcomb, M. and Riederle, M. (1993). *Sexual Abuse and Consensual Sex: Women's Developmental Patterns and Outcomes*. Newbury Park, CA: Sage.

Zimmerman, M., Copeland, L., Shope, J. and Dielman, T. (1997). A Longitudinal Study of Self-esteem: Implications for Adolescent Development. *Journal of Youth and Adolescence*, 26, 117-141.

Zuvarin, S.J. (1989). Severity of Maternal Depression and Three Types of Mother to Child Aggression. *American Journal of Orthopsychiatry*, 59, 377-389.

Index

328